Viceroy
Curzon to Mountbatten

Viceroy
Curzon to Mountbatten

Hugh Tinker

Karachi
Oxford University Press
Oxford New York Delhi
1997

Oxford University Press, Walton Street, Oxford OX2 6DP

Oxford New York
Athens Auckland Bangkok Bombay
Calcutta Cape Town Dar es Salaam Delhi
Florence Hong Kong Istanbul Karachi
Kuala Lumpur Madras Madrid Melbourne
Mexico City Nairobi Paris Singapore
Taipei Tokyo Toronto
and associated companies in
Berlin Ibadan

Oxford is a trade mark of Oxford University Press

ISBN 0 19 577698 4

Printed in Pakistan at
Mas Printers, Karachi.
Published by
Ameena Saiyid, Oxford University Press
5-Bangalore Town, Sharae Faisal
PO Box 13033, Karachi-75350, Pakistan.

CONTENTS

LIST OF ILLUSTRATIONS

DEDICATION

In affectionate memory of Michael Argles and Bill Reader, my companions in the History VIth at Taunton School and fellow officers in the Indian Army: although they were never wholly committed to the military style.

INTRODUCTION

'The true story of each Viceroyalty is in reality written in the weekly private letters which are exchanged between the Viceroy and the Secretary of State'.[1] This very Curzonian claim may be taken as hyperbole, yet the position of the Viceroy of India was certainly unique within the British Empire. The Viceroy of Ireland also combined supreme executive and ceremonial functions, but Dublin being only a hundred miles from the British mainland was susceptible to direct influences from London at all times. India on the other hand was 7,000 miles from Britain, and although the construction of the marine telegraph had diminished the Governor-General's freedom from the control of London, the Government of India remained unique: dependent yet independent. Four Viceroys served as Governor-General of Canada before taking up the post in India, they were Dufferin, Lansdowne, Minto and Willingdon. All were struck by the complete difference between these two grand positions.

We may have had too many studies which focused on the correspondence between the Secretary of State and the Viceroy, but probably a fresh look at the role played by the Viceroy as head of the Indian administration is timely now that fifty years have elapsed since the last Viceroyalty ended. This study is a kind of personal retrospect, completed when a lifetime of writing about southern Asia is almost over. For the most part, the Viceroys were ordinary men in an extraordinary position, only rarely did they possess extraordinary talents, (however sometimes the demands of

[1]The Marquess Curzon, *British Government in India,* Vol. 11, 1925, p.129.

the position rubbed off on the man). The period covered in this book begins with British rule at its zenith and ends with its eclipse.

Research carried out in former days has been drawn upon, and only the most limited new research has been attempted. The book draws heavily upon the work of others published during the last thirty or forty years. Those who must be specially thanked (though their interpretations may not always have been followed) are S. Gopal, B. B. Misra, R. J. Moore, and Stanley Wolpert. Unfortunately *The Viceroys of India* by Mark Bence-Jones (1982) was only discovered after this book was in draft.

Those who have helped in getting this study into a form suitable for publication include Thelma Goodman, responsible for inter-library loans at Lancaster University Library and a former colleague, David Blake, Curator of European manuscripts in the Oriental and India Office collections of the British Library. Also a very special thanks to Professor Z. H. Zaidi, who has been a steady source of ideas to me. As always, my greatest debt is to my very dear wife.

Hugh Tinker

Chapter 1

THE ACTORS

The office of Governor-General became known by the title of Viceroy when the Crown assumed direct rule in India from the East India Company after the so called Mutiny or the 1857 war of independence as it is referred to in the subcontinent. The Viceroy had two different responsibilities; as Governor-General of British India and as the representative of the Crown with the Princely States. His was the most important overseas appointment in the British Empire. The Viceroy was personally selected by the Prime Minister and appointed by the monarch, sometimes the hand of the monarch was strong in the choice, but there was no instance of a Prime Minister being overruled until Willingdon came. The appointment was for five years, and during his tenure the Viceroy was not allowed to depart from the territories of the Indian Empire which included Aden and Burma until 1935, although from 1924 he was able to take one spell of home leave during his tenure.

The incoming Viceroy met his predecessor on arrival usually in Bombay, though occasionally in Aden. However until the departing incumbent left Indian territory he remained the Viceroy, and the new man was Viceroy designate. Soon after being sworn in the Viceroy was surrounded by the panoply of power. As Minto observed, 'An unnatural atmosphere of holy awe surrounds his person, creating an unnatural *gêne*'. This constraint or inaccessibility applied to all, including Governors and Members of his Council so that the Viceroy seldom if ever received the frank opinions of others. The only persons likely to be free of this constraint were his wife and his Private Secretary. The PSV, as his private secretary was called, was usually the personal choice of the Viceroy. Many were members or former members of the Indian Civil Service, but this was not essential. Lord Ripon chose General Gordon to be his PSV, who was not a success. The historian Vincent Smith, formerly in the Indian Civil Service suggested: 'The position of Private Secretary is unlike any other office in any country....To a man of ability and tact the power is vast alike in patronage and in influence upon the ruler's policy'.

The Viceroy made all appointments throughout his domains except for the Governors of Bombay and Madras and later also the Governor of Bengal. Until the introduction of dyarchy these were the only ones designated Governor: the remainder being Lieutenant-Governor or Chief Commissioner. The 'Presidency' Governors enjoyed the right of direct access to the Secretary of State. All the others had to correspond via the Viceroy who might, if he thought fit, pass on their communications to the Secretary of State. The Presidency Governors were selected from English Public life, all the other Satraps were high flyers from the Indian Civil Service although a few rulers of the border regions like Baluchistan and Burma came from the Indian Army. These heads of provinces were almost always chosen from the Viceroy's Council. It therefore behoved them not to cross his path.

The Viceroy's Council which came to be later known as the Executive Council was a small body, six in number with the Commander-in-Chief as an 'additional' member. All except the law member were from the Indian Civil Service. The members were each responsible for one or more departments. The Viceroy was personally in charge of the Foreign and Political Department, dealing with the Princes, the Frontier beyond the administered districts, and India's relations with the neighbours namely Afghanistan, Tibet, and the Gulf States. In the 1930s this Indian Civil Service monopoly was dented with Sir George Schuster (Finance) coming from the British Civil Service and Sir Fazl-i-Husain a politician coming from the Punjab. In Victorian days the executive element was augmented by a legislative element, which in time became much more numerous. The Viceroy presided over this Legislative Council until with the advent of dyarchy this task was given to a professional, the first incumbent being Sir Frederick Whyte, formerly a Liberal MP. Also with dyarchy the overall responsibility of the Viceroy for Legislation was limited as a range of powers were removed from the centre and handed over to the provinces. This did not diminish the unique dignity of his post.

Thus far we have considered what Bagehot called the 'efficient' part of the constitution. In Britain what he called the 'dignified' part is represented by the monarch.[1] The Viceroy had to personify the ceremonial aspects of rule throughout British India, and especially in relations with the Princes. He approved all honours; as well as awarded certain commissions in the army like the Viceroy's Commission. He entertained visiting dignitaries, who before 1914 frequently included royalty, foreign and British. He gave magnificent entertainments, like receptions, garden parties, balls, dinners, invitations to which were prized even by the highest in the land. These entertainments were organized with military precision; each guest being accorded a brief word with the Viceroy or his consort. The ladies curtsied, the men bowed, as to the monarch. It was almost worthy of Versailles.

Every year the Viceroy paid visits to the leading Princes who almost bankrupted themselves to impress their visitor. Such visits occasionally afforded a little comic relief as when the Nizam of Hyderabad, the richest man in the world, reluctantly served the Wavells with flat champagne, not once but twice.

With these varied and exhausting experiences it was not surprising that successive Viceroys found their five years in office more than long enough. When a Viceroy was required to extend his period beyond the limit, the extra time was almost always too much. The most dismal case was that of Curzon who moved from triumph to disaster, but Hardinge's time also ended in sad failures while Linlithgow left India only with the memory of his reactionary policies and apparently heartless indifference to the Bengal famine. Contrasting the record of the two most remarkable Viceroys of the twentieth century, we have to recall that Curzon went on too long while Mountbatten, in his hurry to get results was able to call it a day before the consequences were fully evident. Curzon and Mountbatten had many characteristics in common. Both were aristocrats, as were the great majority of Viceroys (only John Lawrence, Rufus Isaacs, and Wavell were from middle class or professional backgrounds). However, Curzon and Mountbatten were aristocrats, not merely by inheritance but also by temperament. Both exhibited a hauteur which was only occasionally relaxed. Both were appointed at a young age, Curzon was forty when he arrived in India and Mountbatten was forty-seven (Curzon's successor, Minto was sixty on appointment as was Mountbatten's predecessor, Wavell).[2] It is interesting to note that both Curzon and Mountbatten were compulsive workers, unable to delegate responsibility, toiling late into the night, often upon subjects of minor importance. Both had a strong sense of their place in history and were intensely ambitious and ruthless in thrusting their way upward. Because both were imbued with a sense of mission they brushed aside objections and discarded those who did not share their views.

Both entertained a somewhat juvenile concern with uniforms and medals and enjoyed being the central figures on occasions for celebration, such as big parades. However, nobody could question the care with which they had prepared themselves for their heavy task. Curzon had been Under-Secretary for India, 1891-2, and had travelled extensively in Central Asia, writing three books among which *Problems of the Far East* (1894) was probably the most important. Mountbatten, who could not follow such a systematic pursuit of background knowledge of Indian questions had however accompanied his cousin, the Prince of Wales on an extended tour of India in 1921-2, and had become friendly with some of the young princes. He attained a familiarity with the Indian military machine and with leading Indian figures during his period as Supreme Allied Commander South East Asia, 1943-6. All this was subsidiary to his overwhelming determination to get to the top in the Royal Navy. Although Curzon was more drawn to India he also had his eyes upon greater prizes, above all, the premiership.

When heavy decisions had to be faced, neither man hesitated, this was specially true when political boundaries were to be redrawn. Curzon sliced up the unwieldy province of Bengal, creating East Bengal and Assam as a new political unit. He also carved out a new province, the North West Frontier Province. Mountbatten, faced with even graver decisions, accepted the need to create two new entities: East Bengal (not so different to Curzon's East Bengal) and West Pakistan incorporating the North West Frontier Province but also slicing the province of Punjab in two.

Behind the two Viceroys were two remarkable women, Mary Leiter, Curzon's bride and Edwina Ashley, Mountbatten's wife. Both ladies brought immense wealth to their marriages. Both were faithful to their men 'in their fashion', though both introduced puzzlement and some unhappiness into the relationship. Because both Curzon and Mountbatten were so single-minded they did not mix up their personal and public problems.

Of course, the two men were not dual versions of one personality. Curzon was the more conventional in his route to success; Eton, Balliol, All Souls. Mountbatten went through the rougher, tougher route of Dartmouth and the navy. He did not acquire an assortment of influential friends along the way as Curzon did, though access to the royal family made up for a lot.

Whether Mountbatten would have been a success if he had been required to carry out the normal term as Viceroy may be doubted. He on his part made it clear on appointment that he intended to get back to the navy within two years and that he also intended to bring British rule in India to an end. It is therefore impossible to make a direct comparison between these two men, separated by forty years in time. However Curzon remains the outstanding head of the British administration of India.

There were ten Viceroys during the twentieth century out of which three were above average; they were Hardinge, Irwin, and Wavell. The three acquired a deep sympathy for Indian aspirations, somewhat masked by their Olympian manner. Minto and Reading also did useful work in giving life to a somewhat moribund administration. The other Viceroys were mediocrities although their high office helped to conceal their lack of talent; Curzon and Mountbatten remained apart.

What of the men responsible for India in Whitehall? Here, the nominal head of affairs, the Secretary of State, was frequently of less importance than the senior officials.

The top layer of the India Office was provided by the Council of India, established in 1858 to replace the Directors of the East India Company. It had no counterpart in other civil departments, such as the Foreign Office or the Home Office. When Sir Alfred Lyall became a member he found it 'rather depressing...we have all rather the looks of old hulks laid up in dock...the distance between London and India makes one feel as if looking at things as through a glass darkly and not face to face'. The Council had virtually no function under a Conservative Secretary of State, but when the Liberal, Morley, took office they endeavoured to hold him back.

The Council was finally abolished under the 1935 Act when they were replaced by advisers, mainly concerned with the Services. The executive head of the office was the Permanent Under-Secretary. The most permanent was Sir

Arthur Godley, later Lord Kilbracken, who ruled the office, 1883-1909. His successors mainly held the top job for six to seven years, as did Sir Arthur Holderness, the only one to have served in the Indian Civil Service, 1872-1901. He was the Permanent Under-Secretary 1912-19, the period when the reforms were laboriously conceived, while three politicians held the post of Secretary of State. Sir Arthur Hirtzel who entered the office in 1894 was Permanent Under-Secretary from 1924-30, a particularly sensitive period with three changes of government. He was succeeded by Sir Findlater Stewart, 1930-42. The last Permanent Under-Secretary was Sir David Monteath, 1942-8 (for the last six months he was responsible only for Burma).

As a group the officials at the India Office showed a remarkable collective solidarity. It was a peculiar feature of the system that their entire career was passed in London, so that they tended to view India as it was when they first joined the office and regarded any pressures for change as of transient significance. Penderel Moon went to India in 1929, as Gandhi's biggest campaign was starting up. He records his meetings with the sages at the office before his departure: 'The India Office officials were quite sure of their ground. Any misplaced idealism, any doubts about the continuance of British rule were quickly silenced with the curt remark "We have £100 million capital in India. We remain in India to safeguard it not to teach them how to govern themselves". These realists of the desk knew what they were about.'[3]

These cold, calculating men were in charge in London, not the politicians who represented India in Parliament for a few years. Godley wrote of his political chief Lord Cross, 'He was a very pleasant kindly old gentleman, perfectly capable of doing all that was required of him, and with the help of the official machine, which he left pretty much to itself, he got through his six years at the India office well enough'. Among the Secretaries of State who were appointed in the twentieth century, Morley, who inaugurated the reforms associated with his name, was past his prime. He was installed in the House of Lords where Liberals were in short supply. When he departed in 1910 his successors disappointed Indian aspirations. Edwin Montagu, 1917-22, was a visionary but he arrived too late to attract Indian support. Those who followed were devoid of political vision and Birkenhead, 1924-9 was a crass reactionary. Samuel Hoare was the most competent, he also lasted the longest, 1931-5, only to be reviled afterwards for his double dealing over Ethiopia. His reforms were hotly resisted by the last ditch Tories led by Winston Churchill. When Churchill became Prime Minister in 1940, any hope for constitutional advance faded. The post-war Labour government followed the practice of most of its predecessors in placing a mediocrity at the India Office. However, the new Prime Minister and his earnest colleague, Cripps, took the lead in Indian affairs. Their plans were not realized. Indian independence did not proceed according to their intentions.

These persons in formal charge of Indian affairs were probably of lesser importance to India than others who had no recognized standing upon the scene. Apart from the government servants including teachers, forest officers, and railway staff, the largest British group in India were the missionaries. In former days they had been pioneers in the modernization of society. By the 1890s most were conformist and had become part of the Indo-British establishment. However, there were two of exceptional importance, Charlie Andrews and Edward Thompson. Their significance was in providing a bridge between Britain and India. Andrews (1870-1940), formally renounced his missionary vocation in 1914. He went to join Gandhi in South Africa and for several years made the wrongs of Indian labourers exported throughout the British Empire his main concern. His friendship with Gandhi was the deepest of his many friendships. He also wrote several books which made a considerable impact on the religious public in Britain, North America, and other English-speaking lands. Thompson, 1886-1946, gave up missionary work in 1923 and later taught at Oxford. He was the author of many books as well; novels, biographies, and advocacy of Indian self-government. He was the most perceptive interpreter of Rabindranath Tagore to English readers and he was a close friend of Jawaharlal Nehru.

Edward Thompson was something of a loner, in Oxford he found few who were congenial. Andrews on the other hand had a multitude of friends, and he played a leading part in setting up the India Conciliation Group in London to exercise pressure in Whitehall and in Fleet Street. Another pressure group was the India League formed from left wing supporters of Indian freedom, notably Reginald Sorenson, Sidney Silverman, and Fenner Brockway, though its most assiduous member was Krishna Menon, who ardently supported the group throughout his long exile in London. Although most of its members were Labour supporters the League did not have access to the Labour leadership whose attitude to India was pragmatic. Leonard Woolf, influential in Labour's committee on international affairs, was exasperated by the absence of concern for colonial freedom on the Left.

All this suggests the limited impact of India on the climate of British thinking and policy. As the shrewd men of the India Office knew, the importance of India to Britain was measured by its economic contribution to the well-being of the metropolis which was hit by the exports of the United States, Germany and Japan. Britain's place in Indian development was especially associated with the manufacture of cotton. By the mid-nineteenth century, United Kingdom annual cotton exports amounted to more than £30m. India accounted for more than £5m of this total, being the largest single earner. Aware of the benefits of Indian imports, the Lancashire manufacturers were vociferous in denouncing bad labour conditions in Indian mills. British competition against the Indian menace was partially sustained until in 1921 India obtained fiscal autonomy and swingeing tariffs were imposed on British products. British textile exports to India hovered around half the pre-war average throughout the 1920s but by 1937 had fallen to 10 per cent of the pre-war peak. This was what the British in India were really concerned about.

Overall, the transformation of the trading relationship was strikingly abrupt. In the five years up to 1914, India imported an average of goods from the United Kingdom worth 61m and exported goods to the UK to the value of £37.5m. In 1938, the last normal year before independence, Indian exports from the UK were 34.8m and exports in the reverse direction were 43.5m, making a favourable Indian balance of 8.5m. Before 1914, India took 63 per cent of its imports from Britain and sent 25 per cent. In 1938-9, Indian imports from Britain were no more than 30.5 per cent of the total, while the proportion of Indian exports to Britain had increased to 34.5 per cent. All this affected British relations with India as much as political factors.

When India entered the twentieth century the population numbered 294,361,056. This figure was not much greater than ten years before, when it was 287m. The 1881 total was 254m; thus, the 1890s were a period of almost zero growth, marked by a series of famines in Bombay, the Central Provinces, and in parts of the United Provinces, (UP) and the Punjab. Famine was even more serious in some Princely States. The decade showed an actual decrease in their population (5.4 per cent) while in British India the decennial increase was only 4.8 per cent.

These trends were in spite of the massive increase in railway construction towards the end of the century. In 1880 less than 8,000 miles had been built, but by 1900 there were 25,000 miles of line. Most of the financing of this new construction had to come from loans contracted on the London market, and hence the nationalist politicians were critical. They asserted that the railways were mainly constructed for strategic purposes and were not necessary to India. It was true that a few lines were built with military needs in view, such as the railway from Quetta to the Afghan border, but the great majority were for commerce and civilian supply, a necessary precaution against the spread of famine in inaccessible areas.

The other massive public works mainly completed near the end of the nineteenth century were the irrigation canals. The Mughals had been great canal builders but their works had crumbled into disrepair. The British began to restore these fallen achievements, and then to construct new canals, the first major undertaking being the Ganges canals, built 1824-54. As British rule embraced Punjab, plans were formulated for the transformation of the barren tracts between the Five Rivers. The first major project was the Lower Chenab colony, completed between 1892-6, and opening up 2.5m acres. This project was co-ordinated with schemes of social engineering, yet this scheme was only a beginning. The major irrigation works were still to come.

British rule during the end of the nineteenth century was mainly devoted to keeping things quiet. The spectre of the 1857 so-called mutiny still hovered across British minds. The lesson that was drawn was that in the era 1839-50 reform had been introduced much too quickly, without consideration for Indian feelings.

Innovation, particularly constitutional and political innovation, came mainly from Indian sources. Much had been hoped from Queen Victoria's proclamation of 1858, for which the Queen herself had been largely responsible, promising a greater Indian participation in their own affairs. The renewal of the Company's Charter in 1853 had, in name, opened the elite civil service to Indian entry through open competitive examination. Despite the difficulties in gaining entry, via competition in London, an Indian, Satyendranath Tagore, son of the head of the Brahmo Samaj, did gain a place in 1864. In 1869 four Brahmo candidates competed and were successful. The British response was to make entry even more difficult for Indian candidates. One of the 1869 entries, Surendranath Banerjea's, was dismissed on flimsy grounds. This contrast between theory and practice was one of the grievances of the middle class. There were many others such as the restrictions on the press and quasi-political associations were formed to agitate for reform. The reform process received a considerable stimulus when Lord Ripon became Viceroy, 1880-84. He liquidated the aggressive North-West Frontier policy of his predecessors, repealed the restrictions on the press, promoted broad measures of local self-government to provide Indians with a fuller share in their own governance, and supported a bill permitting Indian magistrates to hear cases involving Europeans. This was encouraging to the Indian middle classes and was equally unwelcome to Europeans such as the planters who had been accustomed to having their own way. The rift between the growing Indian intelligentsia and their British rulers opened up ominously.

All this was observed by an Englishman, Allan Octavian Hume, 1829-1912, a senior figure in the Government of India, and the son of Joseph Hume, the Radical politician. A. O. Hume had been at the centre of the tumult in the so-called mutiny and had been made a CBE for his outstanding services. When he retired he continued to live at Simla, devoting much of his energy to ornithology and theosophy. He had remained in touch with Indian leaders and he was impressed, perhaps obsessed, with the danger of another mutiny breaking out. This was to dominate British fears right down to the last days of 1947. Hume wanted an outlet for Indian aspirations. Whereas most of the British looked to the traditional leaders, princes, landlords, village elders, as forming Indian opinion, Hume realized it was necessary to tap into the energies of the new educated middle class. Otherwise, he foresaw that they would be the leaders of the next uprising. Hume hastened to support the efforts of Lord Ripon but he calculated that something more was required than constitutional reforms. He wanted a forum where the 'new India' could advance their demands. He addressed an open letter to the graduates of Calcutta University: 'My friends the game is in our own hands; the ball is at our feet'.

The first response was from the Indian Association at the end of December 1883 while Ripon was still viceroy.

His successor, Dufferin, was a diplomat and former Governor General of Canada, 1872-8, who was also a Whiggish adherent of the Liberal party. He was not prepared to support the Indian cause if it came into conflict with European interests, as Ripon had done. He appeared to favour further territorial expansion by intervening in the residuary Burmese state of Ava. Urged on by Hume, politically minded Indians decided to meet in December 1885. Their first gathering was in Bombay, and came soon after a military expedition had voyaged up the Irrawaddy to Mandalay, in part to pre-empt a possible French intervention. As good Gladstonian liberals they deplored excess expenditure on military adventures. At the Bombay meeting there were seventy-three recognized delegates, and some others who as officials were not counted. Among the seventy-three were two Muslims (both members of Bombay Municipal Corporation) one of whom, Badruddin Tyabjee was to play a leading role in the following years. The most numerous group were the Parsees, including the veteran Dadabhai Naoroji, who came specially from London. The official response was cool but not hostile; indeed it would have been almost impossible to object to the ultra-loyal terms in which the delegates spoke.

The choice of the name 'Congress' was inspired. There is no real evidence that this was in imitation of the United States Congress, rather it was borrowed from Europe where it signified any assembly of like-minded persons, meeting for a common object, but its application in India certainly gave the new body a dignity which the alternative, 'Conference' would have lacked. The third Congress, held at Madras, attracted 604 delegates and the following year at Allahabad 1500 were present. Its claim to be a national organization appeared to be justified. The tone of debate remained entirely rational and moderate. Each year the president of the Congress included a declaration of loyalty, of which the following, quoted in Parliament was typical: 'The keynote of the movement is loyalty to the British Crown and attachment to the British People' (1891 Congress).

Dufferin's impending departure was received with a noticeable coolness by Hume and the Congress leaders. Dufferin's riposte was delivered at the St. Andrew's Day dinner in Calcutta, an exclusively European gathering at which the mercantile and industrial community, strongly Scots in composition turned out in force. At this gathering Dufferin put the Congress in its place, demanding whether 'the British Government would be content to allow this microscopic minority to control their administration of that majestic and multiform empire for whose safety and welfare they are responsible?' he stressed that traditional leaders of India 'are already becoming alarmed' at the claims made by Congress.

This evaluation of Congress was to become standard for many years. Thus, Curzon who was briefly Under-Secretary for India in 1892 introduced the 'India Councils Act, 1861, Amendment Bill' in the Commons to give marginally greater powers to the Legislative Council. Pressed to do more by the Liberal opposition he dismissed the plan to introduce the elective principle as 'in the highest degree premature and unwise'. He enumerated the kinds of organization which might be expected to nominate additional members to the Council - the zemindars, the municipalities, the universities, and 'the great religious denominations'. He had no doubt that actually the British were best endowed to safeguard the interest of the people of India:

> The voiceless millions who can neither read nor write their own tongue...The ryots and the peasants whose life is not one of political aspiration but of mute penury and toil. The plans and policy of the Congress Party in India would leave this vast amorphous residuum absolutely untouched....The constituency

> which the Congress Party represents cannot be described as otherwise than a minute and almost microscopic minority.

What then was the goal of British rule in India? Curzon had no doubts, they were destined to rule India for ever. Others might not be so sure, but most were convinced that it would be a great mistake to move too fast. Thus, Kipling, the poet laureate of British India, wrote in *Naulahka*:

> For the Christian riles and the Aryan smiles and it weareth the Christian down,
>
> And the end of the fight is a tombstone white with the name of the late deceased.
>
> And the epithet drear: 'A fool lies here who tried to hustle the East'.

What of Sir Alfred Lyall, 1835-1911, who joined the Indian Civil Service in 1856, saw active service throughout the mutiny, held a series of appointments, including the Foreign and Political Department, becoming Lieutenant-Governor, 1882-7, and finally serving on the Council of the Secretary of State in London, 1887-1902? Lyall liked to call himself a Liberal,[4] and he published a volume of poetry, *Verses Written in India*, 1889, which reflects his nostalgia for the heroic days of the mutiny, but also reveals his awareness of the brittle character of British rule, as when he projects himself into the mind of an educated Muslim watching a game of badminton near the Kashmir gate in Delhi:

> Near me a Musulman, civil and mild,
> Watched as the shuttlecocks rose and fell;
> And he said as he counted his beads and smiled,
> "God smite their souls to the depths of hell"

He produced a voluminous historical study, *The Rise and Expansion of the British Dominion in India*, 1894, in which there was pride in achievement, and a comparison with the

Roman Empire (which was a favourite theme of Victorian administrators). However there is also an awareness that time cannot stand still: 'The isolation of India from the winds and currents of European politics must soon cease altogether and finally....Although civilization has hitherto gone forward very slowly in Asia the spread of European power is now clearing the ground for rapid movement upon a very extensive line of advance. Government by a clear and scientific body of laws...is the only real security for the progress and prosperity of a country....The problem was to simplify and generalize the civil law and procedure and to enact large principles of equity and morality with the least possible disturbance of the practices, prejudices, and organic institutions of Indian society'. Just so...change judiciously balanced: 'all wide and uniform measures of reform are hindered by the immense area of the country and especially by the number and diversity of its population; and undoubtedly this is an operation of extraordinary difficulty....Now that the English have accomplished the building up, after the High Roman fashion of an immense polyglot empire, the stability of its structure must depend upon a skilful distribution of weight....it was formerly anticipated too confidently that education would provide a sure antidote...but modern public instruction when introduced suddenly and strenuously by the State acts as a strong irritant on certain classes'.

Unsure of his ground, Lyall quotes from a sceptical contemporary historian, Spencer Walpole, 1839-1907, who wrote in his *History of England:* 'Centuries hence, some philosophic historian...will relate the history of the British in India as a romantic episode which has had no appreciable effect upon the progress of the human family' (vol. V, p.433, 1890). Could Spencer Walpole be right? However, Victorian policy makers moved forward cautiously, or not at all. Dufferin adjured one of his subordinates: 'Feel your way, and when you come against anything hard, draw back'. Lyall observed shortly before his death in 1911 'It is not impossible that the twentieth century may see the complete withdrawal of Europe from Asia'.

An influential Indian newspaper, the *Amrita Bazaar Patrika,* came out with the following estimation of the post-mutiny Viceroys:

> Sir John Lawrence was not so good as his brother Henry, still he was sympathetic. The good intentions of Lord Mayo were neutralized by the formidable Strachey brothers: still, he was the best friend the Indian princes ever had. Lord Northbrook was a very noble Englishman, but with one exception he was the last of the good Viceroys. Lord Lytton who succeeded him came out expressly to make the Afghan War which his predecessor had refused to undertake. Lord Ripon was an angel. Lord Dufferin was sympathetic, but violent. Lord Lansdowne and Lord Elgin brought India to a state of despair. As to Lord Curzon, he first of all restored life and hope by his speeches, but he deceived us later on.

The French author of the work in which this estimation was reproduced added that it would be wrong 'to conclude...that the peoples of India are weary of British administration. The loyalty of the great majority is incontestable' although he added that Curzon, by lack of sympathy, had 'excited feelings of veritable hatred'. This verdict was made by Joseph Chailley after visiting India in 1900-1 and 1904-5.[5] It therefore represents a strictly contemporary view. Why did Curzon attract so much criticism after making a favourable early impression? Surely, it was mainly because he insisted on following his own inclination regardless of opinion.

In examining this estimation we have to recall Curzon's previous apprenticeship to the governance of India.

NOTES

1. Walter Bagehot, *The English Constitution*, 1867 (2nd edition 1872).
2. Only Dalhousie (1847-56) was younger than Curzon on appointment: thirty-five years old.
3. Penderel Moon, *Strangers in India*, 1944, pp. 15-16
4. 'Morley states in his *Recollections* that when the shortlived Liberal administration came into office in 1894 he urged the Prime Minister, Rosebery, to make Lyall the next viceroy. This would have been a departure from accepted practice and Rosebery chose another Scottish peer, Lord Elgin, who proved notably inadequate'.
5. Joseph Chailley, *Administrative Problems of British India*, 1910, pp. 185-6.

CHAPTER 2

CURZON: THE MOST VICEREGAL VICEROY

The reaction of *The Times* published on 11 August 1898 to the announcement that Curzon was going to India was ambivalent, almost supercilious. It was, it stated: 'The choice of a rising statesman who has seldom for the last ten years been out of the public eye, and who is always either speaking or writing...and who when not in office...has worked off his superfluous energy by spending his holidays in the Far East or in Central Asia'. This new post was not to be the crown of his career 'but one more success to add to a long line of successes. He goes as knowing something of India...but some might say that he knows too much and that he must have a great deal to unlearn'.

Queen Victoria's response was less convoluted and more sensible: she urged her Prime Minister to ensure that Curzon would 'shake off Red-Tapeism'. He was known as a man of action. His predecessor, Elgin, who *The Times* called 'a courteous, silent Scottish peer about whom politically nothing was known', had not been a success. He was said never to have proposed any innovation and his time 'was marked by political unrest, frontier disturbances, plague, and famine', as *The Dictionary of National Biography* declared, adding that he had 'proved too weak' for his arduous position. He left a mass of unfinished business for his successor.

Curzon landed in India on 30 December 1898: an immediate impression was made by the radiant beauty of

Mary, his young wife. As an American, with an immensely rich father, she was criticized by the *Burra Memsahibs* of Calcutta. As she said herself she stood for hours 'wearing my india-rubber smile'. In her letters she admitted that she hated India, or rather the British façade of India. She specially disliked Simla: she burst into laughter at her first glimpse of the Viceroy's Lodge, 'quite the most amazing and fantastic erection' she had ever seen, which she compared to the mansion of a Minneapolis millionaire while the 'curtains and furniture reek of Maples': it was an apt comment as Lord Dufferin its builder had ordered its contents from the London firm. She gave Curzon all her love and devotion but she had no way of giving him advice or cautioning him against his criticism of all his staff, while she suffered from intermittent ill health throughout all her Indian years. She did not enjoy being Vicereine.

When Curzon turned his attention to the files he was appalled by the labyrinthine methods of the Government of India. In Calcutta the senior members of Government worked together within a small area; and when they moved to Simla, which was the scene of their labours for seven months of the year, they worked within a few hundred yards of each other, yet they seldom conferred. Even though the telephone was already installed in their offices they preferred to address long minutes to each other. Curzon however was a master of this game, he once wrote a thousand word minute on the employment of European barmaids in the Calcutta hotels. But his minutes were designed to reach a decision, not merely to repeat arguments as were those of his Members of Council. Curzon's comments on this method of government in practice were sardonic and sometimes savage, but the civil servants were well aware that a Viceroy's period of office was limited. Curzon's main weapon against the procrastinators was confined to recommending, and in effect selecting, candidates for the post of Lieutenant-Governor. Nevertheless, Curzon had some success in goading his officials into reaching decisions.

Curzon promptly on arrival in India tackled the largest problem bequeathed by his predecessor: the conflict which had engulfed the whole length of the North West Frontier. This was much greater than the sporadic fighting endemic on the frontier. On Curzon's arrival there were ten thousand regular troops confined to forts and encampments beyond the administered districts. He investigated the scene promptly, deciding that neither the civil nor the military control were effective. Several schemes had been suggested for separating the trans-Indus districts from the Punjab administration and Curzon now proposed that four trans-Indus districts and one cis-Indus district (Hazara) be detached from the Punjab and formed into a separate administrative unit directly under the control of the Viceroy. The regular troops were withdrawn to cantonments in the main Frontier centres (Peshawar, Bannu, Kohat) and the tribal areas were policed by an armed constabulary recruited from the local tribes and armed only with rifles. The theory was that by giving them an occupation they would be less likely to make trouble: the theory worked well enough except in times of acute stress.

Curzon cited the 'ladder of delay' involved in subordination to Punjab and the need to liberate the Frontier from 'the complex paraphernalia' of the Indian judicial system. His scheme was sanctioned by the Council of India in London on 20 December 1900, the Secretary of State signifying 'our unanimous and hearty agreement' with the new arrangement. So far so good.

The next major problem for Curzon to tackle was that of famine. It was not on the same scale as in Elgin's time, but was bad enough for three and a half million persons to be receiving relief. Curzon determined to accelerate long term measures by attending to irrigation. However, when Curzon turned to social engineering the difficulties increased.

Also soon after his arrival on 10 August 1899 Curzon wrote 'I'm keeping my eyes and ears open about these great question of abuse of police power...on which our none too stable system rests—and I may require to take it up seriously and on a wide scale before long' (10th August 1899). Irregularities were not confined to subordinates. When A. P. Pennell, an Irish member of the ICS, acting as District and Sessions Judge of Chapra, uncovered and corrected a bad instance of abuse, he was made to regret stepping out of line. This was the case of Nara Singh, a constable on leave in his own village in Chapra district. The district engineer and the assistant superintendent of police were supervising repairs to an embankment. They ordered the constable to do some work, he refused, and was therefore severely beaten so much so that he had to be admitted to hospital. The civil surgeon discovered severe injuries. A hasty conference took place among the senior officials of the district. Nara Singh was arrested and tried on a trumped up charge before a Muslim deputy magistrate, receiving two months rigorous imprisonment. He appealed and the case came before Mr Pennell, who acquitted Nara Singh and censured the European officials. The Muslim magistrate stated in evidence, 'When cases are disposed of and magistrates do not like it they find fault. And so I settled it beforehand'. Pennell paid for his lack of caution by being transferred to Noakhali, a penal station, in a distant corner of the province. Once again he upset the administration. A man was murdered and it so transpired that his killers were friends of the local police chief, Osman Daroga, who joined in subverting the course of justice. Pennell had the murderer sentenced to death and excoriated all the officials who had been involved in the cover-up. These extended even to the Lieutenant-Governor. All this occurred in February 1901: Pennell found himself suspended and with almost inexplicable impetuosity went off on home leave (he seems to have possessed ample private means). Curzon had no option but to order his dismissal, though doubtless he had only a confused account of the affair. This case puts into perspective his efforts to clean up the working of the law. Soon after the Police Commission was appointed with Sir

Andrew Fraser, recently Chief Commissioner of the Central Provinces as Chairman. They visited all the provinces and examined over six hundred witnesses. Their report was chilling. They reported 'The corruption and inefficiency of the great mass of investigating officers of higher grades'. 'Money is extorted as the investigation proceeds...the station house officer will sometimes hush up a case in payment of his terms'. Police were quartered on recalcitrant villagers for several days but they also sometimes associated with criminals in taking gains: 'The commission have the strongest evidence that the police force is regarded as far from efficient and is stigmatized as corrupt and oppressive'. The Secretary of State refused to allow the report to be published until 1905 and reforms were thus delayed.[1] Curzon's changes came mainly from the top—improvements in pay and training and the creation of an Indian police service on ICS lines. However the police as a whole resisted change. While these big improvements were being carried out, smaller innovations were being introduced. Curzon was appalled at the extent to which the British treated Indians as lesser beings. 'My first duty lies to my constituents and they are the people of India. I would sooner retire from my post, than sacrifice their interests,' he told Godley. (17 December 1903). While he sympathized with the silent masses and encouraged the natural leaders, the princes and the aristocrats, he saw no advantage in encouraging the urban middle class and their vociferous spokesmen, the politicians. He considered the Congress to be a mushroom growth, whose rise had been artificial and whose demise might follow equally suddenly. In a private letter to his friend and colleague, Lord George Hamilton (Secretary of State 1895 to 1903) he wrote that in his view 'The Congress was tottering to its fall'; his ambition was to 'assist it to a peaceful demise' (18 November 1900). This assessment was not so outrageous: the Congress of 1900 had run out of steam. For fifteen years petitions had been offered up and ignored. Only five hundred and thirty eight delegates attended the 1903 Congress.

The ruling race went on its way, trampling on Indian feelings without understanding what they were doing: throwing respected judges out of their compartments on trains, blackballing Indian candidates from their clubs, in general blackguarding the Indian professional classes because they found them 'insolent'—unwilling to accept inferior status.

The most obvious abuse of power by the ruling race was the way in which British soldiers behaved. Ignored by the civilians, they turned on those who came into their clutches: servants, coolies, village folk. Whenever Curzon came upon such cases he took drastic action, in one instance dispatching a regiment to Aden as a punishment station when he could not discover those responsible for misbehaviour. A different kind of mistreatment was the manner in which South African colonies tried to exploit Indian workers. Curzon insisted that if additional Indians were to be recruited proper conditions must be laid down. 'If Colonial Governments appeal to us for aid as parts of the same Empire they should treat our people as fellow citizens.' The India Office objected: the Cabinet believed that 'You individually are placing yourself athwart them at a moment of extreme difficulty'. Godley suggested to Curzon: 'I think we must all agree that the real government of India is in the House of Commons...a Viceroy who cannot conscientiously acquiesce in and carry out the policy of the Cabinet has no choice but to resign.' However, Curzon would not retract, and the Colonial Office accepted that their proposal 'should be allowed to sleep'. There was a Department of Archaeology, but its methods were amateurish. Curzon secured the appointment of a professional Director, (Sir) John Marshall. He was able to employ a number of expert assistants and excavation began on an extensive scale. Curzon was less interested in the ancient sites which Marshall's workers began to reveal than in medieval tombs, forts and mosques which had been allowed to fall into ruin. Through his intervention the Taj Mahal was placed in a suitable setting, Fatehpur Sikri was rescued from the desert, the Pearl Mosque in the Lahore Fort was restored to its old glory, many surfaces being rehabilitated from decades of British whitewash. One of his reconstructions of the past was less popular with Indians though approved by the British residents. An area in central Calcutta between the GPO and the Customs House had been excavated to prepare foundations for new public buildings. This work exposed the remains of the old Fort William including the site of the infamous Black Hole. Curzon caused the site to be paved in black marble and enclosed by a railing. An inscription recorded Curzon's responsibility for the work. On visiting Mandalay, Curzon was appalled to discover that the old royal palace was being used in part as a church and also as a club. He gave orders that they were to surrender these halls of audience to permit them to assume their former appearance. It was perhaps typical of the extent to which officials could thwart the great man simply because he could not check on his instructions after he had departed: the club remained for another forty years. He had to assume that he was obeyed.

Although deploring the expenses of the Viceroy, Curzon was not lacking in hospitality; even when he observed his guests departing after a formal dinner their pockets stuffed with cigars. When the still young Winston Churchill came to stay, Curzon had to rebuke him for the 'diarrhoea of talk' with which he had monopolized conversation at the Viceregal table.

Conversing with an artist, Mortimer Menpes, at the Durbar he 'Talked of the art of the country and of the bad influence that had been brought to bear on it. One felt that he had really studied this subject...He realised as no one else seemed to have done that the art of India was slipping away and that if vigorous measures were not taken...we should live to say that there was no living art in India.'[2] Menpes also noted that 'in proportion to the face Lord Curzon's head is enormous...at the back it seems to have burst out into bulges with intelligence'.

During the early part of his time in India Curzon managed pretty well. Perhaps the turning point was reached with the Delhi Durbar of January 1903, which revealed Curzon at his most omnipotent and his most vulnerable. The Durbar was supposedly in honour of the postponed coronation of Edward VII, but in reality it was to mark Curzon's concept of the Viceregal magnificence. Curzon proposed that the great occasion be marked by a reduction in taxation. The Secretary of State, Hamilton, told him this was unacceptable. Curzon responded by threatening to resign (a tactic he too frequently employed). Under pressure, the Cabinet allowed him to make a vague pronouncement on reducing taxes, although this must not be directly associated with the King's name. Curzon called the Cabinet's ruling 'a first class blunder' and asserted that this had taken all the pleasure out of the Durbar. He did not make life easy for himself or his colleagues.

The Durbar camp was planned to have electric light and a light railway. The total cost was three hundred and sixty thousand pounds. One Congress leader, Lal Mohan Ghosh, called it 'a pompous pageant to a starving population'. Those invited included all the rulers, great and small who would render homage to the representative of the King Emperor. Events would include a tottering march past by Mutiny veterans, Indian and British, a guaranteed tear jerker. But the main part of the programme was a procession of regiments, Indian and British. It was here that the proceedings went wrong. In his effort to enforce better treatment of Indians by the British army, Curzon had disciplined the 9th Lancers, cancelling all leave. When the 9th Lancers entered the Durbar stadium they received a hearty and prolonged cheer from the British spectators. It was an intentional, public humiliation for Curzon.

Curzon's first great clash with Indian opinion came over university education. On his arrival he pronounced that although everything was not well with the Indian universities he 'refused to join himself with those who condemned them altogether'. This faint commendation did not assure the graduates. In September 1901 a private conference of civil servants and university officials was convened at Viceregal Lodge, Simla. Not one Indian was invited. Curzon presided at every session over sixteen days. His inaugural speech was an elaborate survey of the whole system and criticism of its adherence to the former London University model, whereby the university function was limited to supervision: 'It is a body that controls courses of study and sets examination papers'. The conference drafted one hundred and fifty resolutions. The conference was followed by a Commission composed of twelve members of whom two were Indians, the judge of the Calcutta High Court and the Muslim Director of Education, Hyderabad. There was an immediate reaction from the graduates: in Calcutta there were crowded protest meetings and Curzon was 'loudly abused as the author of the doom of higher education'. The Commission visited all university centres and submitted a report. This aroused a nationwide protest. It was hard to suggest that the current state of higher education was satisfactory. There were large numbers of colleges (many being private institutions established for profit). In Bengal alone there were sixty-four colleges. No control was exercised over admission. Matriculates were admitted as young as fifteen; equally some were in their late twenties, fathers of families. The next step was the introduction of a Bill into the imperial legislature. This was bitterly contested by the Indian legislators; only two Indian members of the legislature supported the new measure, one being the distinguished archaeologist, R. G. Bhandarker. The affiliation of new colleges to a university became conditional on attaining a recognized standard. The University Senates were reduced in numbers and members were limited to a tenure of ten years. The professors were to have university appointments.

The effect of Curzon's reforms was mixed; an informed writer observes:

> He left education a battlefield. Too scornful in his reprobation of what seemed to him unworthy, too little concerned to search out and develop what was sound and native to the soil in the systems and practices which he condemned he fell far short of that achievement which might have been his had his temperament enabled him to win the sympathies of the population...Nonetheless he left education invigorated in all its parts.[3]

On his departure Curzon reviewed the changes with the various Directors of Public Instruction, observing 'I do not regret the battle and the storm since I am firmly convinced that out of them has been born a new life for higher education in India'. His hopefulness was not well founded: twelve years later yet another commission headed by Sir Michael Sadler was appointed to carry out yet another review.

Educated Bengal regarded the 1904 Act as directly aimed at one of their own special institutions, just as the 1897 Calcutta Municipal Bill had restricted the powers of the Corporation, stigmatized by the Lieutenant-Governor Sir Alex Mackenzie as 'an armoury of talk and an arsenal of delays'. These wounding attacks on educated Bengal were delivered with no seeming awareness of the consequences. Thus addressing the Convocation of Calcutta University on 11 February 1905 Curzon observed:

> Untruthfulness consists in saying or doing anything that gives an erroneous impression either of one's own character or of other people's conduct...I hope I am making no false or arrogant claim when I say that the highest ideal of truth is to a large extent a western conception ...It undoubtedly took a high place in the moral codes of the West before it had been similarly honoured in the East where craftiness and diplomatic skill have always been held in much repute. We may prove it by the

common innuendo that lurks in the words 'oriental diplomacy' by which is meant something rather tortuous and hyper-subtle...There is one thing which we call in England a 'mare's nest', by which we mean a pure figment of the imagination and something so preposterous as to be unthinkable. Yet there is no country where 'mare's nests' are more prolific than here. Some ridiculous concoction is publicly believed until it is officially denied. ...Immoderate adjectives are flung about as though they had no significance. The writer no doubt did not mean to lie. But the habit of exaggeration has laid such firm hold on him that he is like a man who has taken too much drink.

Curzon's detestation of the Calcutta elite was expressed in a letter to the Secretary of State John Brodrick (7 February 1905):

Calcutta is the centre from which the Congress party is manipulated throughout the whole of Bengal and indeed the whole of India. Its best wirepullers and its most frothy orators all reside there. They dominate public opinion in Calcutta, they affect the High Court, they frighten the local government [the government of Bengal] and they are sometimes not without serious influence upon the Government of India. The whole of their activity is directed to create an agency so powerful that they may one day be able to force a weak government to give them what they desire. Any measure in consequence that would divide the Bengali speaking population: that would permit independent centres of activity and influence to grow up, that would dethrone Calcutta from its place as the centre of successful intrigue or that would weaken the influence of the lawyer class who have the entire organization in their hands is intensely and hotly resented by them (2 February 1905).

Curzon was attempting to avert the storm which it was already obvious would be caused by the redistribution of government in India. His regime was subsequently remembered in India mainly, if not entirely, for the partition of Bengal. The province (at one period extended to the Khyber Pass) and although outlying areas were put under separate administrations (Assam was placed under its own Chief Commissioner in 1874) Bengal under the Lieutenant-Governor's rule in 1900 comprised nearly eighty million people. The province had been placed under the 'Permanent Settlement' of Lord Cornwallis whereby there was only a skeletal administration to collect the fixed revenue. Local control was in the hands of the police who (as we have seen) were agents of repression. Proposals for redistribution were many and various. Eventually Curzon found himself confronted by a complicated proposal after it had been vetted and vetoed by numerous authorities. His response was the celebrated 'round and round' minute:

> Departmentalism is not a moral delinquency; It is an intellectual hiatus—the complete absence of thought or apprehension of anything outside the departmental aspects of the matter. For fourteen months it never occurred to a single human being in the Department to mention the matter or to suggest that it should be mentioned. Round and round like the diurnal revolution of the earth went the file, solemn, sure and slow: and now in due season it has completed its orbit and I am invited to register the concluding stage (Minute of 26 May 1902).

Various proposals for redrawing Bengal's boundaries had been suggested since the 1860s. The scheme published in 1903 would have created a greater Assam, with the addition of the districts of Chittagong, Dacca and Mymensingh together with the state of Tripura. The greater part of Chota Nagpur would have gone to CP. Sambalpur district would have been added to Bengal while Ganjam district would have been detached from Madras and given to Bengal. This scheme met with widespread public opposition (three hundred protest meetings were held in January 1904) and was dropped. In its place was substituted the scheme known as the partition of Bengal, announced in July 1905 and put into effect in October.

The Western part of the old province retained the name Bengal, and had its capital at Calcutta, the former Lieutenant Governor of undivided Bengal continued as its head. The Eastern portion, amalgamated with Assam, became Eastern Bengal and Assam with Dacca as its capital. The new province included the Dacca, Chittagong, and Rajshahi divisions, the district of Malda and the state of Tripura: it had an area of 112,000 square miles and a population of thirty-one million, of whom all except six million were Bengalis. The first Lieutenant-Governor Bampfylde Fuller had been the chief Commissioner of Assam. Bengal (West Bengal) included Bihar, Orissa, and small portions of CP. This province had an area of 149,000 square miles and a population of fifty-five million of whom thirty million were Bengalis.

The first proposal had been resisted by all the Bengali leaders, Hindus and Muslims. The partition in its final form was even more obnoxious to the Hindus though agreeable to the Muslim leadership. Many of the zamindars (perhaps most) in East Bengal were Hindu owners of vast estates and mainly non-resident. The bulk of the Tagore estates were in Pabna district, now allotted to the East. Curzon carried out a personal investigation of conditions in East Bengal; while in Dacca he made a direct bid to the Muslim elite: they would have 'preponderant voice'. He was convinced that he had demonstrated the soundness of the proposed changes. He wrote to his wife (then in England): 'My speeches seem simply to have dumbfounded the opponents. The native papers are knocked silly and are left gasping for I showed that all the wild things that they said would ensue are pure fabrications' (22 February 1904).

Curzon may have had administrative considerations mainly in view, but he was also conscious of the political advantages: in a Minute of 1 June 1903 he wrote of 'the advantages of severing these Eastern districts of Bengal which are a hotbed of the purely Bengali movement, unfriendly if not seditious in character and dominating the whole tone of Bengal administration'. Although the whole question was under debate from mid 1903, the formal announcement was not made until 20 July 1905. The Bengali response was vociferous, but not until Curzon had departed did effective demonstrations begin, commencing on 16 October 1905, the day that the partition took effect.

Thus far we have examined the internal effects of Curzon's period in India. But he had arrived as an expert on the regions beyond British control and he remained determined to ensure that none of these areas fell under the influence of the other great powers: with Russia as the principal danger, though the onset of the war with Japan exposed the weakness of the Empire of the Tsar at its furthest extremities.

Curzon's first external excursion was to bring Afghanistan back into line. Regarded as a British Protectorate, Afghanistan had never accepted this situation. The Amir, Abdur Rahman had skilfully walked a tightrope between accepting the British and upsetting them. He died in 1901, and it was anticipated that his successor Habibullah would be more amenable. However, he proved as adroit as his father. Not until 1904 was he persuaded to parley—and then on his own home ground. The treaty signed on 21 March 1905 was virtually a replica of the former document. Curzon was infuriated: 'I should have resigned over this' he told Lord Ampthill, the Governor of Madras (2 April 1905) but he recognized that would not be supported in London. Afghanistan was allowed to retain its semi-independent status.

Persia, so carefully observed by the younger Curzon was the next target. Northern Persia was recognized as within the Russian orbit but Southern Persia was part of the British sphere of influence. It was also about to acquire real importance with its largely unexploited oilfields. Lansdowne, now Foreign Secretary was determined to exclude Russia from the Gulf: supposedly Russia was in search of warm water ports—a figment of the British Foreign Office imagination—into the 1970s and 80s.

Curzon was not altogether and in all circumstances an expansionist. He came under pressure from the Chambers of Commerce—Rangoon, Glasgow and others—to press forward from North Bengal into Yunan, by constructing a railway that would, allegedly, open the potential wealth of China to the British Market. The French had swallowed this temptation and constructed a railway from Hanoi into Yunan. It was always a drain on French resources. Curzon had more common sense: he called the idea 'fanciful political ambition', 'a wild and dangerous hallucination', finally dismissed as 'Midsummer madness'. The India Office more immediately under commercial pressure, was dismayed by this un-Curzonian response.

The Foreign Secretary, Lord Lansdowne, issued a declaration that no naval base would be permitted on the Gulf, and this apparently satisfied Curzon. With most of the Gulf Sheikhs Britain had relations similar to those with the Indian rulers but Curzon felt that these were threatened by other European powers, especially Russia. There was a British resident at Bushire, the most central of these petty states with supervisory powers over the remaining sheikhdoms. Consequently in 1903 he paid a state visit to Muscat, Bahrain and Kuwait. He was accompanied by an impressive naval force but nothing much was achieved: this was 'showing the flag' in the grand manner. Of much more substantial significance was the Younghusband expedition into Tibet. This had remained a closed country to all Europeans though once again Russia and British India eyed each other suspiciously over this almost empty land, nominally under the Chinese suzerainty according to European political ideas. A Chinese official was the resident Ambassador, the Amban. This situation was hardly disturbed by the arrival of Dorjiev, a Buriat Mongol from Baikal in 1880 to attain higher knowledge of Buddhist philosophy. In 1898 he went on a journey to Russia and was loaded with presents for the Dalai Lama. In 1901 Dorjiev paid a much publicized visit to St Petersburg. Curzon decided that this required a counterstroke. In January 1903 he sent a Despatch to London calling for a British mission to Lhasa to regulate diplomatic and commercial relations. With reluctance the British Government consented to a move to meet with Tibetan officials just over the border from Sikkim. A senior monk official arrived, after some delay, with the request that Younghusband's party should withdraw. The months passed: London at last reluctantly agreed to Younghusband proceeding further to Gyantse. The first mission had an escort of two hundred sepoys; this was now increased to three thousand soldiers with seven thousand followers, commanded by a Brigadier-General. By January 1904 they were ready to advance: the Tibetans had built a wall as an indication of how far the British might go. The wall was broken open, a fracas developed, and some three hundred Tibetans were killed and the same number wounded. The British went on to Gyantse, but negotiations did not follow, merely another noisy dispute, and the advance continued to Lhasa where an engagement left three hundred Tibetans dead.

They found that the Dalai Lama, accompanied by Dorjiev had departed but there was an abbot, the Tri Rimpoche who was prepared to negotiate. A convention was signed in September 1904 and the British withdrew. The convention provided for payment of a huge indemnity to cover the cost of the expedition amounting to more than half a million pounds to be spread over seventy-five years: during which period the British would occupy the Chumbi valley, between Sikkim and Bhutan, the main trade route between North East India and Lhasa. These terms were too steep even for the Government of India, and the indemnity was reduced to a third of the agreed total and occupation of the Chumbi Valley was limited to three years.

This reduction was due in good part to Curzon's departure from India on leave. In July 1902 the waspish Balfour had assumed the premiership from his aged uncle. Balfour was one of Curzon's special set, the 'Souls', yet he was in his own way as aloof as his Viceregal friend. Curzon hastened to offer congratulations and at first all seemed well, yet overshadowing their relationship was the question of what would happen when Curzon's Viceroyalty came to an end. He must, surely, be offered a senior Cabinet post and would be a dominant influence in the Cabinet room. The alternative was to prolong his time in India. This he was invited to do, and meanwhile he returned to England on home leave in April 1904.

In December 1902 Kitchener had arrived in India as Commander-in-Chief, being expressly desired by Curzon. He was fresh from his final (if somewhat delayed) victory in South Africa. He had never previously served in India and was accustomed to supreme command. The relations between the Viceroy *(Lat Sahib)* and Commander-in-Chief (*Jangi Lat*, or Lord of War) were somewhat confused in the Indian mind, though constitutionally there was no question. The Viceroy as Governor-General in Council was supreme. His Council included a military member (a General) though the Commander-in-Chief was always included as an additional member. Accustomed to sole authority, Kitchener was dead against the Military Member who exercised no operational function but provided the link between Government of India and the military. Kitchener immediately objected to this 'dual system', as he saw it: Curzon came to its defence as emphasizing the supremacy of the Viceroy and the civil arm. Kitchener was not to be deflected: he at once began to persuade his influential friends in England that he must be the sole and supreme military authority. His allies included the most powerful in the land, especially at Buckingham Palace and Hatfield House.

Soon after Curzon reached London he attended a meeting of the new Committee of Imperial Defence. He was astonished to discover that the agenda included an item put up by Kitchener proposing the abolition of the Military Member and the transfer of his functions to the

Commander-in-Chief. Curzon insisted that this item be deferred.

Curzon fought the battle against Kitchener at long range throughout his time in England. He made no headway, and on his departure to India in November those who bade him farewell noted that he was silent and grave. The Cabinet remained unmoved: Kitchener had enormous popularity with ordinary people, although his relations with colleagues were sometimes strained: Curzon had no support among politicians, the press or the people. Regardless of the merits of the case he had no chance of winning. After Curzon returned to India the whole question came to a head. Curzon in his despatch to the Secretary of State laid weight on the long accepted supremacy of the civil over the military and the need for means to assess advice from the Commander-in-Chief. His Council unanimously endorsed his view. However, Kitchener was still calling on his influential supporters in England: he told Lady Salisbury that in discussing the whole question Curzon had collapsed in tears. Curzon rashly suggested to Brodrick, 'I often wonder if your advisers at the India Office desire secretly to drive me to resign, and I have been many times pondering...whether you also contemplate this as a result of one and a half years of our co-operation. If so, I do not think it will be very difficult to attain that end.' (2 March 1905).

Like other politicians, before and after, Curzon overplayed the resignation threat. He was not indispensable. In a despatch dated 31 May 1905 Brodrick informed the Viceroy that the Cabinet had come down on the side of Kitchener. Curzon categorized Balfour's despatch as 'censorious, immoderate, spiteful and deplorably ill-advised'. These were not the words calculated to advance his case.

The merits of the existing system or of giving the Commander-in-Chief sole responsibility were considered by the Viceroy's Council. It was brought up in the context of a Despatch from Brodrick on the need for the Indian Army to be better prepared for war. The Members of the Council unanimously dissented from Kitchener's proposals: 'Contrary to all expectations Lord Kitchener made no attempt to reply...He sat brooding and silent, except for a brief statement which he read from a paper regretting that he was in a minority of one...At his best in action he was at his worst in discussion'.[4] As Secretary of State for War in 1914 he carried on in exactly the same way, staying silent and then obstinately proceeding with his own plan. Lord Esher observed: 'He would seem to be thinking aloud...[those] who sat round him could make nothing of it or him'. A Despatch was sent from Calcutta on 10 March in which every member of the Council recorded his reasons for disagreeing with Kitchener, who appended a brief note of dissent: 'My assertions have been contradicted but not I think disapproved'.

The whole matter was raised in the House of Lords by the now aged Lord Ripon who declared that Kitchener's reply to the criticism 'was no reply at all'. However, Kitchener did forward a lengthy defence to London without letting his colleagues know. Brodrick convened a meeting which came up with 'a genuine solution' to the problem which would 'stand any amount of hammering' (31 May 1905). Lords Roberts and Lansdowne were present at the London Meeting, but disavowed the compromise, which would create a Military Supply Member in place of the Military Member. The last straw for Curzon was the information that the new Supply Member would be nominated from London.

His objections were overriden. Not until August did Curzon resign. When this was announced (21 August) in London it was simultaneously revealed that Curzon's successor would be Lord Minto. Clearly, the Cabinet were prepared for the final act.

Curzon was induced to delay his departure further by King Edward until after the visit of the heir to the throne, the future King George and his consort. The first proposal was that Curzon should receive the royal party as a private individual, and Curzon's former Private Secretary, Sir Walter Lawrence told the King's Private Secretary that this might produce 'the public breakdown of Lord Curzon. He is ill and sometimes cannot control his feelings and a scene might be very painful to their Royal Highnesses'. Minto agreed to postpone his departure from England.

When Curzon disembarked at Charing Cross Station not one single member of the Cabinet was there to greet him as was the invariable custom. It was true that Balfour was in the process of handing over to his Liberal successor, Campbell-Bannerman, but that did not explain the absence of all his colleagues. It was a shabby performance by a government supposedly of gentlemen.

However, Curzon had succeeded in alienating all his old friends, who indeed were in some disarray. He came back to public indifference and private grief. His beloved wife had never found the Indian climate agreeable; nevertheless she had bravely accompanied him on the return from home leave. She died on 18 July 1906.

For Curzon there were now barren years ahead. His only consolation was his election as Chancellor of Oxford University, but that hardly provided an occupation. He continued with his labour of love, the restoration of historic buildings, Bodiam Castle in Sussex and Montacute House in Somerset. After he entered the House of Lords he intervened twice in significant fashion to persuade his own ranks to accept measures they had vowed to oppose to the death. In 1911 he persuaded sufficient Tory peers to abstain to allow the Parliament Act through the House of Lords. Subsequently, although vehemently opposed to women's suffrage he persuaded the Tory peers to allow through the Suffrage Act of 1918. Mrs Humphrey Ward, a leading opponent of votes for women, recorded in her diary: 'We have been betrayed by our leader Lord Curzon. Coward!' She had misunderstood the convoluted mind of the great pro consul. Henry Dodwell joined the Education Service in

Madras during Curzon's tenure. Writing in the early 1930s while the controversy over the impending Government of India Bill was in full flow, he defended Curzon's aims while accepting that his policies had 'indirect and unexpected tendencies': his measures 'were timed unluckily rather than in themselves ill considered'. His actions 'intensely annoyed the educated classes who claimed that this tutelage was out of date and who were eager to grasp authority in their own hands. To this extent he certainly exasperated the Congress and facilitated the extension of extremist influence'.[5]

NOTES

1. *Report of the Indian Police Commission,* Cmd 2478, 1905.
2. Mortimer Menpes *Durbar,* 1903. Menpes also noted, 'in proportion to the face Lord Curzon's head is enormous...At the back it seems to have burst out into bulges with intelligence'. (p. 187).
3. J. R. Cunningham in *Modern India and the West* (1941).
4. Lord Ronaldshay, *The Life of Lord Curzon* 1928, Vol. II pp. 377-8.
5. H. Dodwell, *Cambridge Shorter History of India,* 1934, pp. 872-3.

CHAPTER 3

MINTO: REPRESSION AND CONCILIATION

When Curzon resigned, three years before the expected date, the prompt selection of his successor had to be made within very narrow limits. Balfour was facing internal party controversy, especially from Joseph Chamberlain. It was convenient that the Earl of Minto, recently returned from a highly successful period as Governor-General of Canada (1898—1904) was available. On the eve of departing in 1898 Curzon and Minto were given a joint farewell dinner by their Eton friends. Minto a former regular soldier fought in several colonial wars, serving under Roberts in Afghanistan. An outstanding rider, winner of the Grand National he was regarded as an agreeable lightweight: 'We have had elderly men as Viceroy' commented Ampthill (Minto was sixty), 'but we have never had an elderly man that was neither brilliant nor hardworking' (Ampthill to Godley 17 October 1905). However, after Curzon India needed a period to recover and Minto seemed to be just the man to carry this out. General Barrow (favoured by the departing Viceroy as Military Member) wrote to Curzon: 'K [Kitchener] and the secretaries run the government, Lady Minto runs the patronage and HE runs the stables'. This derogatory assessment was not altogether unfair. Lady Minto was equipped with brains and in the years to come sprang to the defence of her husband with considerable authority. She was appointed Lady of the Bedchamber to Queen Mary and perhaps more surprisingly a member of the committee convened in 1917 to advise on the new capital and especially on the Viceroy's house—she was the only woman included. In one of his earliest letters from India he wrote 'It takes a very short time in this country to realize how much may be done by a sympathetic appreciation' (3 January 1906). This was written to the new Secretary of State, John Morley, who took over the India Office perhaps not altogether with eager zest. He had given many years to the question of Irish Home Rule, but he felt little empathy for India. Greeting Winston Churchill on the eve of the election which was to give the Liberals their greatest majority he was despondent: 'Here I am in a gilded pagoda,' he observed of the 'highly ornamental circular room' which was his office. While the new Viceroy was sixty, Morley was sixty-seven although still very active. He was one of the most prolific writers of his age, and when he was not composing for publication he was immersed in correspondence with public and private persons. Reserved in personal relations he sparkled on paper.

Morley was no longer a radical though he had recently been a leading opponent of Britain's policy in South Africa. He was aware that he lacked his former resilience. Despite his lack of enthusiasm for his new office he informed Campbell-Bannerman that he would only speak for the government on his own portfolio: 'You sent me to the Ganges and Brahmaputra and I stick to the business of my department' (20 June 1907). Morley frequently indicated his desire to relinquish office, informing Minto of his feelings. Lady Minto felt this might not be undesirable: The Government of India might 'fare very much worse if we have the engaging Winston in the big chair at the India Office'.[1] The idea of Churchill as the Secretary of State for India in the context of reform seems somewhat piquant.

Henry Dodwell found Morley's appointment: 'One of those accidents which characterizes the working of responsible government. He possessed no specific fitness for the office. He never studied Indian affairs...[he had] a deserved reputation for incisive speech and a character for greater honesty than is usual among politicians. His intellect, however, was narrowly doctrinaire...he suffered therefore from all the disabilities which afflict the intelligentsia...He exaggerated the importance of the spoken and written word. He was essentially a critic and a better critic of books and speeches than of action and politics.' Minto by contrast was considered well fitted to be Viceroy: 'He had managed landed estates. he loved fair play with all the earnestness of a true sportsman and would no more have done a dirty thing than he would have shot a bird sitting or pulled his horse in a steeple chase'. Not altogether the assessment that might have been expected from the Professor of the History and Culture of the British Dominions in Asia![2]

Both Minto and Morley had to bear with the consequences of Curzon's policies especially in regard to Bengal. Sir Andrew Fraser, previously Chief Commissioner of CP and Chairman of the Police Commission continued to govern the Western Province; Eastern Bengal and Assam came under Sir Bampfylde Fuller, previously Chief Commissioner of Assam, an excitable Irishman. The new arrangement was promptly challenged by the Bengali intellectuals, mainly if not exclusively Hindu. Their campaign was launched with a mass demonstration on 16 October 1905, the day that partition went into effect. It was observed in Calcutta and elsewhere as a day of mourning. Most went barefoot and fasted.

A ceremony called Rakhi Bandan was observed: yellow threads were bound round the arms of the demonstrators as a symbol of brotherhood and a solemn vow was taken to fight the partition, the principal weapon being a boycott of British goods, especially cloth. Swadeshi, the name of the movement, had a dual object: to damage British industry and to promote Indian manufacture. Markets were picketed to prevent sales of imported cloth and bonfires were made of bales impounded. As many of the cloth traders were Muslims a communal tone entered the controversy. Moreover the slogan of the movement, *Bande Mataram*,

Hail to the Mother, taken from a novel by Bankim Chandra Chatterji, was also Hindu in sentiment. Among the Swadeshi leaders few were Muslims though Ghulam Rasul of Barisal was certainly one. In East Bengal, Fuller issued instructions that it would be illegal to shout *'Bande Mataram'* in public and a number of students were arrested. The leaders of the Swaraj campaign were militants, now assuming the leadership of the Nationalist Movement.

They were Bengalis to a man: Aurobindo Ghosh, Bipin Chandra Pal, Satish Chandra Chatterjee, Aswini Kumar Dutta. Dutta was the principal organizer of the student 'Volunteers' who picketed the shops; Aurobindo was the editor of *Yugantar* ('New Era'), advocating methods of violence (partly modelled on Sinn Fein beginning to challenge the constitutional Irish Nationalists). *Yugantar* argued that the mutiny of 1857 was the first Indian war of independence. S. N. Banerjea while fighting partition had condemned 'rowdyism' but he saw his leadership slipping away. He decided to directly challenge the government at the Bengal Provincial Conference to be convened at Barisal. He would be the main speaker. On his way to the meeting Banerjea was arrested by order of the District Magistrate, Emerson. He was taken to Emerson's bungalow, tried and fined. The response of the Conference was to shout Bande Mataram repeatedly, but no further action followed. The Barisal affair could not be directly attributed to Fuller though Morley fulminated that 'the British Raj must be a sorry affair if it trembles before a pack of unruly collegians' (to Minto, 25 April 1906). The Lieutenant-Governor went further when he personally called for the disaffiliation of two schools in Serajganj, thus cutting off the pupils from progressing to higher education. The Viceroy told Fuller to withdraw his instructions. Fuller objected and rashly asked 'these orders may be reconsidered, or that if I am to give effect to them my resignation may be accepted' (Fuller to Minto, 15 July 1905). His offer was promptly accepted and

Sir Lancelot Hare took his place. British officialdom was not pleased.

As in Ireland, British policy consisted in alternating repression and conciliation. The Indian response became increasingly strident. An attempt was made to sabotage the train carrying Fraser and students called on Banerjea declaring that they would kill Fuller. Militancy was not found only in Bengal, Tilak had long urged the people of Poona to rise up and his influence spread first to Maharashtra and then to India as a whole. Not until 1908 was he arrested and exiled to Mandalay. In Punjab the Arya Samaj developed a militant wing which was led by Lala Lajpat Rai and Ajit Singh, lawyers. Both were packed off to Mandalay (in May and June 1907). It appeared as though constitutional agitation was a dead end.

The older Moderates were still running the Congress, but increasingly under challenge. They had one younger champion, Gokhale. He proclaimed the goal of the Congress as 'self-government within the Empire'. This policy was derided by the militants who declared 'The management of the Congress must be wrested from the hands of the demi-*feringhis* (foreigners). The Moderates managed to retain control of the Congress leadership. In 1906 they persuaded the Grand Old Man of Indian nationalism, Dadabhai Naoroji to assume the presidency (thus forestalling Tilak). Naoroji proclaimed the goal as 'self-government or Swaraj'. This was the first occasion on which this goal was announced. However, the militants worked hard to take control the next year, affirming the boycott challenge and defining its technique to be 'passive resistance' or 'non-aggressive active resistance'. All this was coming about while Gandhi in South Africa was tackling white rule on identical lines, but there is no real evidence that the Bengal militants were influenced by his example. As the leadership came under the challenge of the younger men, the British Government tried to outflank them by offering boons to the Moderates. Morley cultivated Gokhale, the leader most sympathetic to his own political philosophy. Minto responded to the overtures of certain Muslim leaders who might be helpful under the prevailing difficulties.

The fiftieth anniversary of the outbreak of the Mutiny seemed to most Englishmen in India to be a very inauspicious anniversary (the outbreak of 1857 was supposed to be a response to the overthrow of the independent Muslim leadership in Bengal in 1757). There was a protracted correspondence in the Anglo-Indian newspapers, particularly in the *Civil and Military Gazette* of Lahore. One writer declared: 'I wish to lay special emphasis upon the words "subject race" for the native of India'. The writer argued that Indians should not be appointed to government posts with a salary of more than sixty rupees a month. The correspondence flowed on for weeks until the courageous missionary 'Pennell of the Frontier' weighed in with a severe rebuke condemning the 'arrogant spirit of the vae victis', 'the time has gone by when natives can be hectored into submission'. A policy of mediation would attract some support.

However, on the British side there was the conviction that the Empire would last, if not for ever, at any rate for a century or more. All this despite the defeat of Russia by Japan, (but then Russia was backward, its people under an effete autocracy—its defeat was not all that surprising). The neo-Darwinian view of the White races that the White races were hundreds of years in advance of their brown and black wards prevailed. Hence the empathy which Morley felt for the Irish and the Boers could not translate to India. His comments on Indians were frequently racist as of course were those of Minto, who favoured Sinha as member of the Viceroy's Council because he was 'comparatively white whilst Mookerjee [a distinguished judge and Vice-Chancellor of Calcutta University] is as black as my hat'. The notion that India might be safely left to itself was rejected by Liberals of the most advanced school. Lord Bryce, the exponent of democracy in Australia and America observed that if Britain were to leave India 'Its political unity which depends entirely on the British Raj would vanish like a morning mist....To India severance from England would mean confusion, bloodshed, pillage'.[3] This still left the problem of placating the Indian centre and repulsing the militants.

The first step forward was provided by the visit of Gokhale to England from May to August 1906. Morley welcomed him, both to the office and to his home, and they had six meetings together and developed good personal relations. This was despite the efforts of Godley, Lee-Warner (a leading member of the Council of India) and others to denigrate Gokhale. Gokhale told a friend, 'My principal work has now resolved itself into a kind of tug of war between the officials of the Indian Council and myself as to whose views will prevail with Mr Morley'. Morley felt himself to be in the middle: he told Lord Lamington (Governor of Bombay): 'We are obliged to make a move in a liberalizing direction....The risks are pretty plain....The cauldron which is simmering may begin to boil' (24 August 1906).

Morley told the Viceroy of this development (15 June 1906): 'Gokhale came for another interview. Though I don't know that he advances matters much it brings what we call Indian "problems" more vividly before us—a great advantage to a minister groping his way in dark places!...I wonder whether we could not now make a good start in the way of reforming in the popular direction'. He then made a number of suggestions, very tentatively, adding 'Either you write me a despatch, or I'll write you one—by way of opening the ball'. Minto responded by suggesting 'the possibility of a native gentlemen on my Council; he wanted one 'generally looked up to...with a stake in the country [not]...anyone of the purely Gokhale type'. He concluded that the best course would be to begin at the bottom, i.e. by expanding the members of District Councils and Municipalities. There has been much debate about who originated the reforms: Viceroy or Secretary of State. It might be suggested that neither man really pushed for reform: it just happened, as with so many developments in British India. Having fired their opening shots, the two long-range duellists lapsed into silence. In India a small committee was appointed. Morley seems to have assumed that it was up to the Viceroy to make the next move. Minto wired London that a formal despatch could not be prepared before May 1907. Morley wrote: 'I have been studiously considerate of your difficulties....Time is one thing and eternity is another'. There was pressure from some of the more progressive senior officials. Harcourt Butler was to be governor four times (1915-27). At this period he was foreign secretary to the Government of India. He advised the Viceroy's Private Secretary: 'Moderation does not last under the Indian sun. If the Government does not draw them [the Moderates] to itself the Moderates will turn to the Extremists and the pressure of racial feeling will hurry them on their way'. Perhaps stung by this prodding, Minto announced in the Imperial Legislative Council in March that he had addressed the Secretary of State regarding a liberal measure of reform. This despatch dated 21 March 1907 concentrated on the situation of the Muslims and mainly reproduced the recommendations of the small committee presided over by Sir Arundel which had reported in October 1905. They had considered setting up an Advisory Council of Princes, the appointment of an Indian member of the Viceroy's Executive Council, and increased representation on the Legislatures. On the Indian member they could not agree; on the expanded legislatures they suggested separate electorates for Muslims.

The next move was the time honoured ploy of consulting provincial governments, then the Council of India in London had its say. They applauded the idea of a Council of Princes, but otherwise preferred things as they were. The only friend of reform in the Council was Sir Alfred Lyall.

At the end of this long process Morley sat down to write his reply to Minto. He was unhappy with his despatch 'a wretched sort of affair' he confessed to the Viceroy. He felt it spoke 'with two voices' (an echo of Wordsworth?).

Morley's despatch of 17 May 1907 scouted the notion of aristocratic advisory councils, but also minimized the prospect now opened up: the goal was simply 'to improve existing machinery'. The main element was the expansion of the Indian Legislative Councils. The whole approach was reminiscent of parliamentary reforms in Britain in the nineteenth century: a step-by-step development of the existing structure from something like oligarchy to something like democracy. Not until 1 October 1908 did the Government of India submit their response which was an attempt to persuade London to restrict the reform element further. Morley replied irritably 'India can't wait'. When the final draft was presented to the Council in London Lee-Warner and James Thomson (formerly Acting Governor of Madras) dissented. Morley went ahead and introduced his Bill in the House of Lords in December 1908. He repudiated (almost passionately, as Curzon observed) the intention of setting up a parliamentary system for India: 'If it could be said that this chapter of reforms led directly or necessarily up to the establishment of a parliamentary system in India, I, for one, would have nothing to do with it'. As there was a built in Conservative majority in the Lords, doubtless this disclaimer was essential if the Bill was to pass. Among the Council of India was MacDonnell, former Lieutenant-Governor of the North West Frontier Provinces and subsequently Permanent Under Secretary for Ireland (1902-8). He was created a baron in 1908, and hence was directly able to challenge his own Secretary of State. He was instrumental in getting rid of proposals to set up executive councils in the provinces outside those already existing: Morley acknowledged these were 'good sound bureaucratic arguments but it was the bureaucratic system they were going to make a breach in'.

On 11 March 1909 the Bill passed its third reading in the Lords with the Prince of Wales present. In the Commons it passed without difficulty through an almost empty house

(Morley counted fourteen members on the Government benches and eight on the opposite side). He recorded the royal assent on 25 May 1909. Its effect was to increase the 'additional' non-official members of the Imperial Legislative Council from sixteen to sixty, while in the legislature of Bengal the number of elected members went up from thirty-nine to one hundred and thirty-five. The UP and Bombay Councils included twenty one elected members out of a total of forty-eight and forty-nine respectively; in the Punjab Council of twenty-four members only five were elected; the Burma Legislature consisted of seventeen members: one was elected (by the Burma Chamber of Commerce, a European organization). The 'elected members' were all chosen by 'colleges': by groups of municipalities and district boards, by universities, and most contentious in the future—by separate Muslim constituencies. This innovation was even accepted by Gokhale and his associates without challenge. Gokhale told the Imperial Legislative Council in a speech of 29 March 1909: 'It has been urged by some of my countrymen that any special treatment of minorities militates against the idea of the union of all communities in public matters. Such union is no doubt the goal to which we strive but it cannot be denied that it does not exist in the country today'. Neither could the Liberal Party—more vulnerable to the pressure from the right than when they had come in—ignore their problems. As Morley told Minto (30 April 1908): 'The huge majority of two years ago, the result of a sweeping movement of public opinion against Balfour and his manoeuvres gave us a position...which we could not possibly expect to keep up'. Because of the slothful procedures of the Government of India, the Liberals had wasted the first three years during which their political dominance was complete. Morley felt compelled to compromise in the final phase of his tenure. Going back to the Lords, in retrospect the response of the Conservative opponents seems absurdly exaggerated. Lansdowne, the former Viceroy complained that the Bill 'was not a step forward but a plunge forward and a plunge which will lead us we cannot tell where'. To Curzon the enlargement of the Councils was a 'revolutionary change'. And yet, the Bill had only limited intentions; even if it did open the direction to all that was to follow.

From the expansion of the Legislative Councils, minds turned to the question of appointing Indians to the Executive Councils of the Secretary of State and Governor-General. This issue seemed important to British minds, though the Indian politicians saw it for what it was—tokenism. Controversy was most heated over an Indian member of the Viceroy's Council. Minto dismissed the name of the most obvious candidate, Gokhale, without any thought: 'he was the last sort of man we want'. Kitchener led the opposition to any Indian member. There was a fear that secrets would be divulged; there was, of course, the problem that the Muslims would resent a Hindu appointment and vice versa; there was the seldom mentioned but much resented fact that the introduction of an Indian must entail the exclusion of a British official member (this fear was averted by creating a new portfolio on the Council so that no Englishman would suffer). The Law Member had always been appointed from the ranks of the lawyers since the time of Macaulay, the first Law Member, and it was this office which was given priority. There was no lack of qualified candidates. Ashushtosh Mukherjee was a respected judge, currently Vice-Chancellor of Calcutta University where he had shown his strength of character when he warned the university convocation: 'The most strenuous efforts must be made...to protect our youths from the hands of irresponsible men who recklessly seek to seduce our students...and to plant in their immature minds the poisonous seeds of hatred against constituted government'. However, he had a disqualification which Minto found insuperable: 'Mookerjee is as black as my hat'. The choice went to Sinha, a member of the progressive Brahmo sect and Advocate General of Bengal since 1905: he was 'comparatively white' (Minto to

Morley, 9 November 1908). The appointment had to be formally agreed by King Edward VII, who strongly objected, though he had to accept the appointment. Morley reminded the King that Queen Victoria had made a 'famous promise' that race and colour should be no bar to office in India. The King minuted: 'Why he should bring in the name of Queen Victoria I cannot see, nor how it bears on the question....I have had to sign the objectionable paper' (20 March 1909). Morley also announced that he would make an appointment to his own Council, and at once brought up Gokhale's name. Minto dissented strongly: 'I could not trust him...I am very suspicious of the wires by which he is worked'.

After all this fuss, Sinha was only a few months in office before he asked to resign. His wife disliked Simla and he complained that he was not given enough to do. He reported: 'No self-respecting man can remain here now that he sees the Government of India from inside'.[4]

Equally unfortunate was Morley's appointment of an Indian to his own Council. S. H. Bilgrami, brought in to 'balance' the Hindu Sinha, found the English climate inclement (or such was his pretext). He went home. This aspect of the reforms was important only as demonstrating to British officials how unimportant Indians considered access to their deliberations really was.

One last element in the reform process was the appointment of a Decentralization Commission with the Parliamentary Under Secretary as Chairman and five members, one being R. C. Dutt. Its brief was to consider how far administration could be devolved from Simla to the lower levels of power, right down to the district councils and perhaps to panchayats or 'village councils'. These subordinate bodies should endow the non-official members with much greater power. The Report of the Commission was not ready until after Morley was immersed in his reforms. The evidence given by Indian witnesses was illuminating. Gokhale was predictably positive and forward looking:

> We want an interest in the administration around us. The educated classes are only critics of the administration today because the Government does not realize the wisdom of enlisting their cooperation....The problem of bringing the administration into closer relation with the people is essentially a problem of associating the educated classes with the actual work of the administration. With village panchayats at the bottom, District Councils in the centre and reformed Legislative Councils at the top this problem will have been fairly faced.

It was more surprising that Tilak, about to be prosecuted for sedition was still interested in the potentialities of devolution:

> The only way to restore good relations between officers and the people is to create by law the necessity for consulting the people...we must begin with the village system...it should be the aim of the British administration to educate the people in the management of their own affairs.

Besides these contributions from the leading politicians there were many insights into the extent to which the grip of officialdom reached down into the most petty affairs of local government, the Commissioner of Lucknow said:

> I have been at a meeting where the only business has consisted in the formal reading through and passing of twenty resolutions: and the members have complained that they have been brought forty or fifty miles for that simple purpose.

All this revealed how far there was to go before Indians had any genuine measure of responsibility for their own affairs. The gap between British ideas of what was needed to satisfy Indian demands and their actual aspirations was vast. A pattern had been established: after strenuous efforts by Indians, the British accepted the need for a constitutional advance: but the offer was so far short of Indian demands that the satisfaction given was temporary in the extreme. No sooner had the British settled back, imagining that there would be no more protests, than Indian political aspirations soared again. Instead of satisfying the demand British policy only encouraged further and more peremptory claims.

Although nobody recognized that India was at the parting of the ways in the years before the Great War, this was the time when a substantial transfer of power could have succeeded in satisfying Indian political opinion. Those leading the political movement were thoroughly imbued with British constitutional ideas. If a Governor-General and Commander-in-Chief had remained to safeguard the essential interests of Britain, all the rest could have been transferred to the politicians; to Gokhale and to S. N. Banerjea, and the younger men coming forward: Jinnah, R. P. Paranjpye, C. Y. Chintamani, Motilal Nehru and Gandhi. But of course any such suggestion would have been thought of as a 'midsummer madness' by all but a tiny fraction of the British people.

The Congress went through violent convulsions between 1906 and 1908: the 'Extremists' quit in 1907 and the 'Moderates' reconstituted the organization on the lines accepted before 1900. The twenty-fourth Meeting of the Congress in December 1908 took place immediately after the announcement of the forthcoming reforms, and gave them some reason for hope. The President made the following pronouncement: 'Those that have gone out of us were never of us, for if they had been of us they would no doubt have continued with us'. Just so. Much was made of the reforms. Banerjea called them 'the crowning triumph of constitutional agitation' and despite Morley's disclaimers about the goal of parliamentary government hailed him as 'the author of Parliament in India'

Terrorism continued; on 31st April 1908 a bomb intended for the District Judge of Muzaffarpur killed two ladies, Mrs Kennedy and her daughter; the police officer who arrested their assailant was shot in Calcutta in November 1908. Also in November an unsuccessful attempt was made to kill the Mintos. In June 1908 a Newspaper Act was passed under which *Yugantar* and other papers were suppressed. Aurobindo Ghosh was jailed, turned to religion, and fled to Pondicheri in 1910. Lajpat Rai, released from jail, repudiated the attempt to make the Congress intercommunal, declaring: 'In the present struggle between the Indian communities I shall be a Hindu first and an Indian afterwards'. On 1 July 1909, Sir William Curzon-Wyllie, Morley's political adviser was shot at a reception for Indian students in London. The assassin was a Punjabi student, who thought he was killing Lord Curzon. Morley was placed under police protection. On 25 November 1909 the retiring Collector of Nasik 'Pandit' A.T.M Jackson was shot down. Like Curzon-Wyllie he was unusually sympathetic to Indian aspirations.

With the Extremists totally committed to violence and the British in London and Simla hesitant to proceed with genuine reforms the Moderates found themselves (in words later uttered by Chintamani) 'in the unenviable position of the proverbial earthen pot between two brass vessels'. There was a strong move to strengthen even further the British brass: Kitchener had enjoyed influential supporters insisting that he be the next Viceroy. Sirdar of the Egyptian army, and Governor-General of Sudan, commander in South Africa in succession to Roberts, Commander-in-Chief India, 1902-9, Field Marshall, 1909: there were not many more important posts for him to fill (he had no wish to serve in the UK). His qualifications as Viceroy were strongly supported by Edward VII. After Curzon-Wyllie's murder the King recorded: 'The sooner these Indian students are sent back to their own country the better. They fall into bad hands'. He insisted that the firm hand of Kitchener was required in India. Morley wanted to propose the Earl of Inchcape as Viceroy. A self-made man who started work at fourteen, he had twenty years experience of shipping in Bombay and Calcutta and had ended up as Chairman of the P & O, the main shipping company linking Britain with the East. He was not acceptable and Morley countered by recommending another of the King's friends, Sir Charles Hardinge. The monarch retorted that as an expert diplomatist he should 'stick to his last'. Morley promised to give serious consideration to Kitchener, but he had no intention of giving way. He insisted: 'To put our biggest soldier in the post of Governor-General would be to set up the sword as the symbol of our rule over India, and the basis of it; it would be construed as a sign that our policy of the last four years was a failure...it would shake the faith of the Moderate Indian politicians in the stability, consistency and good faith of British statesmen' (Memo 6 May 1910).

The King continued to press the claim of Kitchener: indeed, it was his last theme when he saw Morley almost on his deathbed. Morley received no great support from Asquith who was content to humour the dying King (he had more important claims to make in confronting the House of Lords) but he left the final decision to Morley. He informed Morley: 'Haldane told him the decision would be mine and that whatever my decision might be the PM would back it though I hear that the PM personally would be much better pleased if the lot fell upon Kitchener'. (letter to Morley, 29 April 1910). Edward's death on 6 May released Morley from this pressure. The new King was so much less experienced and accepted the name of Hardinge gracefully.

The Mintos left India in November 1910, to expressions of regret. Minto had less than four years left, he died in 1914. He had aged greatly. Mary Minto lived on into the second World War, she still had much to do. She was appointed Lady in Waiting to Queen Mary, and also became the only woman to be a member of the London committee to advise on the future of New Delhi, especially the new Government House. They began work in 1917. Meanwhile, the Countess was displeased by Morley's *Recollections* when they appeared in 1917, assuming all the credit for the reforms.[5] She encouraged John Buchan to compile *Lord Minto—A Memoir* (1924) and herself published *India, Minto, and Morley, 1905-1910* (1934). It was a remarkable composition by an elderly though spirited lady.

NOTES

1. Lady Minto's Indian Journal: Later deposited in the Bodleian Library, Oxford. A sparkling social history of the little world of Simla and Government House, Calcutta, illustrated by the paraphernalia of her world.
2. Dodwell, *Cambridge Shorter History of India*, p. 873.
3. James Bryce, *The Ancient Roman Empire and the British Empire in India*, 1914.
4. Sir George Clarke, Governor of Bombay, brought in by Morley to tell him about what was going on: 26 May 1909.
5. Lady Minto called upon Morley to allow an impartial critic to examine his manuscript before publication (Lady Minto to Morley, 2 August 1916). He refused.

CHAPTER 4

HARDINGE: DIPLOMAT WITH A DIFFERENCE

Hardinge's period of office frequently appears just as an interlude between one set of reforms, those of Morley and Minto, and another, Montagu and Chelmsford. His period was actually as significant as those of his predecessor and successor. Hardinge was a blue-blooded aristocrat, a member of the ruling elite. At the Foreign Office he was a leading member of a clique which saw Germany as the enemy and regarded a European war as inevitable. But he managed to project himself as a friend of India in ways neither Minto nor Chelmsford contrived. Almost his first major task was to organize the Delhi Durbar of 1911. George V, when Prince of Wales, had visited India in 1906 and was eager to repeat the experience as King. He wrote to Morley (8 September 1910): 'I'm convinced that were it possible for me [to]...hold a Coronation Durbar at Delhi where we could meet all the Princes, officials and vast numbers of the people the greatest benefits would accrue'.

Morley replied (12 September) beginning with the words of a courtier and continuing with a warning: 'This splendour would be very costly as the last Durbar only too abundantly proved'. The proposal was sanctioned by the Cabinet two months later, 'not without a certain amount of criticism'. The decision was communicated to Hardinge the day he arrived in India (18 November 1910). Several difficulties, typical of court protocol were then produced. The King wanted to crown himself, the Archbishop of Canterbury objected, so the King appeared wearing the crown. But which crown? The crown of St Edward might not be removed from England and in any case it was a burden even during the coronation service. A special imperial crown was manufactured (at enormous expense to India) though after the visit it was placed in the Tower of London.

Of greater real significance, a royal visit required to be accompanied by 'boons'. The first suggestion was that the British Government should make a gift to India of a crore of Rupees (£ 666,666) to assist technical education. This was rejected by the Cabinet. The Viceroy then proposed that two separate 'boons' should be announced: the cancellation of the partition of Bengal and the transfer of the capital to Delhi. The first would please the Hindus (at any rate among the Bengalis) and the second was expected to please the Muslims. This idea was widely opposed and Crewe (Secretary of State) was lukewarm. The dual scheme had few supporters: Hardinge later explained that having only just arrived in India he had accepted the advice of his Council, who were the main proponents of the dual scheme. All was done in extreme secrecy.

Then came the renewed suggestion that the partition of Bengal be annulled. Hardinge opposed this, telling Crewe that 'an announcement of this kind would alienate the Muhamaden population....What India requires above everything at the present moment is peace and quiet. We do not want fireworks or any political concessions designed to produce an effect....the idea should be abandoned' (22 February 1911). Yet Hardinge was far from happy with the Bengal situation: 'The fact is there has been no Government of India during the last few years and affairs have been allowed to drift in the two Bengals with the absurd idea that there should be no interference with the local government....I am glad to say I hear less of this theory at present' (Hardinge to Morley, 25 May 1911).

How then did the change come about? It is probable that it was the brainchild of Sir John Jenkins, the Home Member, who suggested to Hardinge that the annulment of partition might simultaneously be announced as a 'boon' along with the transfer of the capital from Calcutta to Delhi[1]. It was about then that the transfer project was communicated to twenty persons or less—not even to the Queen—under the codename 'Sesame' in London. It was known to the Secretary of State, his predecessor and his Private Secretary. Crewe told the Cabinet in November, the Viceroy told his Council but not the Governors, even of the provinces involved.

The despatch proposing the scheme was signed on 25 August 1911 at Simla. Crewe informed the Cabinet in November. Thereafter events moved fast.

Along with Jenkins, Fleetwood Wilson had a major hand in the transfer scheme, advising that the new capital should form an administrative enclave 'on the lines of Washington'. When the King arrived in India, Hardinge ceased to be Viceroy for the next period though continuing to be Governor-General. On 12 December 1911 the King arose in the vast amphitheatre erected for the Durbar to proclaim the momentous changes. The move to Delhi came first but was not treated in the same detail as the annulment of the Bengal partition and its consequences. Also, the King's voice apparently did not penetrate throughout the amphitheatre, despite his quarterdeck tones. At any rate the significance of the restoration of the old Mughal capital went largely unnoted—not just for a few moments but for some time. Muslim dignitaries were heard to murmur 'No bombs, no boons'—or so the Durbar wits declared. Did the transfer signify any real change? Harcourt Butler told a friend 'We are at present organized for inaction and we ought to be organized for action because India is moving so fast' (Butler to Mrs Griffin, 3 August 1911).

The Royal tour continued with appropriate magnificence and also with enormous security precautions. When the King disembarked at Bombay he remarked to the Viceroy: 'You seem very pleased Charlie to be getting rid of us'. Pleased was not the word, but relieved Hardinge certainly was.

Montagu, then Undersecretary for India visited Hardinge eighteen months later and noted: 'He personally is on the right lines....[yet] his policy so often seems slack or wrong or ineffective. The answer is to be found in the fact that he leans on the advice of his counsellors and does not form his own view'.

The Viceroy did not fully comprehend the consequences of this move. When the Delhi territory was taken out of Punjab, Malcolm Hailey, an up and coming star of the ICS was appointed Chief Commissioner. Eighteen months after the Durbar, Hardinge was questioning the way in which the plan was projected: why were six square miles allocated for the accommodation of the Government of India when its total staff numbered 5,630, of whom 2,500 were the employees of the Government printing press? And why were 275 acres allowed for a new university—an area the size of Kensington Gardens? (Hardinge to Hailey, 12 February 1913).

The transfer was especially unpopular with the British mercantile community in Calcutta, who saw the replacement of the 'city of palaces' which symbolized the predominance of British sea trade in the East by a 'city of tombs'. Curzon identified himself with the clamour: he had expected that his Victoria Memorial (not completed until 1921) would be the great symbol of the British Raj. The cost was invoked as an intolerable burden for India and the Government of India estimate that the work of building the new capital could be completed within three years was pooh-poohed (rightly, the work was not finished for twenty years, if, indeed, it ever was finished).

However, the device of the royal proclamation had pre-empted any protest. Hardinge and his immediate staff were installed in temporary accommodation on the site of the Durbar the next year. Because the Viceroy's personal life was simple, the move to what had previously been a backwater was no burden, though doubtless his Council were less satisfied.

A Royal Commission on the Public Services in India with Lord Islington as Chairman was approved in 1911. Fleetwood Wilson urged Hardinge to include Gokhale among the members of the Commission, from mixed motives it would seem: 'If Gokhale drowns himself in it [the work of the Commission] it will make your position as Governor-General in Council so much pleasanter' (Wilson to Hardinge 2 March 1912). Hardinge replied: 'I mistrust Gokhale more than almost any man in India, as he is watching for our mistakes and is the only Indian who knows how to play a waiting game' (Hardinge to Wilson, 18 July 1912). The Secretary of State went against Hardinge's advice and Gokhale became a member, along with Ramsay MacDonald, Chirol and H. A. L. Fisher. Hardinge was very unhappy telling the Governor of Bengal that the aim of the first two 'is simply to destroy the Civil Service, which really means to destroy British administration in India'. (Hardinge to Carmichael, 2 August 1912). Because the war made other developments so much more urgent, the Commission's Report was not published until 1917.[2]

At the end of 1912 came the event which might have changed the direction of the national movement and the attitude of the Government if it had succeeded: this was the attempted assassination of Hardinge. This followed a year of relative calm, when it seemed that the annulment of partition really had succeeded in restraining the nationalists from violence. On 23 December 1912 Hardinge was proceeding down Chandni Chowk in a magnificent procession when a bomb was thrown from a bank, aimed at the elephant on which the Viceroy was seated with Lady Hardinge. He ordered the procession to carry on, but Lady Hardinge perceived that he was grievously wounded in the back while the Indian attendant (Chobdar) standing behind holding the ceremonial umbrella was dead. The Viceroy had to leave, but the procession continued to the Red Fort with Fleetwood Wilson deputizing for the Viceroy.

The attempt was associated with a breakaway group of the Arya Samaj. A former teacher at St Stephen's, Master Amir Chand was the leader. A conspirator in the plot, the militant student, Har Dayal, had decided to depart to California where he received the news of the bombing with delight. Reviving the title *Yugantar* he published a piece about the bomb-thrower: 'He awakened us from sleep it was the only voice in India which was dumb with fear'. However, this response was far from general; the main feeling was of revulsion. The Hardinges retired to Dehra Dun for some weeks while he recuperated, being joined by C. F. Andrews, with whom they had struck up an unlikely friendship. Andrews helped Lady Hardinge to organize the celebration of the Viceroy's recovery from his wounds and induced her to take an interest in his Indian friends, notably Tagore and Munshi Ram an Arya Smaj educationalist. Hardinge hailed Tagore as 'the Poet Laureate of Asia' declaring 'his affections, his intuitions, his emotions were as large as humanity itself'.[3] Surely this was a different man from the one who was so suspicious of Gokhale?

Hardinge intervened in the commotion at Cawnpore over the demolition of a washing-place attached to a mosque in order to widen a road. This controversy showed every sign of exploding. Advised by Andrews, Hardinge made a personal visit to Cawnpore and ordered the release of a hundred detainees arrested by the police. The Muslims were compensated and the potential confrontation was avoided.

His new concern for India and the Indians was revealed over the treatment of the Indian workers in Natal. Others were also moved, Lord Willingdon the Governor of Bombay told Hardinge, 'I wish I could help but fear you won't allow me'. (Willingdon to Hardinge, 8 November 1913). But Hardinge was in full sympathy with the South African Indians now on strike: he cabled Lord Gladstone, First Governor-General of the Union of South Africa to urge 'the use of methods common to civilised societies in dealing with strikes' (20 December 1913). More important he spoke out at a public meeting in Madras (home of most of the indentured labourers) having just read accounts of the flogging of Indian strikers in Natal: they 'have violated, as they intended to violate those laws [banning entry into Transvaal] with full knowledge of the penalties involved....In all this they have the sympathies of India - deep and burning - and not only of Indians but of those who like myself without being Indians themselves have feelings of sympathy for the people of this country' (*Tribune*, 16 November 1913).

It was probably the most extraordinary speech ever delivered by a Viceroy. Crewe cabled anxiously 'I quite understand and share your view....But you ought to be aware that Harcourt [Secretary of State for the Colonies] and possibly others of my colleagues were greatly disturbed by your speech'. Hardinge did not recant, he told Crewe 'some passages of my speech are understandably open to criticism; they came straight from my heart' (29 November 1913). Smuts and other South African politicians demanded his recall. The Cabinet discussed this possibility but realized it would only precipitate an explosion of Indian resentment.

The South African campaign made Gandhi an all-India hero: it also did much for Hardinge's standing with the Indian public. The issue of the abolition of indenture was overshadowed by the outbreak of war in Europe. It had been expected in Britain that a European war would require the reinforcement of British troops in India to hold unrest in check. Unexpectedly, India responded to the declaration of war by an amazing nationwide demonstration of support for Britain in this hour of crisis. Hardinge was able to assure London that India would send forces to fight in Europe. One consequence of the Kitchener reforms was that the army was organized into divisions and brigades, ready to move. Kitchener had envisaged fighting a war in Central Asia, but now the war was in Europe. Immediately two infantry divisions and a cavalry brigade were committed (it should be remembered that the contribution of the army from the United Kingdom was initially limited to four divisions). The first Indian reinforcements arrived in Marseilles late in September. On arrival they were issued with the Lee Enfield rifles standard in the British army but previously withheld from Indian troops. The Indians were rushed up to the front line, still wearing the cotton uniforms in which they had embarked. Two more infantry divisions followed soon after, together with two cavalry divisions: useless in France except to fight as infantry. Through the bitter winter of 1914-15 the Indians withstood the German attack. (They were issued with great-coats but still wore their cotton tunics). The Indian casualties were grim: few of the peasant soldiers ever returned home. However, all was not harmony. Hundreds of Punjabis, mainly Sikhs, had migrated to British Columbia and California between 1905-8. A series of Orders in Council followed to restrain immigration. A shipload of Sikhs arrived in May 1914 on the Japanese vessel, *Komagata Maru*. They were detained off Vancouver, and eventually escorted out of Canadian waters by a gunboat. They arrived back in India after the war had started in rebellious mood. Arrangements were made to transport them back to Punjab: but some escaped. All were disgusted at their treatment, and were made thoroughly anti-British. Their feelings were given form in a newspaper published in California, *Ghadr* (war). Its editor was that same Har Dayal who applauded the bombing of Hardinge. The movement took its name from the title. Dayal was expelled from the United States and went to Germany, but not for long. Proscribed in India, *Ghadr* remained largely a foreign-based movement, but the authorities in Punjab were worried about possible repercussions in the province. However, Punjab was to provide over 446,000 of the 1,097,000 volunteers enlisted in the wartime Indian Army.

These then, were the contributions of the peasants to this war which meant so little to them. But what of the educated, the elite, who had shown such unexpected enthusiasm? In Britain, their counterparts were rushing to enlist and after a few weeks were becoming the junior officers who led their men into action on the Somme and in a hundred other dreadful encounters. In the Indian Army the only officers' positions open to Indians were those of Viceroy's-Commissioned-Officer—a junior category, filled mainly by senior NCOs. Deprived of suitable openings (for even if they had wished the educated would not be accepted in the ranks unless belonging to one of the 'martial classes') the early enthusiasm turned tepid. A few highly motivated young Indians made their way to Britain, at their own expense, and joined up there. But the great majority began to question why they should support an empire in which they were so obviously not fully integrated.

V. S. Srinivasa Sastri, founder of the Servants of India Society, and a leading liberal, compared the presence of the Indian troops in France with the despatch of Piedmontese soldiers to the Crimea by Cavour to put the Italian case on the European agenda: it was hoped that similarly India's military effort would help to bring forward complete self-government. The first visible response was the rejection by the House of Lords in March 1915 of the proposal by the Government of India that an Executive Council should be created in UP similar to those in the three Presidencies. What a slap in the face!

Hardinge realized that political India would be shocked. In 1915 he instructed the Home Member Sir Reginald Craddock to prepare a paper on 'India after the war'. Craddock was no liberal. Montagu called him 'that arch-retrograde' (in the 1930s he was a leading member of the Churchill group opposing the Government of India Bill). His proposals were quite inadequate and Hardinge decided he must tackle the question himself. He was able to draw upon a Note by Sir Claude Hill the most liberal member of his council. Hardinge's forty-one-page memorandum upon questions likely to arise in India at the end of the war, was despatched to the Secretary of State in October 1915, backed up by the endorsement of his Council and the heads of provincial governments. Its recommendations did not amount to an integrated proposal for greater self-government however, rather, it was a shopping list of miscellaneous items, all desirable no doubt. They included commissions (i.e. Second Lieutenants and upwards) for Indians, elected majorities in provincial legislatures and increased representations at the centre, relaxation of the control of the Secretary of State over the Government of India and similar relaxation of Government of India control over the provinces. India's representation on the Imperial Conference, in session in London, the appointment of Indians to the Privy Council, increased employment of Indians in the public services—and abolition of indentured labour overseas. There were other economic reforms. Hardinge followed this up with a speech at the United Services Club in Simla on 8 October. It was a compound of the old paternalism and the new idea of partnership:

> England has instilled into this country the culture and civilisation of the West with all its ideals of liberalism and self-respect....it is necessary for her to cherish the aspirations of which she herself has sown the seed, and English officials are gradually awakening to the fact that...a still nobler task lies before them in the present and the future in guiding the uncertain and faltering steps of Indian development along sure and safe paths. The new role of guide, philosopher and friend is opening before you and is worthy of your greatest efforts....Slowly but surely you must divest yourselves of some of the power you have hitherto wielded. Let it be realised that great as has been England's mission in the past she has a far more glorious task to fulfil in the future in encouraging and guiding the political development of the people. The goal to which India may attain is still distant....but I look forward with confidence to the time when...bound by ties of affection and gratitude India may be regarded as a true friend of the Empire

and not merely as a trusty dependent....It is to this distant vista that the British official should turn his eyes.

This pronouncement which now seems so unreal was held by many British officials as going much too far and by Indian Moderates as 'inspiring'. It was made against a background of bad news from the war. Hardinge was suffering acutely from personal tragedy. His elder son was killed in action in France just before Christmas 1914;[4] then he lost his beloved wife. His loneliness affected his power of decision. He had his younger son as ADC, but he too went off to France and was wounded.

The Gallipoli expedition from which so much had been anticipated had ended in failure (Indian soldiers had been an element in the British Capital Expeditionary Force). Nearer home, the Mesopotamia campaign had suffered a dreadful defeat. The original intention had been to safeguard the oil supplies of Iraq and Abadan from enemy control. But when the capture of Basra went ahead smoothly, the objective became more ambitious: an advance to Baghdad and beyond. The soldiers employed were largely Indian and overall management was under the Government of India. The senior officers belonged to the Indian Army. It was all a test of Kitchener's reforms of the Indian military machine: and it failed totally. Perhaps the worst aspect of the campaign was the breakdown of the medical facilities, all the way from the front back to Bombay.

More attention was paid in India to the revelations of the evils of indenture which appeared in a report by C. F. Andrews and another ex-missionary, W. W. Pearson. One government doctor told Andrews that 'Of course it's next door to slavery; there's no denying that'. Hardinge was very worried; he replied to Andrews' report by assuring him that he would 'further study the question and what can be done' (1 July 1915). A despatch was sent to the Secretary of State (15 October 1915) which upset the India Office who complained that 'Government of India have abruptly thrown over the previous policy'. When the Council of India took up the question on 2 February 1916 they accepted the conclusion that indenture must be abolished.

However, implementation was delayed. Gandhi, now back in India made this a central issue and contrasted the swift response of Parliament to the issue of 'Chinese slavery' on the Rand with the delays over terminating Indian indenture: this intensified the 'unnatural relationship' between British and Indians he said, in which racial inferiority and superiority was systematized.[5] When the issue was debated in the central legislature Hardinge led the attack upon its evils and heralded its termination. A few days later he departed, on 4 April 1916, having delivered an address to the legislature combining caution and hope: 'I do not for a moment wish to discountenance self-government as a national ideal, it...has the warm sympathy of all moderate men'. It was a welcome relief from the worries of Mesopotamia where on 29 April the garrison of Kut was compelled to surrender.

The Mesopotamia tragedy was partly created by Kitchener's changes in the system and partly by the man who had emerged as his chosen successor as Commander-in-Chief. Sir Beauchamp Duff had served in South Africa while Kitchener was gaining his laurels and assisted him in his reorganization scheme in India, 1903-9. He became Commander-in-Chief in 1914 when whatever merits he had once possessed were extinguished. During the Mesopotamia campaign he did not leave Simla; he did not visit Basra or even Bombay. Nevertheless he felt able to state the plight of the British Indian forces in Mesopotamia 'The health and spirits of the troops are excellent'. (One critic declared that Kitchener had not abolished the Military Member; he abolished the Commander-in-Chief). Because Kitchener's changes eliminated the Military Member they also excluded the Viceroy's Council from any part in decision making. The Mesopotamia Commission was to state that 'the Governor-General's Council was never consulted....Their opinion was not asked as regards the advance to Baghdad'.

The Commission also objected that so much of the correspondence between London and India was conducted through the 'Private' channel which excluded the Council from their legitimate functions. The Commission considered that all this prevented the Council from exercising its powers.[6] But the marginalizing of the Council was an almost inevitable consequence of Kitchener's dictatorial methods which both Curzon and Minto had acquiesced in. Hardinge had to bow to the storm which broke after the Mesopotamia Commission reported. Montagu in his biting attack in the Mesopotamia debate acknowledged that when Hardinge departed he was 'by universal opinion of all Indians...the most popular Viceroy of India of modern times'. His regime had 'achieved much for India'.[7] On leaving India he returned to the Foreign Office as Permanent Under Secretary of State. He was under heavy pressure to resign, but despite personal qualms he resisted. He was British Ambassador in Paris, during the critical years 1920-22. Like Curzon, his Viceroyalty was shadowed by the manner of his going. Perhaps his fault was simply that events went too fast for his way of working.

NOTES

1. The main accounts of the transfer by R. E. Frykenberg, *Delhi Through the Ages*, 1986, 'The Coronation Durbar of 1911: Some Implications', R. G. Irving, *Indian Summer; Lutyens, Baker and Imperial Delhi*, 1981, F. A. Eustis and Z. H. Zaidi, *King, Viceroy and Cabinet*, *History*, June 1964. However, Frykenberg observes that the whole episode 'has yet to be satisfactorily explained'. This seems like other momentous developments which 'just growed'.
2. *The Report of the Royal Commission on the Public Services in India*, 1917, cmd 8382.
3. *Civil and Military Gazette*, Lahore, 28 May 1913.
4. Five Viceroys lost their sons in the Great War: Lansdowne, Minto, Hardinge, Chelmsford and Willingdon.
5. *The Leader*, Allahabad, 25 February 1916

6. *Mesopotamia Commission Report*, Cmd. 8610, 1917
7. *House of Commons Debates*, 1917, Vol. 95, Column 2202 DMC.

Chapter 5

CHELMSFORD: LUKEWARM LIBERAL

Hardinge's period in India was extended by a few months, and a further extension was discussed but the unfortunate example of Curzon was fresh in mind. In May 1915, the Liberal Cabinet was replaced by a Coalition. Asquith remained Prime Minister but a Conservative Secretary of State for India was appointed, Austin Chamberlain. He was regarded as a great gentleman: it was said of him 'he always played the game, and he always lost'. Chamberlain proposed the names of several Conservative peers as the next Viceroy, but Asquith made this a sticking point and insisted on a Liberal. All through 1915 he was engaged in a desultory correspondence about the next Viceroy. Willingdon, a potential candidate told the Prime Minister in April that Hardinge was 'tired'. Churchill seemed a possibility, and expressed interest but only if he could postpone his departure until the war was over. The failure at Gallipoli put an end to his hopes. Churchill had a cousin, Ivor Guest, who had crossed the floor of the House of Commons along with him; he was now Viceroy of Ireland as Lord Wimborne. His daughter Frances Charlotte had married a minor Liberal aristocrat, Frederick Thesiger, Third Baron Chelmsford. He had a good brain: Fellow of All Souls as well as captain of the Oxford cricket team, but his experience in public life was limited. He had been Governor of Queensland (1905-9) and Governor of New South Wales (1909-13). At the outbreak of war he joined a territorial battalion (the Dorsets) and was sent to India where he was guarding a radio station near Simla when the Viceroyalty came his way. He returned to England to collect his family and make the customary ceremonial arrival at Bombay: a curious diversion, given the urgency of the time. Everybody said he had a fine presence, also all said he possessed a cold personality, withdrawn and silent. He was frequently shielded by his Private Secretary, Maffey (later Sir John and Lord Rugby) a man of great ability who went on to be Governor-General of the Sudan. As a Frontier officer he was unused to dealing with politicians and when crisis followed in Punjab his instinct was to strike back.

Chelmsford's first year was marked by no government initiative. Sinha, freed from official links, became President of the Indian National Congress in December 1915. His address, though moderate underlined the need for an early statement of policy by the Government. In October 1916 a detailed survey was submitted by the elected members of the Imperial Legislative Council to the new Viceroy. Called 'The Nineteen Members' Memorandum it foreshadowed the reforms to come: they described the Morley-Minto reforms as 'of a very limited character'. They listed a series of moderate changes required to produce 'a government which is acceptable to the people because it is responsible to them'. The Executive Councils (Imperial and Provincial) should be half Indian; the Legislative Councils should have a 'substantial majority of elected representatives'; the Council of the Secretary of State should be abolished; India should be given the same status as the self-governing dominions; the Provincial governments should be 'made autonomous as stated in Government of India despatch dated 25 August 1911'; commissions in the army should be awarded 'under conditions similar to those applicable to Europeans'. The memorandum was signed by the Maharaja of Kasimbazar, D. E. Wacha, Bhupendranath Basu, Madan Mohan Malaviya (all Congress leaders), Tej Bahadur Sapru (the leading

Liberal), and—perhaps most significant—M. A. Jinnah. The memorandum aroused no response from the Viceroy.

The last major event of 1916 was the holding of the joint Congress-League meeting which produced the Lucknow pact. Jinnah had become the dominant personality in the League and was determined to align its policies with those of the Congress. The time was propitious. The Congress was firmly under 'moderate' leadership. Tilak had just been tried at Poona where he was defended by Jinnah and thanks to his advocacy was cleared of bringing the law into contempt. He attended the annual gathering of the Congress at Lucknow where the different branches of the National movement were reconciled. They went on to negotiate with the Muslim League. Jinnah emerged as 'The Apostle of Hindu-Muslim unity' in the words of the poet Sarojini Naidu. Congress met just before the League, marshalling more than 2,300 delegates. The President, A. C. Mazumdar announced that the disagreement between Congress and League 'has been settled and the Hindus and Mussalmans have agreed to make a united demand for self-government'. Tilak responded: 'We are ready to make a common cause with any set of men'. And so at a joint Congress-League meeting in December the famous Lucknow Pact was signed. This represented a further acceptance of existing communal differences by Congress (as acknowledged by Gokhale just before his death) and a formula to settle their differences. Muslims would continue to vote in separate electorates. They would choose fifty per cent of the elected seats in Punjab, forty per cent in Bengal (a notable Muslim concession), thirty per cent in UP (a substantial Muslim gain, when they formed fourteen per cent of the total population), twenty-five per cent in Bihar, fifteen per cent in CP and Madras, and thirty-three per cent at the centre. No bill or resolution should be accepted if seventy-five per cent of the members of either community affected were opposed. All this represented a major triumph for Jinnah, the constitutional lawyer and advocate of compromise, and the Pact clearly challenged the British Government to come up with a credible constitutional response.

Chelmsford adopted the technique he had followed in Australia as a ceremonial governor: he waited to receive proposals from his 'Ministers' or 'Members'. The provincial government were adjured to 'have a free hand to take such measures as they with their local knowledge deem to be necessary'. Under this injunction, the Governor of Madras, Lord Pentland, ordered that Mrs Besant should be interned in Ootacamund. The Government of India's Despatch of 24 November 1916 had not moved the debate much further forward, reviving tried formulae: the introduction of non-official control in local self-government, more Indians in higher ranks of the civil service, expansion of elected element in provincial legislatures, but none of these suggestions altered the fundamental relationship between British and Indians: the former governed, the latter were limited to criticising government measures. This ensured that the Nationalists were a perpetual opposition, denied any opportunity to participate in government.

These proposals were considered by a committee at the India Office headed by Sir William Duke, Lieutenant-Governor of Bengal, (1911-12) and thereafter member of the Council of India in London. Duke was associated with the Round Table group who now began to assume some importance in Indian affairs. The group had emerged from Milner's 'Kindergarten' in South Africa, they produced a journal directed to making the British Empire a more coherent whole—in fact an imperial federation (they were much influenced by the example of the United States). The leading intellectual in the group was Lionel Curtis 'The Prophet' whose technique was to influence those who had influence—politicians, civil servants, senior figures at Oxford and Cambridge. Curtis now departed for India where he stayed with Sir James Meston, previously one of Milner's 'Kindergarten' in South Africa and currently Lieutenant-Governor of UP. Meston was a recognized liberal (he was later President of the Liberal Party in Britain). With introductions from him, Curtis toured the provinces and began to formulate a plan. Meanwhile, the Duke Committee reported in March 1917: another increase in elected members of the legislatures would not lead towards self-government but simply 'perpetuate and aggravate a vicious system which makes it the main function of the Legislative Councils to oppose and criticize the Government while remaining completely free from responsibility for the results of their actions'. Chamberlain, Conservative though he was, went along with these criticisms. 'After all, we want to train Indians in self-government' (2 May 1917). This was a remarkable advance even from the approach of Minto and Morley.

In the Spring of 1917 three delegates from India arrived for the Imperial War Conference, a recognition of the importance of India's contribution to the war effort and also a sign that India would, one day (whether sooner or later) take its place along with the White Dominions. The delegates were the Maharaja of Bikanir, Sinha, and Meston. *The Times* hailed their arrival by declaring that it was time 'for something more than pious aspirations about the future of India: it was time to declare what terms were proposed—that time was now'.[1]

This lumbering progress towards some kind of constitutional formula was not assisted by the confinement of Annie Besant. With everything in suspense, came the publication of the report on Mesopotamia, and the subsequent debate in parliament, on 12 July 1917. One of the most powerful speeches came from Edwin Montagu. By now the Asquith coalition had been replaced by Lloyd George's war-winning coalition. However, in mid 1917 there seemed no prospect of victory. France was rent by military mutinies and virtually out of the war. Russia had just witnessed the abdication of the Tsar and a revolution—to be followed in October by the Bolshevik revolution. Another of Haig's murderous offensives was beginning and its name

'Paschendaal', was to become synonymous with the uselessness of war. Lansdowne, former high Tory Viceroy of India, had challenged the war cabinet to consider a negotiated peace and was shortly to repeat the challenge in the *Daily Telegraph*. The year 1916 had been bad; 1917 was worse. The Mesopotamia debate gave Montagu the opportunity to launch a biting attack on the Government of India: 'Too wooden, too iron, too inelastic, too antediluvian to be of any use'. The House of Commons took no interest in India. The Secretary of State 'can be over-ruled by a majority of the [India] Council!...The whole system of the India Office is designed to prevent control by the House of Commons for fear there might be too advanced a Secretary of State'. The office was 'the apotheosis of circumlocution and red tape beyond the dreams of any ordinary citizen'. He went on to outline a federal structure for India and hammered home the message that 'You should give some instalment to show that you are in real earnest'. Josiah Wedgwood had been a member of the Mesopotamia Commission and submitted a minority report even more damning of the Government of India.[2] In the debate he claimed that the time had arrived to declare that their goal was 'complete Home Rule for India'. He added 'the spirit of bureaucracy in India has been particularly vicious'.

Chamberlain decided that he must resign: though his responsibility for the Mesopotamia disaster was remote. Lloyd George immediately tendered his post to Montagu, who pondered the offer, having already had the Ministry of Reconstruction put before him. Lloyd George left him to choose between the two posts, though on 17 July the Prime Minister virtually compelled Montagu to accept India, even though Curzon and Balfour were objecting that after his House of Commons speech it would be concluded that this was now Indian policy. Montagu's letter of acceptance was somewhat guarded: 'Home Rule for India is not possible....The goal for which we were aiming should be stated to be a federation of great self-governing provinces and principalities....The policy should be safeguarded as to time. Before that goal is achieved many years, and indeed many generations will have been spent....I have not the slightest intention of urging my colleagues if I become a member of your Government to embark upon precipitate action'.

Was this letter designed to be shown by the Prime Minister to his Conservative colleagues? It was soon outdated. Montagu at once came forward with a draft for an announcement of the Government's intentions. This was not too soon for the more progressive senior civil servants. On 17 August, Meston wrote to Robertson (Chief Commissioner of the Central Provinces) 'At the present moment there is no government in India; we are forgetting the way to rule. It is perfectly childish inviting each province to take whatever measures it considers necessary and abdicating the whole business of ruling the whole country'. This was an obvious dig at Chelmsford. But in London things were starting to move.

On 30 July, Montagu placed a draft before the Cabinet. He was supported by the former Secretary of State who retained his influence with senior Conservative colleagues. Despite all the urgent questions requiring consideration, on 14 August Montagu put his draft before the Cabinet and had it accepted subject to one amendment. Montagu's draft included a phrase about 'the gradual development of free institutions with a view to self-government'. Curzon had agreed to this formula, but later objected that this would mean different things in Britain and in India. He proposed instead the term 'responsible government', which Montagu accepted, believing that the historical use of this term was even more specific than 'self-government'. Curzon gave an account of the meeting to Chamberlain writing all went 'as merrily as a wedding feast' (25 August 1917). The decision was communicated to the House of Commons on 20 August, Montagu said that 'substantial steps in this direction should be taken as soon as possible'. In the usual style, having given with one hand the Government took back with the other: 'The British Government and the Government of India on whom the responsibility lies for the welfare and advancement of the Indian peoples must be judges of the time and measure of each advance, and they must be guided by the co-operation received from those upon whom new opportunities of service will be thus conferred'. How this could be reconciled with Montagu's fulminations against the Government of India and the Council of India on 12 July, is hard to understand. In part it was this tendency to speak with different voices which eventually brought about his undoing.

The August declaration was steadily opposed by Balfour, now Foreign Secretary; though his own declaration (or that to which he gave authority) on the Jewish home in Palestine which appeared in November 1917 was to create much greater confusion than the Indian declaration (Montagu was a persistent opponent of the Balfour declaration).[3] Anyhow the Cabinet found themselves in an atmosphere amicable to democracy and national self-determination, partly in response to President Wilson who as early as January 1917 called for a League of Nations. Curzon wrote of 'almost incredible development', adding that the application of these ideas to India were included because they had 'become the common shibboleths of the Allies' (memorandum to War Cabinet, 27 June 1917). If the Government did not take the initiative they would give way to the Nationalists 'who might bring the mission of the West in India - itself an ennobling duty - to an abrupt end'. (Cabinet Minutes, 29 June 1917). With uncharacteristic candour Sir John Simon was to speak of the August declaration as issued 'when we had our backs to the wall, when the Indian war effort on the side of the British was of great importance'. There was much talk of devolution, of increasing the democratic element at provincial level. Everyone denied that change would mean introducing the Westminster model at Delhi, as Morley had done before:

but this was just what Indian politicians were determined to claim.

In London Sir William Duke made a start, and in Lucknow Curtis produced a long paper under the heading 'Diarchy', advocating a dual system of government, part under Indian politicians, part still controlled by officials. On 10 November 1917, Montagu arrived in Bombay. He spent several weeks in Delhi and then toured the Presidency cities. He was accompanied by a small mission, consisting of Lord Donoughmore, Conservative peer, Charles Roberts MP, former Under Secretary at the India Office, Duke and Malcolm Seton, Secretary of the Public and Judicial Department at the India Office, as well as Bhupendranath Basu, one time President of Congress and now a Member of the Council of India. C. H. Kisch, a rather grey bureaucrat, was to draft much of the forthcoming report. Chelmsford claimed that a report was prepared before the Commission arrived, drafted by Sir William Marris under his aegis. On 7 August Montagu wrote to his predecessor: 'The Viceroy and various people in India have become more and more insistent about an immediate pronouncement'. However, Chelmsford made no attempt to bring change over the heads of the provinces who mainly remained hostile to further reform.

One well-informed though establishment-minded writer contrasts 'Chelmsford's lack of ideas of his own, his sound if cautious judgement, his coolness in all circumstances and his respect for orderly administration, [which] contrasted sharply with Montagu's under-disciplined initiatives and constant state of excitement'.[4] Perhaps a state of excitement was required to galvanize torpid thinking at Simla. The Report was drafted according to Montagu's account with the contribution of Chelmsford being confined to 'speculations as to whether the Government of India is a plural or singular noun'. The draft report was first considered by the Viceroy's Council. In the initial stages those concerned with the draft endeavoured to move away from the system of communal electorates. A note by Marris argued that if the system was perpetuated for the Muslims it was likely to lead to demands from other minorities and the fragmentation of the electoral process. Against this was the acceptance in the Lucknow pact of this arrangement by Congress. At the provincial level an advance to an elected majority was accepted as inevitable; but what if the legislatures blocked essential financial demands? The solution proposed by Montagu was that Governors could 'certify' whatever bills they regarded as essential. Under the new system certain departments, mainly concerned with law and order would be 'reserved'—outside the authority of the legislature, while others would be 'transferred' to full control by the politicians. These were designated the 'nation building departments' such as local self-government, education, and health. Here the authority of the legislature would be complete. At the provincial level there was to be a definite change: but what about the work of the Viceroy and the central government? To limit political demands Montagu proposed two chambers in the legislature. The upper chamber—the Council of State—would be elected under a very narrow franchise, restricted to landlords and big business. The Legislative Assembly, a much larger body with a substantial elected membership, was in effect the House of Commons of India. Despite its disclaimers about taking Westminster to India the new system was going that way.

Other features of the Montford Reforms (as they rapidly became known) were the liberation of local authorities from official control: but without equipping them with the substantial financial resources required to give them greater powers. A more important advance in the long run was the acceleration of Indian participation in the superior Civil Service. In 1919, according to the Islington Report there were 1305 Europeans in the ICS and seventy Indian members, with three Eurasians. The Islington Commission recommended that a quota of twenty-five per cent Indians should be introduced, but the new proposal was that thirty-three per cent of the intake should be Indians.

While the report was being hammered out between Montagu's committee and the Viceroy's Council, the war entered its final phase. Desperate to mobilize greater Indian support, Chelmsford convened a conference of Indian political leaders (on 29 April 1918). There were six delegates from the Bombay Presidency. Gandhi was a natural choice, Jinnah somewhat more controversial, and Tilak altogether too extreme. On his way to Delhi, Gandhi was told by C. F. Andrews that the liberal *Nation* had reported the disclosure by the new Soviet Government of secret treaties carving up the Balkans and the Near East among the Allies as the booty of war. Gandhi became very doubtful about attending the conference, but was persuaded by Chelmsford that these reports had no firm foundation. Chelmsford asked Gandhi to second a resolution moved by the Gaekwar of Baroda on behalf of the non-official delegates endorsing a renewed war effort. Gandhi agreed, asking if he could speak in 'Urdu' (Hindi). Subsequently Gandhi wrote to Chelmsford: 'It is clear to me that we should give the Empire every man available for its defence' (29 April 1918). He then went off to Gujarat to run a one-man recruiting campaign, which was a lamentable failure. He explained this to C. F. Andrews: 'moral force is not in us today'. Charlie Andrews was pursuing his own campaign to compel the Government of India to free all labourers overseas who were still bound under indenture. He bombarded the Viceroy and his Private Secretary with letters, receiving no acknowledgement. However, this literary barrage at length produced a response. Even the India Office accepted that indenture must be ended. Moving with its usual lethargy the official machinery did not finally terminate indenture until August 1920.

Long before then, Montagu and Chelmsford had put their names to the Montford Report. They insisted that concessions had not been wrung from the British: 'We are not setting about to stir up ninety-five per cent of the people out of their peaceful conservatism...merely at the bidding of the other five per cent...our reason is the faith that is in us'. However, Montagu still had to satisfy the war Cabinet, the inner Cabinet of five of whom Curzon was the member to whom Indian questions were referred. In their correspondence both Ministers were addicted to interminable letters. Montagu informed Chelmsford that Curzon complained that the Report was 'confused' and 'complicated'. Yet he reflected (31 May 1918) that Curzon's criticism was 'in the manner of the Grand Mogul' (he added that 'Lady Curzon complains that she is not even allowed to engage her own under-housemaids'). The Report was published on 1 July 1918. It received a mixed reception in India. Annie Besant in *New India* wrote 'The scheme is unworthy to be offered by England or to be accepted by India'. Tilak said the scheme 'is entirely unacceptable'. Though disappointed, other leaders were not so uncompromising. The most responsive members of Congress met separately to consider their position. A Moderate conference met in Bombay in November 1918 with S. N. Banerjea as President, Tej Bahadur Sapru and Sastri as leading members. This example shows the Moderates' position in Indian politics: they were eminent individuals, but commanded no grassroots support. Sastri and others continued to attend meetings of the Congress in England. Montagu had to back down on some issues: thus, in the proposed upper house, the Council of State he conceded a continuing official majority. Curzon remained doubtful: 'Why is it necessary to proceed at breakneck speed in a case which constitutes a revolution' (23 July 1918).

Montagu had the steady support of Chamberlain and the Liberal Ministers such as H. A. L. Fisher (Education). When the war ended unexpectedly in November 1918, Lloyd George decided to call an election on the basis of the wartime Coalition, which meant that the opposition would be confined to the Asquithians and the small group around Ramsay Macdonald. In order to be assured of the support of the Coalition Liberals, Lloyd George gave an undertaking to his Liberal colleagues (Montagu, Fisher and Addison)that the Indian reforms would get high priority, support for reform was also forthcoming from Lloyd George's old crony, Lord Reading (his confederate in the Marconi scandal and recently Ambassador at Washington though presently back in his substantive post of Lord Chief Justice) and perhaps more surprisingly from Churchill, once again a Liberal Cabinet Minister. Montagu went ahead to draft the reforms legislation, but constitutional advance was only part of his strategy. He insisted that as the White Dominions had been given separate representation at the Peace Conference India should be accorded the same status: India was to sign the Treaty and become a founder member of the League of Nations. For the purpose of getting his reforms through Parliament, Montagu invited Sinha to be Parliamentary Under Secretary with a seat in the House of Lords (much to Curzon's distaste).

The Bill went through the Commons in all its stages as an agreed all-party measure without a division. The Bill reduced the power of the Council of India. Their number was reduced, their term of office came down to five years, and weekly meetings gave way to meetings once a month. Montagu maintained that Parliament was ready 'to grant with enthusiasm to India as soon as may be the surrender of her trusteeship to a well-qualified Indian government'. The Commons welcomed the measure and from the opposition front bench Sir Donald Maclean welcomed 'this great Liberal measure'. Replying, Montagu declared that this was the proudest moment of his life.

Montagu was exceptionally lucky in his timing. Already in India the situation had dramatically deteriorated. The bogey of the hour was Bolshevism. Indian army units were deployed around the Black Sea and the Caucusus to contain the danger. More urgently, Bolshevism was feared to be spreading in India. A committee had been set up with Sir Sidney Rowlatt a judge of the King's Bench Division as

Chairman to investigate the spread of sedition. They recommended that when the special wartime powers lapsed there should be continuing measures to safeguard public order. A Bill was introduced into the central legislature to implement these measures. The Bill made it clear that the measures could be used to repress almost any political activity. All twenty non-official members voted against, but were over-ruled by the thirty-five official members. Jinnah took the lead by resigning. His letter of resignation informed the Viceroy that the Council was merely 'a machine propelled by a foreign executive'. He added 'A government that passes or sanctions such a law in time of peace forfeits its claim to be called a civilized government'. All the other non-officials departed after him.

When Montagu received the report he noted (10 October 1918) 'There is much in its recommendations which is most repugnant to my mind'. He predicted that the Government of India would not be able to invoke the Rowlatt powers. Critics have questioned why Montagu did not veto the legislation: but no Secretary of State had imposed a flat veto on a Government of India measure since the 1890s. (Morley insisted on the supremacy of Whitehall over Simla but he did not veto a Press Law of which he thoroughly disapproved.) The stage was set for the most disastrous period in Chelmsford's Viceroyalty.

The Amritsar Massacre occurred on 10 April 1919. It followed Gandhian demonstrations against the Rowlatt legislation. Gandhi asked for Sunday 30 March to be observed as a Day of Humiliation and of Prayer to achieve 'purification and penance'. His call caught the country unprepared and only in Delhi was the day observed in traditional Indian fashion by a hartal (a closure of the shops). Next day a crowd of about 1,500 gathered in Delhi's Peepul Park; the atmosphere was tense and the military were called in, resorting to shooting. Six persons were killed and sixteen injured.

The hartal was observed generally on the following

Sunday, with the greatest response in Punjab, especially in central Punjab the Sikh homeland. At Amritsar the local brigade commander responded to attacks on Europeans by staging a show of force. A mela or fair was taking place in the city and was exploited by local Congress leaders. Doubtless without their direction an English woman doctor who had worked in the city was left for dead. The small European community was evacuated into the Fort. The scene was reminiscent of the Mutiny, a young British officer recalled 'A barrack room of women and children who had been brought into the Fort from the Civil Lines for safety. There was a terrible quietness in that barrack room. The ladies seemed so bemused and sad'. Next day, (13 April) General Dyer arrived. He had fifty men at his disposal from the 59th Rifles and 9th Gurkhas. They marched into the city and proclaimed by beat of drum that any gathering of more than five persons was illegal. Rioting had occurred, and the town hall had been burned out. Dyer marched his fifty men into Jallianwalla Bagh in the city centre and instructed those present to disperse. Few could have heard the order; and Dyer's fifty soldiers opened fire. Within a few minutes Jallianwalla Bagh was cleared: next day (14 April 1919) a count of the Gurkhas' ammunition revealed that nine hundred and twenty-three rounds had been fired.

The extent of the killing (over four hundred were dead) was known to the Lieutenant-Governor, Sir Michael O'Dwyer within hours and to the Viceroy at Simla the next day. Chelmsford showed no inclination to go to Amritsar, though it was only two hundred miles distant. Punjab was virtually sealed off from the rest of India. The news which emerged was distinctly one-sided: the murder of Europeans and destruction of public property was described. Martial law was proclaimed in the Amritsar and Lahore districts on 16 April. Receiving these versions of the situation, Gandhi announced on 18 April that the campaign of civil disobedience was suspended: he had 'underrated the forces of evil'. On 10 May Gandhi wrote a long letter to Maffey in which he pledged that 'The whole of my weight will be thrown absolutely...on the side of preserving internal peace. The Viceroy has the right to rely upon my doing no less, but my weight will be absolutely nothing if I receive no support from the Government'. He asked for withdrawal of the Rowlatt legislation and a declaration of British policy towards Turkey and the Middle East. He added 'My weight will be absolutely nothing if I receive no support from the government' (10 May).

C. F. Andrews fired off a letter of protest to the Viceroy and his Private Secretary, mainly concerning reports of whippings of students and others; Maffey sent a lofty reply. C. F. Andrews dashed up to Simla and was received by Chelmsford, 'cold as ice with me and full of racial bitterness'. C. F. Andrews applied to enter the Punjab, and believed the Viceroy had agreed, but when he took the train for Lahore he was turned out at Amritsar. O'Dwyer informed Chelmsford (13 May) that 'his presence...could have a disturbing effect'. Martial law was extended throughout the central Punjab. The first response came from Tagore who asked Chelmsford to relieve him of his knighthood, bestowed by Hardinge ('for whose nobleness of heart I still entertain great admiration'). He was ashamed of 'badges of honour...in the incongruous context of humiliation' (31 May). Martial law was lifted on 12 June. Subsequently, a Committee of Inquiry into the trouble at Amritsar was announced. It proved difficult to find an appropriate judicial chairman. Eventually, Lord Hunter a Scottish law lord was appointed, though he could not go to India until October. He was joined by a panel of assessors, two Indians and three from the British Establishment in India.

Montagu was increasingly unhappy with Chelmsford's handling of affairs. 'He had attempted to justify Dyer's actions' which, he argued 'saved the situation from being infinitely worse...very notable services which he rendered at an extremely critical time'. 'It was the savage and inappropriate folly of the order which arouses my anger'

(11 June 1919). Montagu replied 'I cannot admit that any services that Dyer has rendered anywhere can atone for action of this kind' (17 July 1919).

When called to give evidence, Gandhi insisted that the leaders of the uprising be released: this was refused. In its report, the Committee split down the middle: Hunter and the two Indian members condemned Dyer, their colleagues (a general, a judge, and a civil servant) exonerated him. Dyer was recalled to England (he was due for retirement anyway) and was not re-employed. His 'punishment' released primitive forces in the Conservative party. In a debate on 8 July 1920, Carson led a savage attack on Montagu, whose reply was unwise: he accused Dyer of 'a doctrine of terrorism': 'are you,' he accused the bellowing Tories, 'going to keep your hold upon India by terrorism, racial humiliation and subordination and frightfulness?' Those who came to his rescue were mainly opposition Liberals, such as Wedgwood Benn. On his own side, Montagu was most indebted to Winston Churchill who as Secretary of State for War had dealt with Dyer. He observed: 'Frightfulness is not a remedy known to the British pharmacopoeia'. Asquith (from the opposition benches) declared that the Punjab authorities 'had abdicated their functions' and shown 'gross dereliction of duty'. At the end of the debate, a hundred and twenty Diehards voted against Montagu and two hundred and thirty MPs supported him. These included Sam Hoare (future Secretary of State for India) and Edward Wood, who as Lord Irwin was later to be Viceroy.

In the Commons, a majority had supported Montagu. In the Lords a motion was put down by Viscount Finlay, supposedly a Liberal, to exonerate Dyer. Sinha replied for the Government: the debate would 'Fan the flames of racial animosity': Amritsar was 'a deplorable chapter in the history of British rule in India'. Finlay was supported by Salisbury and Ampthill, who had acted as Viceroy during Curzon's absence in England. But Curzon and Birkenhead defended the government and the Archbishop of Canterbury, Randall

Davidson warned of the damage the motion would cause. Nevertheless, a majority of peers (a hundred and twenty-nine in all) voted for the motion. India was informed that their Lordships condoned the massacre at Amritsar.

Despite conducting their own investigation into the events at Amritsar, when the Congress met in December 1919 Gandhi asked the delegates to work the reforms scheme. His conversion to non-cooperation was gradual. On 2 August 1920 he returned the Kaisar-i-Hind medal bestowed by Hardinge, 'not without a pang' as he informed Chelmsford but his 'light hearted' attitude to the massacre had 'disabled me from tendering, as I have hitherto tendered, my loyal cooperation'. Non-cooperation was the policy of the Khilafat Committee, the combination of Muslims (led by the Ali brothers) and the Congress to reverse the abolition of the Khilafat, the leadership of the Turkish Sultan over the world's Muslims. They drafted 'the fourfold scheme' as it was called: withdrawal of all students from government schools and colleges, boycott of British Courts, refusal of soldiers and others to serve in Mesopotamia, boycott of foreign goods.

Most of the leaders of the Congress were highly sceptical: C. R. Das, Mrs Besant, Pandit Malaviya, and most significantly, Jinnah, all rejected the Khilafat scheme and endorsed the Reforms with varying enthusiasm. Tilak, at the end of his life, formed an alternative Congress Democratic Party. Gandhi threw in his lot with the Ali brothers and with Lala Lajpat Rai, the fiery Punjabi militant. A special Congress was convened in Calcutta in September 1920. This was the first thoroughly rigged meeting with trainloads of delegates arriving from all over India—paid for by financial interests. In his keynote speech Lajpat Rai (a member of the puritan Arya Samaj) gave a clear warning: 'If they suspected the least danger the Hindus would not only withdraw co-operation with the Mussalmans but they would take steps to counteract that danger'. He warned against an Afghan invasion (there had been a half-hearted war with Afghanistan in 1919) 'Hindu-Muslim unity would...break up as soon as they felt that the Afghans were making a move towards India'. All this was reflected in the vote on the fourfold scheme: 5,814 delegates were registered for the conference; only 2,735 actually voted, 1,852 for Gandhi and 883 against him. Even Lajpat Rai did not regard this as a decision for action. He was by no means committed to all the resolutions of the special Congress; he urged their application only in gradual form and expressed his disapproval of the move to withdraw students from schools and colleges.

Gandhi had not lost his faith in the British Empire: 'I am not prepared to reject the possibility of an honourable equality' (23 November). At the regular annual conference held at Nagpur Gandhi declared (28 December 1920) 'There is room in this resolution for both: those who believe that by retaining the British connection we can purify ourselves and purify the British people, and those who have no such belief'. The Nagpur Congress was the last major event of Chelmsford's Viceroyalty, though the Moplah rebellion (21 August) and the Bombay riots (21 November) were its consequences. The Moplah rising stemmed from complex economic pressures but it was projected as a bloody protest by Muslim tenants against Hindu landlords. The tenuous Hindu-Muslim unity was already under severe pressure.

The first elections for the new legislature took place at the end of 1920. The electorate comprised about ten per cent of the population. Following Gandhi, the mainline Congress boycotted the elections, leaving the field to the Moderates—now calling themselves Liberals—to certain provincial parties, and to a large number of independents. The average population of each rural constituency was over half a million, of whom 14,000 would be electors. In the urban constituencies the average population was 126,000 with 9,800 electors. The transferred sides varied from province to province. Only one member on the reserved side was an official: hence three of the four responsible under the Government for policy-making were Indians drawn from public life. In Madras the two sides met together under the Governor and functioned more or less as a Cabinet. Elsewhere they remained separate. Liberals emerged as Ministers in Bombay and UP. In Bombay the leading figure was Dr R. P. Paranjpye, a mathematician and a disciple of Gokhale. C. Y. Chintamani, a newspaper editor dominated the UP legislature. Elsewhere, provincial parties emerged. In Punjab, Fazl-i-Husain was a Congress member who was also important in the Muslim League. He set himself to form a party based on agricultural interests to counter the Urban Congress party; attempting to bring Muslims, Hindus and Sikhs together as Unionists. The Justice Party swept to power in Madras, with a clear majority over all other groups (including the officials). Previously the tiny Brahmin minority had dominated the administration and all aspects of public life. But even the restricted Montford franchise gave the non-Brahmans the advantage.

At the Centre there was now a bicameral legislature, greatly enlarged in numbers but still dominated by the official bloc. The Legislative Assembly, the lower chamber contained 145 members of whom 105 were elected; the Council of State numbered 60 of whom 34 were elected. The Viceroy ceased to preside over the legislature although he continued to exercise supreme authority over the government, its legislation and its finances. In accordance with the Lucknow Pact formula Muslims received thirty per cent of the elected seats.

All this was less important than the move by Congress towards an active policy of non-cooperation. At the Nagpur Congress of December 1920 the Congress constitution was radically altered with a Working Committee to sustain political activity throughout the year. The consequences of the Gandhian revolution were still unrealized when Chelmsford laid down his charge on 2 April 1921. Before he left he had become almost totally isolated. The Heads of Provinces had given up writing, as Chelmsford's own letters were so barren of information. Even the Presidency

Governors corresponded with Montagu rather than the Viceroy. Willingdon complained that he had 'Little power to lead', and the next Governor of Bombay, Lord Lloyd compared him to a block of marble. His successor, Lord Reading found him unable to communicate, 'singularly lacking in charm and geniality'. Montagu had a long talk with Chelmsford on his return to London on 21 April 1925. He described the ex-Viceroy as 'just rather sloppy ice'.

He did make a brief reappearance in government as First Lord of the Admiralty during MacDonald's minority Labour Government of 1924. He was no socialist—indeed he first consulted Baldwin before accepting the appointment. Otherwise, his chief consolation was to be appointed Warden of All Souls, Oxford for the last year of his life (1932-3). He ardently wished his record in India to be recognized and applauded but according to the general verdict he had failed.

NOTES

1. *The Times,* 2 May 1917.
2. H. C. Debs, 1917, Vol. 95, Cols, 2208, 2306, 2378.
3. He told Morley 'I have been striving all my life to escape from the Ghetto'. He told Lloyd George 'If you make a statement about Palestine as the National Home for the Jews every anti-semitic organization and newspaper will ask what right a Jewish Englishman has to take foremost part in the Government.
4. Sir Algernon Rumbold, p. 107, *Watershed in India.*

CHAPTER 6

READING: CAUTIOUS COUNSELLOR

As so frequently happened, the search for a new Viceroy was protracted. Montagu wanted to go but Lloyd George was unenthusiastic. Pressure was put on Chamberlain to accept, but he resolutely declined. The names of Churchill, Fisher, Buckmaster, and Islington were suggested, but failed to persuade the Prime Minister. Among those with experience of India, Willingdon was vigorously promoted by the King and he received 1,500 premature letters of congratulation. In the end Lloyd George chose Reading. As that knowledgeable commentator Sir Algernon Rumbold observes 'It was a sound instinct that led Lloyd George to choose one of the acutest politicians at hand'.

Nearly sixty-one, Reading was the most elderly politician to go to India as Viceroy: he was also the most unusual. His family were in trade and in the East End of London, only just middle class, and most unacceptably, they were Jewish. They might have lived in England since 1700 but this did not count for much in English society before the Second World War. Asquith had accepted Montagu into his circle, but his correspondence is filled with anti-Semitic jibes and Montagu was always referred to as 'the Assyrian'. Lloyd George was not much bothered by anyone's antecedents and appointed Montagu as his Secretary of State. He was beholden to Rufus Isaacs, and he knew that he was not satisfied with his position, elevated though it was, as Lord Chief Justice. Isaacs had been a tower of strength during the war and after and now they needed a Viceroy. Late in March 1921 he accepted Lloyd George's invitation, though the new position was fraught with difficulties. Most worrying was the precarious health of his wife, though he was assured that Simla was as healthy as Britain. Also, though Reading was familiar with the ceremonial side of high office he had no previous experience comparable to that of the Viceroy. He went about acquiring familiarity with the new situation most conscientiously. He regularly went riding in Hyde Park, he and his wife took dancing lessons for when they had to lead off the Viceregal ball. He practised clay-pigeon shooting in preparation for shikar with the Maharajas. He consulted Churchill about what he had to do when he had to inspect troops on parade ('Look each man straight in the eye'). None of this really mattered though, when his big task was to try to restore confidence in British rule and get the reforms off to a good start.

Within a few days of his arrival Reading visited Lahore and then he announced that he would go on to Amritsar. Sir Edward Maclagen, the Governor and Vincent the Home Member, strongly opposed the visit, but the Viceroy insisted. The visit being improvised there was none of the customary pomp: he told Montagu 'The fact that I had visited Lahore and Amritsar, not withstanding the great heat, made some impression'. He described the local people as 'quite friendly', 'no untoward incident': he added that he was 'prepared for criticism' from the Anglo-Indian newspapers.

Reading dominated his Council, though he conscientiously sought their views. He did not intend to initiate new reforms: those so recently launched were enough to occupy his five years. The Council now included three Indian members: Sapru, Mohamed Shafi, a Punjabi, and B. N. Sarma from Bihar. All three were lawyers. The first major problem faced by Reading was a series of labour disputes, among tea garden workers and then on the railways. On top of all this there was a visit to India by the Prince of Wales pending. It was postponed on account of the disturbed conditions.

Among Reading's first meetings was his encounter with Gandhi, within a month of his arrival. He told Montagu (19 May 1921): 'There is nothing striking about his appearance...my first impression...was that there was nothing to arrest attention in his appearance and that I should have passed him in the street without a second look at him. When he talks the impression is different. He is direct and expresses himself well in excellent English with a fine appreciation of the value of the words he uses. There is no hesitation about him and there is a ring of sincerity in all that he utters, save when discussing some political questions...his religious and moral views are admirable and indeed on a remarkably high altitude but I must confess that I find it difficult to understand his practice of them in politics'. Reading first met Gandhi in May through the mediation of Malaviya. His visits were 'very frequent and very lengthy', as Lady Reading noted. Reading openly brought up the subject of Amritsar and found Gandhi very bitter against O'Dwyer and Dyer. Nevertheless, the Viceroy secured a pledge that the Ali brothers would cease preaching violence. They prevaricated—in September the Ali brothers were arrested and given two years imprisonment. Believing that the political climate was easing, Reading suggested that the postponed visit of the Prince of Wales should go ahead. When he eventually arrived his reception was mixed: in Bombay there was an ugly confrontation between Congress volunteers and 'loyalists', mainly Parsees. Fifty-three were killed and nearly 400 injured in the melee. At Poona he was well received. Then at Allahabad he passed through empty streets. Calcutta was closed down by a hartal. The Prince had received tumultuous receptions in the White Dominions and he was upset by his inability to meet the people. The visit was a great worry to Reading, though of the most limited importance in Indian politics. The Prince wrote to Reading (28 December 1921) 'I am not at all happy about the results of the tour as far as it has gone. Twenty-five thousand pounds of English money and goodness knows how many lakhs of rupees are being spent over it and I must honestly say that I have not been able to justify that vast expenditure....As regards the police and the hopelessly exaggerated police precautions which surround me and do not give me a chance....They take their responsibilities very much to heart because...of the very strict orders they have from Delhi....Money and time are being absolutely wasted.'

The joint Gandhian Khilafat movement continued, with the treatment of Turkey by the allies as its main concern. Reading accepted that Muslim sentiment had been ignored by the Lloyd George government and on 9 February suggested to Montagu that he should state formally that the Treaty of Sevres, which had humbled Turkey, was unacceptable in India. Montagu ardently agreed and on 1 March 1922 Reading cabled London outlining the objections to British government policy. He ended by telling Montagu 'So important is it for the Government of India to range itself openly on the side of Muslim India that we press for permission to publish the foregoing...forthwith'.

Montagu circulated Reading's protest to his Cabinet colleagues (3 March). The Cabinet met on 6 March and were told that Montagu had sanctioned the publication of Government of India telegram. Curzon exploded: 'The part that India has sought to play...passes my comprehension'. On 9 March Lloyd George returned to London and demanded Montagu's resignation, which was tendered the same day. Reading was appalled to think that his demand had precipitated this result. He deliberated over his own course of action , though he did not communicate with Montagu until 30 March. He averred that 'the Government at home have accepted the Government of India's action and my action as legitimate'. This was reasonable inasmuch as Reading's telegram had not been a demand but a request for Cabinet permission to go ahead. Actually, more persuasive was Reading's suggestion that for two Liberal leaders to leave the government would alarm political India. At any rate, Montagu departed into oblivion and Reading survived unscathed.

The new Secretary of State was Lord Peel, an easygoing Tory peer; his Parliamentary Under Secretary was another Tory, Lord Winterton, so no Liberal influence remained in the India Office. There was a debate on India in Parliament on 2 August 1922, initiated by Hoare, expressing 'The grave anxiety and discontent in the ranks of the [Indian] Civil Service'. Replying, Lloyd George insisted 'Britain will in no circumstances relinquish her responsibility for India. If Britain withdrew her strong hand nothing would ensue except division, strife, conflict and anarchy'. He went on to produce his celebrated aphorism that the ICS—'was the steel frame of the whole structure'. The opposition Liberals were appalled, as were Labour, among whom was now Josiah Wedgwood. He demanded 'What evil genius inspired the Prime Minister with the necessity to make this speech today?' Montagu had laid down a 'perfectly steadfast, settled policy'. This was now replaced by 'alternate threats and concessions' and would prove fatal in India as it had in Ireland. Reading told Peel 'The Prime Minister's speech has upset things tremendously here'. A major reason for Lloyd George's illiberal speech was the absence of enthusiasm among young Englishmen for an ICS career. In the years after 1918 a number of war service candidates were recruited by nomination (127 between 1919-21). Thereafter, there was a return to entry by examination, and numbers dropped dramatically (19 between 1921-4). Meanwhile, Indian recruitment was rising fast, (143 between 1919-24) and it increased further between 1925-35, after the Lee Commission recommended equal recruitment of Indians and Europeans: two hundred and fifty-five British recruits were accepted and three hundred and eleven Indian recruits. All this was to reverberate in Indian politics in years to come, but immediately the main pressure was the waxing and waning of direct action by Gandhi and the Congress.

By 1921 it was obvious that the Mahatma was the principal inspiration for nationalist hopes. For his part, Gandhi was concerned that many were joining his movement for the wrong motives and non-violence was being forgotten. He planned mass civil disobedience in the Bardoli District, and on 1 February 1922 informed Reading of his intentions. However, on 8 February in Gorakhpur District in Eastern UP a mob attacked a police outpost at Chauri Chaura. Having set light to the building, they forced the constables to emerge, and twenty-two were murdered. Gandhi was appalled—he called this 'a Himalayan blunder'—and prevailed on the Working Committee to call off the campaign. Many of his supporters were flabbergasted. The young Jawaharlal Nehru objected: why stop because of a minor deviation? Gandhi gently put him right (19 February 1922). This was not the first act of aggression and would have served 'to ignite the gunpowder', and spread 'the foetid smell of violence'. Gandhi may have detected that he had lost control of the movement. Reading was perplexed about tactics. He was dissuaded from arresting Gandhi by Sapru, but finally took the plunge in March 1922: he told the Secretary of State 'Not a dog barked'. When Gandhi was arrested and tried, his judge, Broomfield realized the prisoner could not be indicted for crimes in the customary fashion. He accepted Gandhi's admission of responsibility for his actions and his admonition to Judge Broomfield to inflict 'the severest penalty' made this a unique occasion. Broomfield sentenced him to six years simple imprisonment and expressed the hope that circumstances would enable the Government to release him sooner.

Others were already incarcerated—Jawaharlal Nehru from 5 December 1921, and C. R. Das since 6 January 1922. The movement declined after Gandhi ordered the suspension of non-cooperation in February 1922, leaving most of the groups involved in uncertainty. Das was released in July, and indicated his intention of contesting the next provincial elections. He assumed the presidency of the Gaya Congress and reiterated this intention. His proposal was defeated by a majority of the Congress but he went ahead. His most formidable partner was Motilal Nehru, uncomfortable with the sterile politics of Gandhi: they announced the formation of the Congress-Khilafat Swaraj Party on 1 January 1923, declaring that 'the immediate objective' was 'the speedy attainment of full Dominion Status'.

One aspect of politics in 1923 which seemed only incidental involved Reading in a head-on collision with his counterparts at the India Office. Kenya had a small but powerful European community and a much larger Indian community which supplied most of the colony's professional and commercial infrastructure. The Europeans demanded a substantial instalment of self-government and the Indians put in similar demands: the Africans, the overwhelming majority, were assumed to be too backward to participate in the processes of government. A strong Indian delegation travelled to London to urge the Indian case and Reading gave them all his support. The Cabinet decision went against the Indians in Kenya: a Memorandum was published on 25 July.[1] The main parliamentary debate followed next day in the House of Lords. Both Hardinge and Chelmsford spoke to support the Indian case. Reading reacted strongly to what he saw as a climb-down by the British Government to European threats. In a telegram to Peel (28 July) he condemned 'The subservience' of HM Government to 'the threats of the settlers', adding 'I trust that you and HMG understand the difficulty in future in impressing upon the Indians the benefits they derive from associating with the Empire'. On the same day he told the Legislative Assembly 'They [HM Government] have announced their decision and the Government of India must consider it, and arrive at its conclusions. If submission to Whitehall must be made then, with all due respect to HM Government—it can only be under protest'. The speech was assessed by the *Daily Telegraph* as comparable to Hardinge's denunciation of South Africa. The Under Secretary, Winterton, read the telegram and the *Telegraph* article on 30 July and immediately addressed a confidential note to his chief: 'I feel that it would be impossible to allow these two sentences to pass without a severe rebuke to their author. Their constitutional impropriety can hardly be questioned'. He realized that this might induce Reading's resignation, but though this might cause 'inconvenience' they could not overlook the offence. Peel was made of less inflammable material and he gave a reassuring reply to a question in the Lords. As parliamentary spokesman for Labour on India, Josiah Wedgwood repudiated the communal provisions in the Kenya White Paper and declared that if Labour took office they would reverse the decision.

As a sequel to this 'betrayal', Reading sent a personal telegram to Peel (2 September): 'Indian opinion is becoming more consolidated in determination to hit out against the Dominions and England, even though India itself may suffer....The wave of anti-Empire sentiment is gaining strength'. But Kenya was only at the start of the long campaign to assert White dominance. Reading received no such applause as was awarded to Hardinge for his protest in 1913. He lacked charisma, but it was insensitive of the Indian leaders to ignore his efforts on behalf of their countrymen.

When the second elections to the reformed legislatures were held in September 1923, the Swarajists made considerable gains. In Bengal they put up fifty-seven candidates, both Muslim and Hindu and of these forty-seven were elected (including twenty-one Muslims). The Governor, Lord Lytton, invited Das to nominate the Ministry; he declined, arguing that they were elected 'to put an end to the system of Diarchy' Subsequently the Swarajists formed a coalition with the 'National Party'; the object was to wreck the new system. The Governor was obliged to take responsibility for the transferred subjects from September 1924. In the CP the Swarajists won an absolute majority (forty out of fifty-four seats) but refused to operate the system. Elsewhere their successes were less impressive, although they formed the largest group in UP and Bombay. They were motivated more by caste and religious motives than by nationalism. The Justice party was again returned to power in Madras, though with a reduced majority, and in the Punjab the Unionist hold was not shaken. The Central Assembly (where, of course, the non-officials were still restricted to an opposition role) included a strong Swaraj group numbering forty-two out of the total of one hundred and five. They were aligned with sufficient independents (who included Jinnah) to form a 'National bloc' of about seventy members, 'a party based on compromise and adjustment' as the best informed Indian scholar observes.[2] The electorate for the Legislative Assembly was about one million: that of the Council of State merely eighteen thousand (less the representative of Burma). This contributed to the unreality of the all-India legislature.

Reading was not just a conscientious Viceroy, he genuinely wanted to further India's progress towards self-government. He encountered an entirely negative response except from the Indian Liberals. India had embarked on that form of passive resistance which was to continue until 1947. Never again would an imaginative gesture (like Hardinge's) or a programme of reform (as with Morley and Minto) evoke a positive response from the Indian leaders. Any favourable response would be tactical and temporary only. However, Reading was not discouraged. He plodded on. An opportunity seemed to open up with the installation of a Labour Government in January 1924. MacDonald had long demonstrated a concern about India. However, his situation in 1924 was precarious: not simply because he relied upon Liberal support but in his own party he was under pressure from militants, and he had other and greater priorities. If Wedgwood as the Parliamentary Spokesman on India had been given office he would certainly have pressed for constitutional advance, but MacDonald gave the post to Sydney Olivier, ennobled to strengthen the Labour team in the Lords. Olivier was a former civil servant, Governor of Jamaica, 1907-13. Reading hoped that progress might be made. In February 1924, Motilal introduced a motion in the Legislature embodying the 'National Demand' calling for revision of the 1919 Act recognizing India's right to self determination, Reading responded to this demand. Montagu's reform programme had laid down that there must be a review of the 1919 legislation after ten years but also that there might be a review earlier. Reading hoped that by advancing constitutional change he might open up a response from a wider circle of nationalists: 'It is quite impossible for me to speak [to] the central legislature without referring to constitutional advance, for it is being pressed in one form or another upon us from various quarters both in the legislature and outside it' (15 February 1924). Olivier replied that no change outside the 1919 Act would be permitted. Reading retorted that this handed the initiative to the non-cooperators: 'For the present the Swarajist has it all his own way...there is none to compete with him'. He continued to urge an advance, which Olivier refused: 'To do this would be tantamount to admitting that the grant of full responsible self-government...has become a question of immediate practical politics, an admission which I have not sufficient material to sustain'. Motilal Nehru cabled Wedgwood, insisting 'the guiding motive of the British in India is to serve the selfish interests of their own country. MacDonald seems to have realized that Olivier was being heavy handed. He told Olivier 'I feel that I must strongly advise you not to be too rigid in your telegrams to the Viceroy, as we would like, on matters of internal policy, to make the Viceroy feel responsible'. At any rate in March 1924, Gandhi was released from jail after an operation for appendicitis. The *Manchester Guardian* reported (15 March) that his release had created 'a new spirit of Friendliness'. The Labour Government allowed the opportunity to pass without any gesture. Accepting that his release was an act of clemency, Gandhi resolved not to resume political activity until his original sentence would have ended. Reading seems to have lost patience with Labour. He turned down a proposal for a conference to include Government of India officials and Swarajists.

Having eased the political situation, Reading now found that terrorism was again making ground in Bengal. One, Day, was shot dead mistaken for the Calcutta Police Commissioner; the murderer was hanged and became a martyr—C. R. Das extolled his patriotism. Lord Lytton, Governor of Bengal called for emergency powers, but Reading fearing another Rowlatt Act urged caution on the Secretary of State: 'I view these proposals with grave anxiety'. When a bomb killed three more people, and a bomb factory was discovered, the Viceroy changed his attitude and on 25 October 1924, a Bengal Ordinance created new emergency powers. The first Labour Government abruptly came to an end with Reading in a less flexible position than ever before. He was not helped by the appointment of Lord Birkenhead as Secretary of State when the Conservatives came back to power. Birkenhead was frankly no longer interested in the details of government. Birkenhead wrote to Reading (4 December 1924) 'I think you know that alone in the Cabinet I distrusted, and to some extent opposed the Montagu-Chelmsford Report. To me it is frankly inconceivable that India will ever be fit for Dominion self-government. My present view is that we ought rigidly to adhere to the date proposed in the Act for a re-examination of the situation'. Later Birkenhead decided to appoint the Commission required under the Act not later than mid-1927. Reading urged the announcement of the review of Dyarchy in December 1925, but Birkenhead ignored his advice. Another opportunity to enlist progressive Indian opinion was lost. Motilal's response to the question of a constitutional commission was delivered in the Legislative Assembly (7 September 1925): he pooh-poohed their probable line of inquiry: 'What is the state of education in India? What progress have representative institutions made? Whether these people deserve any further progress or whether it is necessary to send them down a form or two to learn their lessons better...? Now that is the sort of thing that we are objecting to. We say we are absolutely fit for self-government as fit as you are in your own island. This is what we say here. We are occupying that position and you tell us as you would tell schoolboys: "Be good boys and you will be promoted to a higher form"'.[3] Reading and Birkenhead had been friends and rivals at the Bar. The Secretary of State invited the Viceroy to attend the Imperial Conference in London in October 1926, but he declined. His time in India was coming to an end.

A bill to enlarge the scope of the Bengal Ordinance was introduced into the Indian Legislative Assembly in March 1925 by Sir Alexander Muddiman, Home Member. The Bill was rejected by the Assembly but was restored by the Council of State and the Viceroy. In April, Reading paid a brief visit to England at Birkenhead's invitation, to discuss future constitutional change. Indian politics remained in ferment. In the Central Assembly the coalition between Swarajists and Independents began to disintegrate. Jinnah seceded and formed a separate party, the Independent Party. His intention was to consider 'the possibility of...balancing the vote of the Government and the Opposition'. When the budget for 1925-6 was debated the Independents 'declined to join the Swarajists merely to pursue a policy of obstruction for its own sake'.

The last major contribution of the Reading government was to launch the Indian Sandhurst Committee to give substance to the decision of the Government of India made in 1918 to award the King's Commission to Indians in the Indian Army. Indians were admitted into Sandhurst for officer training but during the first ten years, 1918-28, although one hundred and thirty-four Indians were accepted at Sandhurst, only seventy-seven were commissioned. The environment was not friendly. Indian politicians called for a more positive policy. A Committee for the Legislative

Assembly was constituted with a British general as chairman (Sir Andrew Skeen) and including Jinnah and Motilal Nehru. Their proposals did not appear until after Reading's departure. They recommended that 'a substantial and progressive scheme for the Indianization of the Indian Army be adopted without delay'. They called for the establishment of an Indian Sandhurst and this was taken up, but Indianization of the officer corps still had a long way to go.

Reading had a lot of trouble with the Princes. The noisiest hubbub was created over the attempt to blackmail the heir to the State of Kashmir, Hari Singh. The husband of the temptress who enticed him sued his bank. Reading was instrumental in persuading the judge to refer throughout the case to 'Mr A', though his real name was soon widely known. Reading also had to remove two Maharajas—Indore and Nabha—from their thrones; but the most difficult issue which confronted him was the claim by the Nizam of Hyderabad to be given back Berar, formerly under the rule of the Nizam but handed over to British administration in 1893; when Hyderabad was heavily in arrears over payment of the subsidy allocated for the upkeep of a force at division strength, known as the Hyderabad Contingent. This had always been resented by the rulers of Hyderabad and in 1925 the Nizam put in a cleverly argued claim for the return of Berar, insisting that this did not fall within the area of foreign policy in which British paramountcy was acknowledged. He asked that the question be referred to an independent commission of inquiry. Reading absolutely rejected the 'claim to absolute equality with the British Government except in foreign affairs' and his interpretation was upheld by Birkenhead. He insisted that 'even though a Court of Arbitration may be appointed in certain cases, its function is merely to offer independent advice to the Government of India with whom the decision rests'. This categorical rejection of the Hyderabad claim alarmed other states which wished to enlarge their power in relation to British paramountcy. Reading might have wished to depart on a more amiable note, but he was largely remembered for his severe handling of the Berar issue.

During their last year, Lady Reading was diagnosed as háving cancer. She underwent an operation in Calcutta and insisted on staying with her husband until his term was completed. Among their guests at Simla they entertained Lord Lee of Fareham, a former coalition colleague of Reading. Lee's wealthy American wife noted in her diary:

> I went to lunch by myself with Miss Stella Charnaud Secretary to Lady Reading. She is a nice girl. Clever and hard working, whose job is by no means an easy one looking after anyone so ill yet so imperious as the Vicereine....She was very sweet to me as always and is certainly a remarkable woman....But for her passionate ambition for him I do not believe that in spite of his ability he would have risen to any heights at all. He...has a sweetness of nature which would have been satisfied with very much less. They say he consults her on every question and when he does make up his mind it is often she who has made it up for him'.[4]

Reading departed in 1926, and this was accompanied by his elevation to the rank of Marquess. He greeted his successor at Bombay with the observation that he might hope for a relatively calm period during his first eighteen months in office but that later he must expect trouble and anxiety. The wife of that successor, Lady Irwin, observed that Lady Reading was drawn and haggard. She had another four years to live. After her death, Reading married Stella Charnaud in 1931.

Reading's last major contribution in Indian affairs was as leader of the Liberal group among the British delegates to the Round Table Conference convened by MacDonald and Benn, commencing in November 1930. At first, Reading's attitude was cautious, but increasingly he warmed to the plan for a federal India which Indian delegates had suggested. On 5 January 1931 he announced that 'he was prepared to agree to a responsible Federal government', declaring 'English Liberals were the lawful inheritors of the democratic tradition'. As Benn informed Irwin, Reading 'was the hero of the conference and creamed the milk the Prime Minister was due to deliver'. Lloyd George had earlier been critical but now he fulsomely congratulated Reading and on 4 February 1931 said to Reading: 'It was a triumph of historic Liberal doctrine guided throughout by your great knowledge of Indian affairs, by your statesmanship, and by your great personal influence and prestige'. After all that, it was unfortunate that the federal plan came to nothing.

Soon after the conference the Labour government fell apart. In the 'National' government which MacDonald formed in August with a Labour rump and Conservative plus Liberal support, Reading became Foreign Secretary, though not for long.[5] When a second National government was formed in November 1931, Simon took over at the Foreign Office. Thereafter, Reading enjoyed only the honorific post of Lord Warden of the Cinque Ports, 1934-5. He had retained a romantic feeling for the sea, ever since he had shipped as a cabin boy in his youth. He died on 30 December 1935 aged 75. Few men have lived such a full life.

NOTES

1. Indians in Kenya: Memorandum by the S. S. for the Colonies, Cmd. 1922, 1923.
2. B.B. Misra, *The Indian Political Parties,* 1976, pp. 224-5.
3. Ind. Leg. Assy Debs, 7 September 1925
4. Lady Lee's Lunch: H. Montgomery Hyde, *Lord Reading; the life of Rufus Isaacs, 1st marquess of Reading,* 1967.
5. He was the third ex-Viceroy to go on to be Foreign Secretary in the 20th Century—Lansdowne, Curzon, Reading and Irwin (Halifax) all held the office.

CHAPTER 7

IRWIN: REFORMING CONSERVATIVE

The Hon. Edward Wood, newly elevated as Lord Irwin and later remembered as the Earl of Halifax was forty-five when he arrived in India. His grandfather, Sir Charles Wood was President of the Board of Control for India, 1853-5 and subsequently Secretary of State for India, 1859-66. He was created Viscount Halifax in 1866. The father of Edward Wood, the second Viscount Halifax was the leading High Churchman of his day and conducted conversations on union with Rome, which of course led nowhere. He bequeathed his son (the only survivor of four sons) his great personal piety. Edward Wood was elected Conservative MP for Ripon in 1910. In spite of being born with a withered left arm and with no hand, Wood was a fine horseman and marksman and went to France with the Yorkshire Dragoons in 1914, returning to London in 1917 to a post in the Ministry of National Service. He became President of the Board of Education in Bonar Law's Ministry (1922) and subsequently Minister of Agriculture under Baldwin, 1924-5. When the time for Reading's return to India drew near, there was 'a difficult problem in personalities'.[1] When consulted George V proposed the name of Earl Haig (then sixty-five years old) but since Kitchener no soldier had been considered, (none appointed after the Mutiny, except Minto who had only served as a regimental soldier). The King then suggested Edward Wood, who was not particularly attractive to Birkenhead. Birkenhead informed the departing Reading 'He is a man of the highest character, of very considerable ability, great courtesy of manner and of distinguished appearance'. Birkenhead wrote the same day 'Wood is the best man we could have got'.

The Irwins landed on 1 April 1926, at Eastertide. The programme arranged for them was modified so that they could attend religious services on Good Friday and Easter Day. It might have been expected that Irwin's personal spirituality would appeal to Indians, especially to Gandhi, but this was masked by the grandeur which seemed natural to him as the heir to a great landed family. There has always been controversy over how far Irwin's piety represented his whole character. His nickname was 'The Holy Fox'. Perhaps his difficulty in establishing rapport with Gandhi was due to his being a Holy Fox also. Both men were slow to accept the bona fides of the other. He never really achieved terms of intimacy with many Indians: nor, of course, with his own subordinates. His relations with his Secretary of State were formal and increasingly distant. Later, he was to tell R. A. Butler 'I remember so well how bloody it was serving under F.E.'.

The Irwins moved into the 'temporary' Government House which had been constructed for Hardinge. No greater contrast could be found between the Viceroy and the Secretary of State. The building of the new capital had been halted during the war and was only now moving forward to completion. Certain changes had been introduced after the Montford reforms. A separate Parliament building was under way, though set on one side from the Secretariat and the Viceroy's residence, the real seat of power.

One of the problems Irwin inherited from Reading was the hostility of South African governments to the Indian community in that country. In February 1926 a deputation was sent from India to give evidence about a proposal to repatriate the Indians to a country which most of them had never seen. It was led by G. F. Paddison ICS, Commissioner of Labour for Madras. They managed to persuade the South

African Government to postpone punitive actions and to see another delegation from India. C. F. Andrews was in South Africa, independently, and on his return to India Paddison told Irwin how Andrews had been instrumental in bringing round the government. Irwin passed this on to Birkenhead, emphasizing 'the favourable impression that he made generally in South Africa' (26 May 1926). In June Charlie Andrews was given four interviews by the Viceroy who reported to Birkenhead 'I think Andrews may be useful in keeping Gandhi more or less straight'. After these Simla meetings, Andrews told a friend that Irwin was 'Modest and unassuming...without the slightest tinge of racial prejudice'. At the urging of his new friend the Viceroy paid a visit to Santiniketan and enjoyed a long talk with Tagore: 'I completely fell in love with him...and was much taken by his overflowing goodness and simplicity. What a different place the world would be if there were more like him' (18 December 1928).

During 1927, India was plunged into ferment by the publication of *Mother India* by Kathleen Mayo. This went through eight editions between July and December. The book concentrated on the most sensational evils of caste—untouchability, child marriage, temple prostitution, and other horrors. In all this Gandhi was portrayed as an evil genius. Not surprisingly he described the book as 'A drain inspector's report'. Miss Mayo declared in her foreword 'this book has not been submitted to any member of the Government of India'. Yet most Indians suspected that *Mother India* was inspired by the Government and for many years it remained a deep grievance to them, although it was really just a piece of sensational journalism. Numerous replies appeared which simply served to give the book continuing importance. This was Irwin's introduction to the nature of the Indian debate.

One of the first questions to be placed before Irwin by Birkenhead was that of the composition of the statutory commission to examine the working of Dyarchy and make recommendations for the future. Irwin insisted that it must be composed exclusively of British parliamentarians: if Indians were included they would have their own policies and a unanimous report would be impossible. Mischievously, Birkenhead suggested that by including both a Hindu and a Muslim member they could guarantee disagreement and thus prevent the Commission from recommending any 'very considerable advance'. Irwin's view prevailed, and in the Spring of 1927 Sir John Simon was invited to become Chairman. It was not so easy to get together the rest of the Commission. Geoffrey Dawson, editor of *The Times* told Irwin that he had discovered its membership 'and I am bound to say that I am just a little shocked....The chairman may be very good indeed, but he has a terribly weak team behind him....The best that can be said is that they may be tame and harmless, it is really a one man show'. In a *Times* leader Dawson reflected that the personnel were less important than the Chairman whose 'Intellectual predominance gives it a definitely Liberal character' (19 November 1927). When the membership was announced (7 December 1927) there were four Conservative and two Labour members. Among the Tories, E. C. G. Cadogan was a friend of Baldwin, Colonel G. R. Lane Fox was Irwin's brother in law. There were two peers: Lord Strathcona and Lord Burnham, proprietor of the *Daily Telegraph*. The two Labour MPs were Vernon Hartshorn, Postmaster General in the shortlived 1924 government, and Major C. R. Attlee.

As could be expected, the exclusion of any Indian caused a storm in India, though Irwin did his best to lay the ground by meeting Gandhi in November 1927. There was general condemnation at what was seen as a racial selection. Irwin quickly regretted his previous advice; relying on his senior advisers he had assumed that there would be no Muslim boycott of the Commission and therefore no Congress boycott. Both assumptions were wrong: 'The mistake was perhaps evidence that some new force was working of which even those whose knowledge of India went back for twenty or thirty years had not yet learnt the full significance'.[2]

During the first visit (3 February to 31 March 1928) the Commission was confronted by the boycotters chanting 'Simon go back'; however, the ban on relations with the Commission was not yet total. When they returned for the second tour (11 October 1928 to 13 April 1929) the atmosphere was much more violent. The Commission began to feel that they were the object of attack, not just their mission, and when a bomb was hurled into the central assembly in Simon's presence in August 1929 the hostility was unmistakeable. Gradually Irwin was compelled to involve himself in these hostilities. The President of the Legislative Assembly, Vithalbhai Patel, elder brother of the future Deputy Premier of India, made no secret of his involvement in the national movement and time after time gave rulings which he knew not to be impartial. However, his acceptance of office under the British system was condemned by the hardliners among the Nationalists. Divisions became ever sharper. Irwin remained above the battle for as long as he could. When a no-tax campaign was mounted in the Bardoli tahsil in Gujarat by Vithalbhai's brother, Vallabhbhai, the government worked to arrive at a compromise. Looking forward to a change of government, the Labour leader, Ramsay MacDonald made a guarded commitment to study the realization of Dominion Status for India. Irwin's comment to Birkenhead was sarcastic (May 1928): 'I hope that he has no serious doubt about our party coming back to power....It would sound an unprincipled statement for him to have made, because he knows too much about it all, I should have thought, seriously to believe his own statement'. Within eighteen months, Irwin was to make his own commitment on the same lines—a complete about-turn. At this critical moment the Conservative government was defeated; there was a general election in May 1929 in which Labour emerged as the largest party (though receiving

300,000 votes less than the Conservatives). With Liberal backing MacDonald formed another government, and chose for his Secretary of State for India a new recruit to the Party from the Liberals, Wedgwood Benn, whose light stature inclined some to underestimate him, including Beatrice Webb who recorded in her diary 'an insignificant little person'. However, he proved better than his predecessor.

The Indian political leaders hoped to outflank the Simon Commission by drafting their own report under the chairmanship of Motilal Nehru. This attempted to overcome known divisions and difficulties; some were content with Dominion Status, while others demanded complete independence. Even more contentious was the question of communal electorates, agreed under the Lucknow Pact. The Nehru Committee rejected this formula. With almost everything in suspense, Irwin departed for the customary mid-term break in London. His views had advanced considerably, and were now in tune with what he understood MacDonald and Benn to intend. He had decided to re-read the Instrument of Instruction issued when he became Viceroy, and drafted by Montagu. These stated that 'It is His Majesty's will and pleasure that the plans laid by parliament in 1919 should be the means whereby British India may attain its due place among his Dominions'. This was clear enough: why not make a statement reiterating this pledge?

Irwin was conscious that he would face another massive campaign of civil disobedience unless he could utilize the Nehru report to defuse the growing tension by a reference to Dominion Status. He arrived in London on 13 July and made contact with the Labour leaders with a view to persuading Simon to agree to a statement on Dominion Status. The problem was handed to the India Office who proceeded to draft numerous proposals which further complicated an already complicated situation. The Simon Commission had been functioning alongside two other constitutional bodies. There was the Indian States

Committee, the 'Butler Committee', whose report had appeared in March 1929. Following Reading's reassertion of paramountcy Sir Harcourt Butler and his team had considered the states' claims to be in treaty relationship with the British Government and had concluded 'paramountcy must remain paramount' (just so). Another question to be resolved was the conclusion being reached by the Indian Central Committee whose chairman was Sir Sankaran Nair, a somewhat shadowy body created when political India rejected the composition of the Simon Commission as excluding any Indian. The Central Committee was composed of Indians, not necessarily central to Indian politics, who had been meeting in India and had now arrived in London, ostensibly to hear evidence, though actually to have a good time. At this critical moment, Sir Samuel Hoare wrote to Irwin about the state of his party, that is the Conservative Party: 'Politics here are in a most unsatisfactory state. Stanley gives no lead to the party either in the House or in the country. The modus vivendi which we fixed up with Beaverbrook looks like breaking down, each side accusing the other of having destroyed it....I have tried to do what I could...and at present I am disheartened with the result' (17 May 1930).

On 18 July the Secretary of State met Simon and Irwin. Irwin put up a draft declaration to 'set India on the path to a status...similar to the great self-governing Dominions'. Simon responded with a draft letter asking for a reply for the Viceroy which would 'enable the Commission to deal with the relationship between the states and British India'. Simon asked the Government to approve this exchange of letters, to obtain the approval of Baldwin and Lloyd George, and to associate the Central Committee with this procedure. A further draft was produced by Sir Malcolm Hailey which referred to a conference to follow publication of the Commission's report and stating 'His Majesty's Government regard it as implicit in this statement of policy that India should ...be enabled to attain in due season the full status of a self-governing Dominion'. On 21 July, young Mr Monteath of the India Office saw Baldwin in Bourges and showed him the drafts of letters between the Prime Minister and Simon. The letter referred only to the Butler Committee and to 'some sort of conference' to take place after the Commission reported. There was no reference to Dominion Status. In a long and rambling letter, MacDonald reminded Simon of the declaration of August 1917 and added that the Government 'regards it as implicit in this statement...that India should...be enabled to attain in due season the full status of a self-governing Dominion'. Nobody was deputed to see Lloyd George, perhaps because he might prove awkward. All this activity was suspended on 27 July when all the leaders left London for the country. On 17 September Simon was notified that he would meet MacDonald two days later. A revised draft followed when Simon realized his Commission was being used as a stalking horse to endorse the Viceroy's announcement. He met with his colleagues on 24 September. The unity which had thus far marked their efforts was weakening. Almost all opposed any reference to 'Dominion Status' in the proposed letters. Lord Burnham was against the whole proposal; Colonel Lane Fox 'did not think the letter should go unless the Commission were unanimous'—which clearly they were not. Mr Hartshorn was prepared to support a letter to help the Viceroy, though 'it would certainly be regarded as a surrender to the boycotters'. Attlee recalled that the 'original plan was...to give the Commission the opportunity of making the gesture. The letter as now altered would remove the object of our writing. He was strongly in favour of the Government taking action without our coming in'. The dissent of the Commission was not passed to the Prime Minister.

Two days later, MacDonald met Simon and told him 'the Government had decided that the Viceroy should make a statement shortly after landing in India which would include a formula regarding Dominion Status, but that it was still open to the Commission to have an interchange of letters with the Prime Minister on the other points'. On 24 September Simon saw Benn and told him the Commission refused 'to write the letters at all if it was to evoke any statement about Dominion Status in the Prime Minister's reply'. Both the Labour members now 'agreed with the decision recorded above'.

When MacDonald told Simon 'the Government had decided' this was true only inasmuch as a few ministers had been consulted. On leaving the India Office Simon happened to meet Sankey, the Lord Chancellor, in the Street and 'in a few minutes conversation gathered that he was under the impression that the Commission agreed to the proposed statement on Dominion Status'. Simon informed him otherwise and Sankey departed saying 'I will see Benn at once'. There was no record of this brief meeting. Two days later MacDonald sailed for the United States of America and on 10 October Irwin sailed for India.

The Viceroy made his announcement on 21 October: despite its lack of reference to dates, the statement was hailed as a breakthrough as Irwin hoped. On 2 November the 'Delhi Manifesto' was issued by a panel of politicians representing all the main groups in Indian politics. Some were politicians of yesterday like Annie Besant, others belonged to the future like Jawaharlal Nehru. However, they all insisted that if the conference was held it must 'meet not to discuss when Dominion Status is to be started but to frame a Dominion Constitution for India'.

Parliament was not slow to respond. In the Commons Lloyd George rose having put a parliamentary question on the previous day. He asked if the Commission had been consulted on Irwin's statement, Benn conceded that they had not, adding that the goal of British policy remained that stated in the 1917 declaration. Was there no change, 'either in substance or in time?' inquired Lloyd George. The Indian leaders appeared to believe there was a 'fundamental change'. On 7 November the debate was resumed. Baldwin declared that 'every statement of fact and every implication' in the

Viceroy's statement was 'untrue'. He had no support to offer to 'the scheme which Lord Irwin was concocting with the Socialist Government'. He had only heard the previous week that the Simon Commission 'disassociated themselves' from the speech: it was a 'blunder'. Regarding responsible government or Dominion Status, no one knows 'whether that date be near or distant'. It was a classic Baldwin performance.

Lloyd George was more hard hitting; he had received no advance notice of the statement though he was leader of the Liberal Party. Quoting the Delhi Manifesto he observed that India expected 'a very great deliverance', yet in the Lords, Passfield had declared that there was 'no change at all'. *The Times* had called Irwin's statement 'prolix and confused': Lloyd George agreed.

Benn attempted to deflect criticism by abusing the Liberal leader whose remarks were 'lamentable and mischievous'. The object of Irwin's declaration was to provide a 'restatement and interpretation of the Montagu policy'. There had been doubts in India: 'Sympathy was gone...the days of Mr Montagu were gone'. The expected conference would be held when the Simon Report was published. Simon followed with a restrained statement. He emphasized that the Commission was a 'completely united body' and asked for time to finish their work without parliamentary controversy. Simon had done well to keep his people together amid all the fuss.

Years later, the Viceroy, now Lord Halifax, wrote in his memoirs 'I had not reckoned with and have never been able to understand the violent political explosion in Parliament'.[3] However, politicians of each party had been devious—unholy foxes—and it was all for nothing. On 23 December, Irwin had a meeting with Gandhi, Motilal, Jinnah, Sapru, and Vithalbhai Patel. The moderate Motilal was angry. He claimed that 'there was no difficulty about having full Dominion Status at once'. Irwin had no answer; his initiative was over. When the annual Congress met at Lahore, Gandhi rejected any idea of a Conference. On 26 January 1930, led by Jawarharlal Nehru Congress celebrated 'Independence Day' and hoisted the Indian tricolour. It might have been like 1776, except that Congress could raise no military power.

The Irwins had returned to Delhi for the meeting with the Indian leaders. Their Viceregal train was bombed just by Humayun's Tomb, but the attack was mistimed and the train stayed on the rails. They now moved into the new Viceroy's House, Lutyens' masterpiece which was finished at last. The House of Assembly (Parliament) was also ready and was opened though without much sense of purpose. The original estimate of the cost of New Delhi was Rupees 1,270 lakhs. By 1931, the new capital had cost Rupees 146,389,669 lakhs (more than eleven million pounds or forty-four million dollars at prevailing rates of exchange). The bill for the Viceroy's House was Rupees 18,173,766, for the Secretariat on Raisina Hill Rupees 18,483,145, and for the new parliament Rupees 8,892,054. The Viceroys were to occupy their splendid residence for just eighteen years before independence overtook the capital and the nation.

The British and the Congress were now at the parting of the ways. There was a pause before Gandhi launched his campaign; the most effective of them all. He announced that his object was to end the salt tax; a minute levy, but one that affected the whole population. On 12 March 1929, Gandhi left his ashram at Ahmadabad to march to the sea for the purpose of collecting or manufacturing salt. He kept up a cracking pace, tiring out much younger men. Sometimes he rode on a donkey, and there was much in the symbolism of the march which recalled Christ's journey to Jerusalem. He expected an early arrest, but The Holy Fox was prepared to wait. Gandhi reached the sea at Dandi on 6 April after covering two hundred and forty-one miles in twenty-four days. Still the Government did not intervene, and when people all over India began to manufacture salt they were not arrested. The foremost Indian writer on these events, comments: 'Civil Disobedience was always treading on the brink of violence'[4] and the movement was infiltrated by terrorist elements. The worst incident occurred at Peshawar in the North West Frontier Province. Always volatile, it had been incited towards political action by Abdul Gaffar Khan and his Red Shirts. The Chief Commissioner, Sir Horatio Bolton, stayed his hand but on 23 April he ordered the arrest of the Khan Sahib's War Council. Armoured cars penetrated the city and fired; two platoons of 2/18 Royal Garhwal Rifles refused to move, after enduring a day under bombardment from bricks and bottles. The situation was retrieved by a Gurhka battalion but was so grim that Bolton ordered all troops out of the city that same night (24 April). British control was not restored until 4 May. Bolton lost his grip and suffered a mental breakdown. In October he retired (he had held the post since 1924).

This situation in conjunction with the continuing ferment throughout India was too much; Gandhi was arrested on 5 May. The provincial authorities now took stern action. By July, Congress was in retreat everywhere. Defiantly, Jawaharlal Nehru wrote to Gandhi 'For myself I delight in warfare' (28 July). His was not a majority view. While these momentous events were unfolding the Simon Report appeared in May 1930—Volume I *Survey*, and Volume II *Recommendations*—two weeks later Reading commented: 'The two volumes of the Simon Commission Report are a splendid achievement and will rank among the most valuable of State Papers. The unanimity of the members of the Commission...is in itself a great tribute to him...The publication of Volume I a fortnight before Volume II was a truly brilliant idea, and I strongly suspect that it emanated from Simon. Both volumes are remarkable for clarity of vision and lucidity of exposition and for sympathy for Indian national ideals....analysed with judicious impartiality...a series of constructive proposals...of highest importance'.[5] It did not impress Indians, nor C. F. Andrews who rapidly produced a reply (published by Allen and Unwin). The report deals, he wrote, 'Much more with that old India which I knew when I went out nearly thirty years ago...it shows no understanding of the young India which we see rising today'. Irwin expressed his disappointment that the report made no reference to Dominion Status, but it was well received in Britain.

Meanwhile, plans were in hand for the Round Table Conference. In a telegram to Irwin, Benn declared: 'Questions of Indian policy are to be free from subjection to the exigencies of parliamentary politics at home' (11 July). Irwin announced that the purpose would be to provide a solution 'that both countries and all parties and interests in this can honourably accept'. The Cabinet considered the question on 15 July and agreed that the opposition should be included in the British delegation: all those 'with a genuine purpose of cooperation'. The Viceroy informed Benn that the inclusion of Simon in the conference would be 'interpreted to mean restriction of liberty of conference to discussing of his report' (23 July). Benn told MacDonald that 'the Viceroy is much opposed to his [Simon's] inclusion and all the Governors hold the same view' (25 July 1930). Benn told Irwin that the Conservatives would take part: 'a definite success for Baldwin in his fight against the old stagers' (12 September). Benn was very sensitive to who should, or should not be included. Reading would be an unknown quantity ('in the dark'). 'Samuel's inclusion would be very welcome, and I suppose Crewe couldn't matter. But with Simon out of it and Lloyd George a possible non-starter we may get a decent team'.

Irwin maintained his fox-like reputation over the Simon Report and the Round Table Conference. He told King George V: 'I am very sorry that anything I should have said about the Simon Report should have caused Your Majesty any uneasiness. I have never had any doubt that it would in fact be the principal basis of discussion at the Conference'. He did not admit that he had opposed Simon being a member of the British delegation. The first Round Table Conference was opened by George V on 12 November 1930. One week later the Government of India published proposals on constitutional reform (19 November). They accepted provincial autonomy and a form of Dyarchy at the centre with the elected members handling all subjects except defence, finance and the Princely States. The timing was odd. The British side at the conference was represented by eight members of the Government, four Conservatives and four Liberals. Peel was the nominal Conservative head but Sir Sam Hoare was the real leader. Reading headed the Liberals, among whom was Philip Kerr, who had just inherited the Lothian peerage. He had been Lloyd George's private secretary (1916-21) and was a prominent member of the Round Table Group. The Indian delegates included leading Liberals—Sapru, Sastri, Jayakar. There was a strong contingent from the Princely States—some princes came themselves—Patiala, (Chancellor of the Chamber of Princes) Baroda, Bhopal and Alwar, though the largest sent their Dewans, or other representatives: Hyderabad, Mysore, and others. The Aga Khan was there—but most significant was the presence of Jinnah. He was to observe: 'There are four main parties sitting round the table now. There are the British party, the Indian princes, the Hindus and the Muslims'. Hailey wrote to Irwin: 'Jinnah was always the perfect little bounder and as slippery as the eels his forefathers purveyed in Bombay market' (14 November 1930). An unexpected description of the suave, elegant lawyer.

The full sessions of the conference were just a series of set speeches but the subcommittees considering specific subjects were more fruitful. Gradually the goal of an All-Indian Federation emerged. On 19 November a Cabinet memorandum encouraged the idea. As leader of the Liberals, Reading seemed cautious but on 5 January 1931 he announced that he 'was prepared to agree to a responsible Federal Government in India'. His speech carried the day, the Tories did not dissent for fear of being isolated. Benn told Irwin he was 'the hero of the conference and creamed the milk the Prime Minister was due to deliver' (15 January 1931). On this note the conference closed on 19 January 1931 with a speech by MacDonald, promising 'to recognize the principle of the responsibility of the Executive to the Legislature'. The following week, Gandhi and his principal colleagues were released from jail and the Congress Working Committee was again recognized as a lawful organization. At their first meeting on 7 February, Gandhi told Irwin 'how can I sever my connections with you? I have so many English friends...Andrews keeps sending me cables from Cape Town asking me to arrive at a settlement....Is it possible for me to sever all these relations? And yet if cooperation is not possible I shall have to do so'. This banter was the cloak for prolonged and trying negotiation. Both the Viceroy and the Mahatma were more inclined to reach agreement than their advisers. On the British side a major consideration was the Indian boycott of Lancashire cotton goods. It was agreed that this would be discontinued though the encouragement of Indian textiles was also agreed. Slowly, a modus vivendi was evolved, though without much support, British or Indian. Jawaharlal complained 'Was it for this that our people behaved so gallantly for a year? Were all our brave words and deeds to end in this?' On the other side, Baldwin was under pressure, and the officials were disgusted insisting that 'The Civil Disobedience Movement was practically on its last legs'. The Gandhi-Irwin Pact, often called the Delhi Pact, was concluded on 4 March. There were concessions to Indian feeling: all political prisoners not convicted of acts of violence were released. It was agreed that Congress would attend the next session of the Round Table Conference. However, much credit redounded to Gandhi who had negotiated with the Viceroy and the British government on terms of absolute equality, or so it was assumed. However, when Gandhi pleaded for the life of Bhagat Singh, the young

Sikh who had thrown a bomb in the Assembly, Irwin was unable to concede his request. The Pact was a tribute to his personal ascendancy.

Just before his departure from India, Irwin wrote a long letter to Benn (9 March):

> I regard it as a very astonishing thing that Gandhi should have been so far persuaded to come into line....On Sunday the 1st I had made up my mind very clearly that we must break....Although many people are giving me a share of the credit, I don't think very much is really due. I believe that the broad forces that were at work were working very hard in the direction of peace, and it may even be that we could have got something more stiff through. But I do not think that we should have been as successful...in carrying Gandhi on the sentimental side.

He also wrote, as he regularly did, to his father:

> I kept asking myself all the time "Was the man completely sincere?"....I came to have no doubt that if Mr Gandhi gave me his word on any point, that word was absolutely secure and that I could trust it implicitly. On the other hand...in some matters he was the victim of unconscious self-delusion.

This assessment might have been delivered on Irwin himself. As his biographer Birkenhead comments: 'The Viceroy was aware that he was risking his own future but....every day it was borne in on him that repression led nowhere'. Just before Congress met in Karachi, Bhagat Singh was due to be executed. Gandhi and others beseeched Irwin to commute the sentence. Irwin remained adamant and the assassin was hanged on 25 March. Meanwhile, the Princes were having second thoughts. There was unrest in Patiala and an official inquiry was held. The Maharaja, previously a supporter of federation now proposed an alternative scheme.

On this note of uncertainty, Irwin departed from India on 18 April: five days earlier Irwin met with the delegates to the first Round Table Conference to discuss forthcoming arrangements, Gandhi was present. He was to meet the Viceroy again in Bombay on the eve of his departure.

He returned to a welcoming committee which included Stanley Baldwin. He went on to Windsor to be appointed a Knight of the Garter. However, he was quite unsure about his future. His correspondence seems to suggest that he contemplated adhering to the Labour Party. Any such move was pre-empted by the great economic crisis which now overtook the Labour Government. Unable to cope, they resigned and MacDonald formed a 'National Government', mainly Conservatives with Liberal participation and with the inclusion of a few Labour MPs. In this gallery, Reading became Foreign Secretary, though not for long. Sam Hoare went to the India Office. Irwin was outside the government, and still in the margin of politics, still suspected by the Conservative party. In November 1931 there was a general election in which the Conservatives scored an overwhelming majority. Simon replaced Reading at the Foreign Office. Still Irwin was not included, but the President of the Board of Education, the Liberal Sir Donald Maclean died suddenly and the post was offered to Irwin. He had found this little to his taste ten years previously, but he accepted, remarking to his Parliamentary Secretary 'I shall be able to have two days hunting every week'. He seemed to have reached a dead end, but fate, and Hitler still had much in store for him.

NOTES

1. Harold Nicolson, *King George V, His Life and Reign*, 1952, pp. 504-6. The information is conveyed in a somewhat elusive manner.
2. Earl of Halifax, *Fulness of Days,* 1957, p. 116.
3. Ibid. p.118.
4. S. Gopal, *The Viceroyalty of Lord Irwin 1926-1931,* 1957, p. 67.
5. Reading to Sir Godfrey Collins, 8 July 1930.

CHAPTER 8

WILLINGDON: MARKING TIME

Irwin's successor knew India better than most incoming Viceroys, having been Governor of Bombay, 1913-19. On his departure he had served as a delegate for India at the League of Nations. Born Freeman Freeman-Thomas, in 1866, he went to Cambridge where he made friends with E. S. Montagu. He served in the Rifle Brigade until he went out to Australia as Aide-de-Camp to Lord Brassey, Governor of Victoria, 1895-1900. He had married Brassey's daughter, Marie Adelaide in 1892 and in the language of the day they made a 'remarkably handsome pair'. On their return from Australia, Freeman Freeman-Thomas became a Liberal MP. He was elected despite the Conservative landslide, he supported the war against the Boers. He became Joint Secretary of the Liberal League, the organization of the so-called Liberal Imperialists who had supported the Boer War. He lost his seat in 1906 but was elected for Bodmin. He remained Secretary of the League until 1910 when he again lost his seat. He became a Lord in Waiting to George V in 1911, and was said to be the King's favourite tennis partner. Having some influence with Asquith he was then offered Bombay in 1913.

His reputation was that of a pleasant, progressive politician; but he was outclassed by his lovely wife (as Minto had been). She was both gracious and on occasions domineering. She had almost an obsession with the colour mauve which she employed in clothes and furnishings. On his appointment to Bombay Lord Willingdon succeeded in breaking down racial exclusiveness in the city. He quickly made friends with Gokhale. On 14 November 1913, Hardinge wrote 'I am glad that you saw Gokhale and that you like him. I like him too.' As the need to respond to Indian aspirations became clear, Willingdon got in touch with Gokhale (26 January 1915) writing 'I have told the Viceroy that you were going to prepare some notes of your views to me. He expressed a great desire to see them, if you don't object'. The outcome of this request was a draft which Gokhale prepared two days before his death. Its provisions bore a remarkable resemblance to Montagu's forthcoming scheme: an Executive Council of three Indians and three Europeans; all laws to be passed by the Legislative Council (enlarged) but the Governor to have final powers. Control from London over the Government of India was to be relaxed and the Council of India abolished. Gokhale hoped that this scheme might gain official acceptance.

When his old friend, Montagu became Secretary of State, Willingdon was among the few to give him whole hearted support. On 24 January 1918, Montagu told his wife: 'I had a divine letter from Willingdon saying that I had cheered him up by coming to see him, that everything was coming right'. Willingdon's emollience failed to impress Jinnah. After the Delhi Conference on the war effort, Willingdon convened his own gathering (10 June 1918). Jinnah attended, and adopted a very independent line: 'They wanted a national army, or in other words a citizen army and not a purely mercenary army....You must make the educated people feel that they are citizens of the Empire and the King's equal subjects. But the Government do not do so'. Jinnah's social relations with the Willingdons were equally tense. Invited to Government House, his wife Ruttie wore a low-cut Paris gown; she had the figure to set it off. Perhaps out of envy—certainly not out of prudery—Lady Willingdon ordered her servant to bring a wrap to cover up Mrs Jinnah 'in case she felt cold'. Jinnah was furious; he informed his hostess, 'When Mrs Jinnah feels cold she will say so and ask for a wrap herself.' They then walked out.[1] This must have been a unique event at Government House. When in November 1918 Willingdon's time in Bombay ended, coinciding with the end of the war, the Bombay loyalists organized a public meeting in the Town Hall to thank the Governor for his work. Jinnah organized a counter demonstration and drowned out the speeches of the platform party. The police had to clear the hall. All this was unfortunate inasmuch as Willingdon at this period really was a progressive. After a conference of governors to discuss the Montford scheme, the Secretary of State recorded: 'Willingdon quite agreed with me: the others looked very gloomy'. When Montagu told Chamberlain about the reception given to his report he remarked 'Willingdon will think it does not go nearly far enough and has too many constitutional safeguards' (4 July 1918).

The Willingdons returned home on leave and almost immediately went back to Madras. Here he made an even better impression. When the Diarchy Constitution came into force, he operated his government as a single ministry with a 'Chief Minister', accepted by the Legislature and the Governor.

When Chelmsford's time in India was coming to an end, Montagu wrote to Lloyd George putting forward the names of possible successors: 'Willingdon, excellent in temperament and a rare exception to the rule that there is no political interest [but] is not a good administrator and cannot be expected to put his back into getting through the innumerable changes still wanted in India' (14 February 1920). Many expected Montagu to recommend his old friend and Willingdon received hundreds of letters prematurely congratulating him on his appointment as Viceroy.

Willingdon was among those who urged a further postponement of the Indian visit of the Prince of Wales: probably thinking about the effects in Bombay rather than in sleepy Madras. His last years were somewhat was uneventful. On his return from India, Willingdon was created a viscount in 1924: next year he led the 'Indian' delegation to Geneva.

Appointed Governor-General of Canada in 1926, his time in the office spanned the period of formal constitutional change between the Balfour Report and the Statute of Westminster. When Irwin was due to depart, Ramsay MacDonald, the new Prime Minister, decided that the next Viceroy should be Lord Gorell who wrote poetry and detective fiction and who had served briefly as Under Secretary for Air under Lloyd George. Through Gorell's publisher, the news came to Lady Brassey (Willingdon's mother-in-law) who passed it on to the King's Private Secretary, Lord Stamfordham, thinking it must be official. Stamfordham complained to MacDonald that the King's constitutional right to be consulted had been ignored. Despite resentment, MacDonald paused before going further. He mentioned Gorell's name to the King, who replied that he had never heard of him. Baldwin announced that the Conservatives would never accept him. MacDonald tried another unconventional name, that of Jimmy Thomas, a former railwayman who was Colonial Secretary, but this too came to nothing and King and Prime Minister between them decided on Willingdon. King George wrote in his diary: 'I had proposed him to Lloyd George nine years ago when he sent Reading'.[2] Benn was notified later of the appointment; it came as news to him. When the appointment was announced, the editor of *The Times,* Geoffrey Dawson observed in a letter to Irwin that this was 'a thoroughly bad choice...he never had very much stuff in him' (2 January 1931). Was it just a coincidence that Jinnah decided not to return to India?

All this took place within a storm of gathering difficulties. On 21 September Britain went off the gold standard. The Cabinet decided that India must follow suit in order to peg the rupee to sterling. Willingdon protested: either the rupee should be left to find its own level or else Britain must guarantee sterling credits to India up to fifty million pounds. Schuster, Finance Member of the Viceroy's Council objected that India must be left to run its own economic policy. Willingdon and his Council signalled that they were prepared to resign if overruled. Hoare cabled Willingdon on 24 September imploring him not to go. 'Anything like resignations upon the scale which you indicate...would present the appearance of an open conflict of interest....You have given a lifetime of service to the Empire and we are sure we can count on you to stand by us now in the greatest Imperial emergency since the war' (24 September 1931). In the face of this appeal, Willingdon and his colleagues (including three Indian members of the Council) withdrew their resignations. The cuts in public service pay which were enforced in Britain (precipitating the naval mutiny at Invergordon) were introduced in India. In Britain there was a general cut in the pay of ministers and civil servants of ten per cent. In India there were similar cuts in official salaries. Willingdon set an example by awarding himself a cut of twenty per cent and asked his Council to accept a reduction of fifteen per cent. Some might have commented that the Viceroy holding the highest paid appointment in the British Empire could well afford this reduction.

Even afterwards his annual salary was Rupees 2,50,800 or nearly 19,000 pounds when the Prime Minister received just over half that amount.[3]

Where did all this leave the Round Table Conference? Hoare predicted to Willingdon that wider questions would be shelved so that they could go ahead with provincial autonomy (25 October).

This formed the substance of the speech which MacDonald delivered to Parliament (2 December 1931) after the Conference was closed. MacDonald announced that it was the Government's intention to prepare a new constitution based upon the Simon Report. Among the questions raised at the Conference the most important concerned the extension of the franchise: how should this be effected? The debate provided the first occasion when Attlee publicly considered the Simon Report. He reflected that their report had revealed the 'enormous complexity' which was India: 'problem seems to overlap problem'. The Simon Report 'has been utilized as a jumping off place for further advance, as one always expected it would be'. Stanley Baldwin concluded the debate, claiming 'We have got to the point that we have reached with still a practical unity of parties'. To test this assertion, Winston Churchill forced a division and forty-three of his supporters opposed the motion. However, three hundred and sixty-nine were in favour, including Attlee and many Labour men. The hardline Winterton commented that the Prime Minister 'spoke somewhat listlessly and for a very important occasion to a not very full house'. His statement was 'not calculated to produce much enthusiasm', and Winterton concluded that the whole question was 'in the same position in which we have been for the last two years'.

Willingdon was created an earl, he was sixty-five years old, older than Minto or Reading had been. He arrived in India promptly on 18 April 1931. Willingdon related the situation to his son in England (16 May 1931):

> I have had my first talk with Gandhi yesterday and renewed our acquaintance of many years ago. He was at the top of his form, most friendly, most eager to cooperate with me (so he said). Indeed no one could be more desirous to be helpful. But the trouble of it all is that he has roused his movement of Civil Disobedience and having done so, I'm much afraid he can't control it....and this settlement between Irwin and Gandhi is a serious handicap to all our Government for in order to preserve the settlement we have to some extent got our hands tied: on the other hand it is a great advantage to Gandhi's extremists for they openly say that they are using this truce time before their next assault....I don't think we shall get through without some serious outbreak, but we shall get through all right for the army and police are splendid....I own that I feel we are trying to aim very high in our efforts for peace. We are sitting

> on the top of a tinder box and I only hope it won't blow up. Every day that passes in peace is all to the good, but if we have to strike we are going to strike hard...I see that Benn has said that Irwin is the best Viceroy ever known!...He has left me with a baby to bring up which is a squalling and unattractive little devil: let us hope he will improve with years. Mum is hard at work and as usual has made us most comfy. She is a wonder. We found things very sloppy here. The Irwins had allowed black tie always except at really big occasions: all this is being changed, much to the disgust of the staff officers we have taken on.

A few days later he told his son (25 May 1931):

> I'm having a hell of a time over the start of this conference work. First, the members of the committee out here all want to go on different dates, and second that damn fellow Gandhi who was full of cooperation and goodwill when I saw him, directly I ask him to go over and join them in their work in London refuses to go!...I am told by those who know him that he may still change his mind, but to have to deal with a man who is a mixture of a saint and a 'bania' is very trying indeed....Your mother is at the top of her form and reorganising us all magnificently....The Military Secretaries seem to have run things exactly as they seemed inclined: doesn't suit Mum at all. But we shall have everything straightened out very soon...

They were the first Viceregal couple to occupy the Viceroy's House, and Lady Willingdon proceeded to alter the decorations to her favourite mauve. Lady Willingdon was to leave her mark on the new capital in small but significant ways. At her initiative an Olympic stadium was built at the Purana Qila end of Kingsway, obscuring the majestic old fortress much to the disgust of Lutyens, who was further outraged when the Vicereine insisted that chattris be dotted along the outline of the stadium—even over the protests of the Government of India chief architect. Similarly, the Anglican Church of the Redemption (later the cathedral) was given a tower in plastered brick, instead of the sandstone used elsewhere in New Delhi on Lady Willingdon's instructions, so that its height could be increased: this was when the architect was absent in England! On a smaller scale she changed the plans for several of the Princes' mansions. When the Willingdons arrived, Jaipur House was already half built: Lady Willingdon visited the site with the Maharaja and insisted that the whole design be altered and amplified. The Maharaja protested in vain; as he later told Mountbatten, 'no one could stand against her when she decided on something'.

The Viceroy was quite different, as he acknowledged in a speech to the Chelmsford Club, Simla on the 27 June 1931: 'The work that a Viceroy has to do is much too heavy for a gentleman of my mature years.' He arrived with two highly competent aides, (Sir) Eric Mieville as his Private Secretary and General (then Colonel) Ismay as his Military Secretary. Mieville had spent four years as Private Secretary to the British Minister at Peking, and then became Private Secretary to the Governor-General Canada, 1927-31; Ismay had started in the Indian cavalry and had worked for the Committee for Imperial Defence before becoming Military Secretary to the Viceroy, 1931-3. Both were to return on Mountbatten's staff in 1947. Willingdon had no intention of doing their jobs for them. When a complicated case was put before him, Willingdon would ask who had made the recommendation: 'If it was someone he knew to be sound he refused to bother himself with the details': 'He had regular weekly interviews...and it was during these personal discussions that he kept himself up to date'. This was all very well, but it left a lot of the power in the hands of his staff. On his arrival as Viceroy Linlithgow complained that he seldom came across a file with 'W' inscribed in red ink, as was Viceregal practice, let alone an actual Viceregal minute. Sir Fazl-i-Husain was a member of his Council, and a shrewd operator, the Viceroy leaned a lot on his advice. Willingdon inscribed a photograph of the two of them: 'It was taken by

Victor Sassoon after lunch...and clearly shows you and me settling everything for the good of India' (23 February 1936). The next Civil Disobedience campaign had none of the intensity of its predecessor. Willingdon insisted that it was not the Government's intention to destroy the Congress: 'We should treat them not vindictively but coldly'. When Willingdon arrived in India in 1931 the Delhi Pact had been concluded ending Civil Disobedience. What next? It was hoped that Gandhi would attend the Round Table Conference, but as late as 15 August he informed Andrews that 'It was God's Will that I should not go'. At this moment the international economic crisis overtook the Labour Government; lacking any financial plan it was dissolved and a 'National' government was formed. MacDonald was still Prime Minister, but the sympathetic Benn was replaced by the chilly Hoare. After meeting Willingdon, Gandhi decided on 27 August that he would go to London. He was accompanied only by Sarojini Naidu believing that he would speak for India. Willingdon told Hoare (28 August 1931): 'You will find him, I think, amenable and anxious to help with a real desire to work out a satisfactory constitution. I do not think you will find him in any way a violent extremist, or that he will be likely to walk out in order to create a demonstration. I must confess to a sense of extreme relief at having got rid of the little man for a few months, for while we are the best of friends he certainly is the most difficult man to pin down in the matter of negotiations. He may be a saint...but this I am perfectly certain, that he is one of the most astute politically-minded and bargaining little gentlemen I ever came across'. Pandit Malaviya of the Hindu Mahasaba, V. S. Srinavasa Sastri and Tej Bahadur (Liberals), Dr Ambedkar (leader of the Scheduled Castes Federation) and Zafrullah Khan for the Muslim League with intermittent attendance by Jinnah were also members of the conference. Instead of discussing self-government for India, they were back on the familiar questions of the minorities and the Princes. Early in November there was an informal gathering at Oxford attended by Gandhi to meet Lord Lothian, Under Secretary for India and Malcolm MacDonald, son of the Prime Minister. Also present were C. F. Andrews and Edward Thompson. But Gandhi's difficulties were mainly with his Indian colleagues. On 30 November Gandhi made the claim 'The Congress alone represents the whole of India, all interests'. Three days later he returned home, though he had one last meeting with Hoare and promised that before he returned to Civil Disobedience (which he did not then contemplate) he would get in touch with Hoare and Willingdon.

Once again, there was a standoff. Willingdon explained to Hoare: 'If I did agree to see him...they would say again "This is the old story—Gandhi going along to do a deal with the Viceroy"' (20 December 1931). He added 'The Delhi Pact is at all events dead and gone, murdered by Jawaharlal Nehru and Abdul Ghaffar. Edward Irwin certainly made a great and gallant effort but it has proved unsuccessful' (26 December 1931).

A confrontation came almost immediately in the Legislative Assembly. Irwin's last fiscal measure had been opposed and he had been compelled to 'certify' the Finance Act and extend its working for eighteen months. In Willingdon's first legislative session the bill was slightly modified, but this did not satisfy the opposition. It was defeated by sixty-three votes to forty-eight, and once again had to be certified by the Viceroy. Resentment at this case extended to those counted as loyalists. Sir Hari Singh Gaur declared: 'Those of us who believed the principle of autocracy was really dead countered the opposition we received in the country and came to this House to cooperate with the Government....It [the Bill] is the best refutation of the hopes and aspirations of those who came...to see that a new order would take the place of the old'. Sir George Schuster the liberal Finance Member replied 'Their objections are felt with equal, possibly with even greater strength by us....But we feel that we have been forced into this position by the nature of the present constitution'. Willingdon defended his measures not very effectively, arguing 'The Assembly failed accurately to reflect the attitude of public opinion on this question'. He produced the hoary argument that the poor were understood better by the Government than by the politicians.

It was hard to plan any long term initiative in India when policy was in the pending tray in London. Hoare was not his personal friend: they did not meet until Willingdon returned for the customary mid-term leave in 1934, and he was not specially outgoing. Willingdon pressed Hoare 'for some immediate measure to show the constructive side of an imperial policy which was currently demonstrating more success in suppressing Indian political activity than in widening it'. Willingdon told Hoare (10 January 1932): 'I am perfectly clear, as I have always been, that Gandhi is a sort of Jekyll and Hyde, and while he may have his saint-like side on the other he is the most Machiavellian, bargaining little political humbug I have ever come across'. 'Gandhi's vanity is such that he looks upon himself as a parallel ruler in India and cannot understand my refusing to admit it' (22 July 1933).

While the policy for India was in suspense, there were problems to be faced. As always the South African Indians were under threat. An impressive delegation went from India, headed by Sir Fazl-i-Husain, then the member of the Viceroy's Council responsible for Indians overseas. Negotiations were difficult and the Indian delegation did no more than obtain a reprieve. On their return to India the delegation met the Viceroy on 28 February 1932. In his diary Fazli wrote: 'We met HE the Viceroy and had a talk. HE had not informed himself as to the nature of the agreement, legislation, etc. and his talk with the delegates made some howlers which created a very bad impression on the delegates—Sir Darcy Linsay, Mrs Naidu, Sir Kurma Reddi and Sastri, while Bajpai, the Delegation Secretary, and I felt much embarrassment and it was a great relief when it was one o'clock and we went into lunch. Lady Willingdon was her usual charming self and helped me to make the delegates forget the talk during our one hour interview'.[4] In Britain the National Government attempted to maintain some momentum in the reform process by sending three committees to India to investigate aspects of the political framework. The most important was the Franchise Committee with Lord Lothian as Chairman. They proceeded swiftly. They recommended the extension of the vote to all householders, persons with a minimum educational qualification and all who have served in the armed forces. The effect was to increase the electorate from less than six and a half million to about thirty-five million (or twenty-seven per cent of the adult population). Female voters, less than three hundred and twenty thousand under the 1919 Act would now number more than six million.

Less fruitful was the Indian States Enquiry Committee whose Chairman was J. C. Davidson who was familiar with Argentina but knew virtually nothing about India. However, he was an intimate crony of Baldwin. Several wives accompanied the delegates and it was all more like a sightseeing trip than a serious investigation. Davidson told Baldwin, 'I have been most deeply impressed by the exceedingly low standard of the Indian political service'. Late in March they stayed in the Viceroy's House; they had decided that federation had not really been considered by the Princes. Davidson reported (28 March): 'HE is in a very difficult position. He has undoubtedly been anti-federal...but has discovered that in my private conversations I have in fact been pursuing an exactly contrary line of argument....Federation is not the policy of the Government of India and they dislike it. However, he has been playing up splendidly during the last week...and with admirable grace has been pressing the Princes to federate'. Lothian was also dubious about federation: when Davidson tried to pressure the Prime Minister of Hyderabad into accepting federation: 'Lothian intervened to say that was not good enough, and if the states didn't make up their minds quickly he was going to recommend an elected centre....Unfortunately Willingdon intervened in his usual way, saying to Lothian, 'I quite agree with you my dear fellow'. I had to point out to Lothian rather sharply that I was a member of the House of Commons, which he was not and that the House of Commons would not approve an elected central assembly in which the Princes were not represented....Then of course Willingdon agreed with me'. Whereas Lothian's recommendations were adopted (and formed the framework from which the Constitutional Assembly was created in 1946), Davidson's recommendations proved a failure.

Gandhi was due for release from jail on 19 May, but he announced that from 8 May he would fast for three weeks against Untouchability. He was released the same day. He sought an interview with the Viceroy and this time the meeting took place. Lady Willingdon met Gandhi to escort him to the meeting: she urged Gandhi to bring his wife to meet her. Kasturbai plucked up her courage and came; she brought a gift of khadi, dyed mauve (a small example of Gandhi's sensibility). Lady Willingdon was delighted and used the fabric in furnishing her personal drawing room. Gandhi then announced a campaign of selective *satyagraha*. He was arrested on 16 August, and was released one week later because of his physical state. On 16 September he announced that he would abstain from *satyagraha* until 3 August 1934, the date when he had been due for release.

Gandhi was doubtful about further moves, and the Viceroy was content to hold fast. Political development was limited to the activities in Parliament, where Sam Hoare worked to hammer out a plan acceptable to a Conservative party, reinforced by an electoral landslide in which they and their allies won five hundred and twenty-one seats. This enormous majority had a double-edged effect: there was no need to worry about the opposition and their own dissidents could rebel without pulling down the Government. The revolt was headed by Churchill supported by the Tory right wing, notably by Lord Salisbury and Lord Lloyd.

Cautiously, Hoare placed his draft before a Joint Committee of both Houses of Parliament chaired by Lord Linlithgow. This took evidence and heard objections over an eighteen month period. The out-and-out opponents of change declined to serve on the Committee, reserving their fire for the debate on the Bill. The Joint Committee laboured from April 1933 to November 1934; they held a hundred and fifty-four meetings and examined a hundred and twenty witnesses.

There was a pause in India while they awaited events in London. Willingdon told Hoare: 'We have released that intolerable little man Gandhi. He has declared a fast for twenty-one days...on account of the impurities he finds all around him. He also says that he insists on going through with this unless he gets a message to give his fast up!...I'm afraid I feel about him that his purpose in doing this is to strengthen his waning influence by doing something spectacular. His vanity is quite his worst quality....Why Providence had troubled the British Empire with two people like Gandhi and De Velera I can't think....The country is very quiet and the people are at last believing that we are sincere in our intentions as to constitutional reforms. Of course the difficulty now is to get the Bill through Parliament. Hoare has to give assurances to his Conservative friends who, Indians say, show that we British don't trust them at all. What a pity it is that the truth should be decided by the House of Commons and the House of Lords, ninety-nine per cent of whose members know nothing of India'.

When the Bill was debated on the floor of the House (commencing 10 December 1934) there was still substantial agreement between the parties, echoed by Simon who affirmed that their report was drafted 'without a single dissident minute': indeed, he added, Attlee was 'responsible for a good deal of what is in those volumes'. When the house voted on 12 December, four hundred and ten MPs were in favour of the Bill and a hundred and twenty-seven against. These were a curious alliance of Tory Diehards and Labour.

The Diehards had launched their main assault in another place. The Central Committee of the Conservative National Union was much more representative of the rank and file Tories, with four representatives from each constituency. A wrecking motion was proposed by Sir Henry Page-Croft. He told them, 'It is positively your last chance to influence the situation'. He averred: 'It is proposed to...risk the fate of one-fifth of the human race, and, I say it deliberately, to risk the final ruin of Lancashire and the destruction of our greatest market. Why? Because a few agitators with goat and loin cloth make a row in India and your representatives over there have not the will to rule'. Against this a motion against Baldwin and Hoare was moved: this carried the day by five hundred and forty-three votes to five hundred and twenty. By this narrow margin Baldwin and Hoare were reprieved.

At its second reading the India Bill was accepted on 8 February 1935. Churchill pointed out that the absentees included both Lloyd George and MacDonald. Wedgwood insisted that the Bill put India 'under the control of the Princes'; Lansbury declared 'This is the most contemptuous House of Commons I have ever spoken in'. Tempers were short. Those for the Bill numbered four hundred and four; those against, a hundred and thirty-three: a curious combination of the Diehards (Churchill, Brendan Bracken, Lord Hugh Cecil, the Marquis of Hartington) and Labour (Attlee, Bevan, Cripps, Lansbury, Maxton, Wedgwood).

They then proceeded with the Committee stage. On 20 March Churchill suggested that as the Princes were against any further proceedings, he would propose an amendment which effectively suspended further consideration of the Bill; ninety-four members voted in favour, two hundred and seventy against. Meanwhile, in Bombay a conference of the Princes was held on 25 February and a resolution passed denouncing the Bill. The King was appalled. Like many others he had hoped that they would provide a conservative element in the new federation. He told the India Office he was 'disgusted by their vacillations' and suggested that instead of flocking to London for the Silver Jubilee celebrations they might attend to the needs of their own subjects.

The House of Commons went wearily on. On 28 May, Attlee admitted: 'After seven and a half years of the subject I am not so ready to dogmatize as I was when I started. I realize only too well the objections to any attempted solution of the problem'. Isaac Foot for the Liberals acknowledged, 'I knew more about India when I was a member of the Round Table conference four years ago than I know today'. He protested that the safeguards were 'too many and too onerous'. He went on, 'my main apprehension about this bill is as to the unity of India...Federation in a certain sense adds to that danger'. The Liberals had been faithful supporters of the Bill; Churchill had not budged from outright opposition, he insisted that the Bill added nothing of value to the conclusions of the Simon Commission. The last vote was taken on 5 June; those for, numbered three hundred and eighty-six; those against, a hundred and twenty-two: once again a strange amalgam of Left and Right, Bevan and Bracken, Craddock and Cripps. Simon abstained. The Bill became law on 2 August 1935. By then MacDonald was no longer Prime Minister and Hoare had moved from the India Office to the Foreign Office, but Willingdon was still in the Viceroy's House. Willingdon was not just a ceremonial Governor-General. When Quetta suffered its devastating earthquake in May 1935, both the Viceroy and Lady Willingdon visited the stricken city within a few days, despite the heat and discomfort. At the end of Willingdon's tenure of office, the tenuous links between the Congress and the Government of India which had been created by Gandhi and Irwin (now Lord Halifax) had left almost no trace. On 9 December 1935 Nehru wrote to Lothian in highly charged tones, as was his style, but despite the excess of expression his complaints have substance: 'I must confess to you that I feel a certain hesitation in meeting people who have been officially associated with the Government of India during the past nightmare years. That period is full of horror'.

Yet in the short run, Willingdon's policy of inaction was really quite successful. The Congress had suspended all its mass campaigning. When Nehru opposed the 1935 Act as 'a Charter of Slavery' the proposal was put to the annual Congress session in mid April 1936 for Congress to boycott the forthcoming elections. It was defeated by four hundred and eighty-seven votes to two hundred and fifty-five. Congress was back on the course of co-operation. An official announcement appeared in August 1935 that Willingdon's successor would be Lord Linlithgow. The takeover took place as was customary, on 18 April 1936, with pomp and ceremony, the Viceroy stepping through the Gateway of India, erected to commemorate the visit of George V in 1910. This was the last Viceregal departure to take place in the old style.

Few can have regretted Willingdon's passing. On his return to England he was created a Marquess, like Reading, though with somewhat less cause. He was also appointed Constable of Dover Castle and Lord Warden of the Cinque Ports, like Reading. Unlike his more illustrious predecessor his active political life was finished on his return. He died in 1941. His dynamic consort outlived him nearly twenty years. Lady Willingdon died in 1960. She had been amongst the first to predict that Mountbatten would be a good choice for Viceroy.

NOTES

1. Stanley Wolpert, *Jinnah of Pakistan*, Oxford University Press, 1984, p. 56.
2. In December 1930 MacDonald wrote to the Canadian

Premier, R. B. Bennett, asking him to release Willingdon: 'A solution to this problem is essential to the future government of India, and it must now be sought in India itself. I know of no man who can conduct these negotiations better than Willingdon.' (23 December 1930).

3. Rs 45,000 sumptuary allowance Rs 1,60,469 'Contract Allowance', and Rs 52,000 for transport. The pay and expenses of the Private Secretary and Military Secretary were also allowed for in the staff.
4. Azim Husain, *Fazl-i-Husain, A Political Biography*, pp. 211-12.

CHAPTER 9

LINLITHGOW: ICE-COLD AUTOCRAT

Willingdon may be called a 'service' aristocrat; his whole life from the time he left Cambridge was spent in public service of different kinds. Linlithgow was different. He was a landed aristocrat, his life centred on the ancestral home, Hopetoun, on the Firth of Forth. Like most members of his class he was ready to serve his country in time of need; but otherwise his interests were centred upon his estates. Eighteen of his kinsmen are listed in *The Dictionary of National Biography*, starting with Sir Thomas Hope, first baronet who, we are told, 'maintained the King's temporizing policy'. They were created Earls of Hopetoun, and the father of the Viceroy of India (who was the first Governor General of the Commonwealth of Australia) became Marquess of Linlithgow. Despite selling the site of the Rosyth naval base to the government (1903) he left his estates much encumbered.

Victor Alexander succeeded his father in 1908 when he was twenty-one. He went to France with the Lothians and Border Horse, though he had to be invalided home. He tried politics, briefly holding minor office, 1922-4, as Civil Lord of the Admiralty. The family were short of funds and Hopetoun House was closed. Linlithgow's first major quasi-political task was to act as Chairman of the Royal Commission on Agriculture in India which laboured from 1926-8, taking sixteen volumes of evidence. As one of the biggest landlords in Scotland his views favoured the promotion of scientific agriculture. The main recommendation was for an Imperial Council of Agricultural Research. While this task was unfolding, the Donoughmore Report on constitutional progress in Ceylon appeared. Linlithgow told Irwin that this had 'fairly put the wind up me': 'I am still steady in my view that we are fighting a rearguard action in the East, and I am for giving as little ground as possible' (23 September 1928). This seemed like a solidly Diehard response, but Linlithgow was not one of those who believed that no change was possible.

Linlithgow's next big assignment came almost out of the blue. When Hoare decided to endeavour to draw the teeth of his Diehard critics by appointing a Joint Select Committee of both Houses of Parliament he invited Lord Peel, the former Secretary of State to act as Chairman. Just when proceedings were due to begin Peel went down with an attack of phlebitis. Hoare feared that the absence of the Chairman would give the Diehards a field-day, and he asked Linlithgow with his Indian experience to fill the role. The Committee sat from April 1933 to October 1934. The main pressure was directed at Hoare and officials of the India Office, but the Chairman was required to exercise control, often under trying circumstances. Their report was published in November 1934. All this unexpectedly made Linlithgow a central figure in the India debate, associated with the reform programme. When Baldwin took over as Prime Minister from MacDonald, in his Cabinet reshuffle (June 1935) he invited Hoare to succeed Willingdon. This would have given him some months rest before he need go. However, Hoare had long coveted the Foreign Office and he was appointed (with dire consequences for him and for Europe). Hence Linlithgow was invited to succeed Willingdon.

The new Viceroy was little known outside a limited circle. He was aloof and haughty. Halifax wrote 'I have often thought...that a good part of the trouble and delay [in implementing reform] came from the fact that Freeman liked the Princes and really disliked the British Indian leaders anc Hopie had not much use for the Princes and did not reall get on human terms with anybody'.[1] 'Hopie'; what a sobriquet to labour under! 'Wise, cautious Hopie' as R. A Butler called him. Linlithgow's constitutional adviser, H. V Hodson, when invited to analyse the failure of Britisl initiatives put his finger on 'the cautious character and publi reserve of Lord Linlithgow whose...heaviness of style beliec the vigour of his mind'. Ian Stephens, editor of the *Calcutt* *Statesman* who saw him regularly could establish 'no rapport he was 'cold, cautious, self assured...an inscrutable rathe unpleasant figure: stiff, unsmiling, physically very large...anc in some indefinable way uncouth'. Perhaps the mos penetrating of these assessments was by Jawarhalal Nehru who in *The Discovery of India* saw him 'surrounded by al the pomp and ceremony befitting his high position. Heavy of body and slow of mind, solid as a rock and with almost a rock's lack of awareness, possessing the qualities and failings of an old-fashioned British aristocrat, he sought witl integrity and honesty of purpose to find a way out of the tangle. But his limitations were too many; his mind workec in the old groove and shrank from any innovations'.[2]

How much of this coldness and distance had physica causes? Linlithgow was 6'5" in height. He had suffered fron polio in youth from which he made an almost complete recovery, but he was left unable to turn his head withou turning his whole body. His wife was exceptionally tall, jus under 6' and his daughters were also of unusual height. Al this gave an impression of a family apart from the rest o mankind. 'Wise, cautious Hopie' was faithfully concerned tc steer through federation. His principal helper was his Private Secretary, Gilbert Laithwaite, who had become attached tc the India Office after wartime military service and whose abilities had been recognized by his employment on specia tasks with the power brokers: he was Personal Secretary tc the Prime Minister during the Round Table Conference anc Secretary to Lothian's Franchise Committee. Now, he was to work in close association with Linlithgow throughout his Viceroyalty, so closely, that they were jointly called 'Linlithwaite'. This urbane and suave functionary channelled most of Linlithgow's communications with the rest of mankind. As against all these adverse opinions, Wavell wrote on the eve of his departure from India: 'I have the greatest admiration for Linlithgow, he is a wise strong man and very human really' (19 October 1943).

It was an example of how far London and Delhi were from the realities of the 1930s that the Secretary of State Lord Zetland wrote to Linlithgow on 2 March 1936 about plans for a Durbar to mark the new reign. The new King was lukewarm: 'I found that he was at present not much inclined to favour the suggestion as he still remembers his tour of India in 1921-2 with a certain amount of distaste'. This hesitation disturbed the Princes, and the Maharaja of Patiala, Chancellor of the Chamber of Princes was very upset. He told Linlithgow 'the very idea...that His Majesty may be prevented from coming out to India is likely to cause consternation'. Linlithgow was embarrassed and told the King's Private Secretary, Hardinge, that an early decision was needed: the most that Edward VIII would concede was 'A sentence in his speech from the throne' (27 May). Then Mrs Simpson intervened.

Linlithgow had two immediate priorities: to set up the new wholly elected provincial legislatures and to induce the Princes to swallow their objections to federation so that the central federal legislature could be formed. Neither goal was achieved without procrastination on both sides. Linlithgow issued a statement: 'I am convinced that the shortest road to that fuller political life which many of you so greatly desire is to accept this Constitution and to work it for all it is worth'. His words largely fell on deaf ears. Within Congress those of Nehru's persuasion were totally against having anything to do with this 'badge of slavery', though others like C Rajagopalachari ('Rajaji'), were ready to make a success of it. Many officials believed that the Congress 'townees' would be rejected by the peasants, but just to make sure, they used their influence as they had always done. The Congress were specially strong in the United Provinces, and an official circular went out urging the 'agricultural interests generally to inflict as crushing a defeat as possible on the Congress with its avowedly socialistic principles' (December 1936). When this came to Linlithgow's attention he sternly repudiated this advice.

Elections were held during the cold weather, 1936-7. Few predicted the gains which Congress made (though the CID got it right), and many within Congress were surprised at the size of their vote. They were assisted by the multiplicity of candidates, mainly independents, who split the vote. Congress formed the majority in nine of the eleven provinces and was the largest single party in two others. It is notable that Congress did best in Madras, with seventy-four per cent of the seats and least successfully where provincial parties were well set (twenty-two per cent in Bengal and ten and a half per cent in Punjab). Nehru had campaigned against acceptance of office, but with the greatly enhanced powers which the provincial governments would command the old ban on office acceptance no longer seemed convincing. Leaders such as Rajaji in Madras and Prasad in Bihar (where at sixty-five per cent they scored second after Madras) urged acceptance. Gandhi preserved a Delphic ambiguity. So what should be done? Congress played for time (and prestige) by putting in a demand that the Governors be instructed never to exercise the special powers which the Act provided for the Governor to overrule the Ministers. Meanwhile, the Congress refused to take office. This move was thwarted by the Governors installing Ministries from the non-Congress opposition; those who might be called the Liberals. But this could only be a temporary device as the legislatures had to meet and sanction financial measures. In London, Halifax was in favour of making a gesture—mainly to help Rajaji and the moderates. The Viceroy was opposed to anything so defeatist, calculating, correctly, that the Congress desire for office was stronger than any non-cooperation attitudes. There followed a long drawn out and somewhat artificial confrontation. Linlithgow did not retreat, but he gave Congress a way out. There was a moment when London almost overruled the Viceroy. Zetland tried to find common ground with Congress: 'Gandhi's latest formula, as I understand it is that he would be satisfied if we agreed that the Governors should dismiss their Ministers only if the disagreement was of a serious character....It might be possible for us to consider meeting them'. Linlithgow wired back that sooner than acquiesce he would resign. Linlithgow was in a dilemma; he announced: 'You may count on me in face even of bitter disappointment to strive untiringly towards...the principles of parliamentary government'. Who was giving way to whom? The Governors played fair with their unfamiliar Congress associates. Thus, in UP, legislation was introduced to extend land reform. The landlords expected the Governor to block this, but it went through. Congress intimated that their people would take office. In this first exercise in brinkmanship, Linlithgow had kept his nerve and won through. It was not always to be so. If the object was to show who was boss it was a shrewd approach, but if the British wanted to demonstrate that the 1935 Act represented an entirely new regime it was ill-judged. When the Congress governments at last took office in March 1937 they commenced by offering their own supporters a major share in governing. The District Congress Committees were invited to be the channel for decision making and no longer the district officers. However, the whole government machine rapidly became clogged and ministers returned to working through the district administration. In different provinces there were very different results. Rajaji, Chief Minister of Madras started a wholesome programme of social reform, including prohibition on alcohol; he also encouraged instruction in Hindi as the language of national unity. Elsewhere there were less harmonious results. Of Bengal, the Governor Sir John Anderson told Linlithgow (8 February 1937): 'Opinion in the Congress is divided, roughly, as between B. C. Roy's group and Sarat Bose's group on the question of office acceptance...Fazlul Huq's loyalty whether to position or principle is completely unreliable'. However, the Viceroy's main interest lay in inducing the fifty per cent of the Princely States needed to inaugurate Federation to make up their minds. The 1935 Act had envisaged a forum for all the 660 odd states within the federal structure. Later, Mountbatten was to get the states to adhere to the Indian Union in quick-time: but that was not Linlithgow's way, nor would it have been accepted in London. Zetland was influenced by the cool response of the India Office to federation. In the most detailed study of this period, Dr Rizvi declares that 'The India Office was indifferent to the federal scheme and showed no sign of wishing to expedite it'.[3] Zetland told Linlithgow (25 September 1936) that the Princes were 'shy birds...and might easily take flight (or 'fright'?) Linlithgow's strategy took account of this hesitation.

Three high level emissaries were sent to tour the states and explain the advantages of federation. However, they 'had no instructions to try and persuade rulers to join the federation'. One of them, Sir Francis Wyllie, related that he discerned 'an air of complete unreality' about his task. After the visits the emissaries' reports had to be collated: there was no sense of urgency, although Linlithgow pressed harder now: 'The market will not improve with delay': he was 'very apprehensive that the consequences of delay will be most unhappy' (13 January 1938). Nothing had been settled when war broke out in September 1939. The Princes' belief that they were sovereign rulers who had relinquished some of their powers—for an unspecified period—to the King of England was confirmed. Federation could only mean a diminution of their powers. They did not have the wit to discern that they were being offered a superlatively good deal with 104 representatives in the Upper House, the

John Lawrence with his Council in 1867. Left to right (seated): Mr H.B. Harington, Additional Member of Council; Sir Charles Trevelyan, Finance Member; Sir Hugh Rose (Lord Strathanain) C.-in-C.; Sir John Lawrence, (afterwards Lord Lawrence) Viceroy and Governor-General; Sir Robert Napier, Military Member (afterwards Lord Napier of Magdala); Sir Henry S. Maine, Law Member; Sir William Grey, Home Member. *Inset* — John Lawrence.

Governor-General's House, Viceregal Lodge Simla. Summer seat of the Government since 1888.

Lord and Lady Curzon on a Tiger hunt in April 1902. With first day's trophy. Lord Curzon looking characteristically enigmatic.

Lord and Lady Hardinge seated with Diamond Hardinge and two others; summer 1913.

Left to Right: Lady Willingdon, Lord Reading, Lady Reading, Lord Willingdon, Madras 1923.

Left to right: Lady Irwin, Lord Irwin, Lady Willingdon, and Lord Willingdon, 1931.

Members of the Cabinet Mission, May 1946. Left to right: A.V. Alexander, Lord Pethick-Lawrence, Lord Wavell, Viceroy and Governor-General of India 1943-7, and Sir Richard Stafford-Cripps. As in all his pictures with the Cabinet Mission, Wavell looking distinctly quizzical.

Lutyen's Palace, the Viceroy's House, New Delhi. As designed by Sir Edward Lutyens.

Lord Mountbatten seated with Lady Mountbatten and Sir Hugh and Lady Dow, 1947.

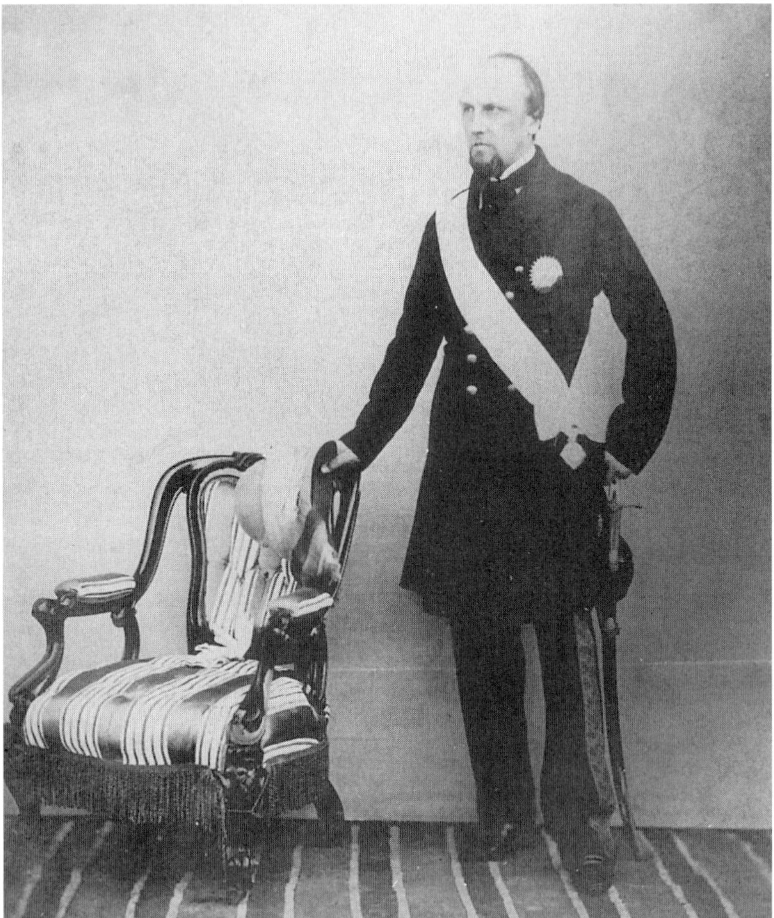

Lord Charles John Canning, Governor-General and Viceroy of India, (1856–62), 5 November 1861.

Lady Canning, 1860.

Sir Hugh, Governor of Sind and Lady Dow.

Council of State, in a total of 260, and 125 in the Lower House out of the total of 375. Given that the minorities would almost certainly join the Princes in voting down any proposal by the majority party (presumably Congress) which threatened their interests they would be in an unassailable position. By September 1939, over a quarter of the Princes had signified their willingness to join the federation. However, most of the Princes could see that they would be handing over their authority to the centre. Hence, federation died in the womb.

Congress had been lukewarm about federation all along, but now they became active opponents: they would accept the accession of the Princely States only if their representatives in the Central Assembly were chosen democratically. The left wing of Congress remained implacably opposed to the 1935 Act; as President of Congress Subhas Chandra Bose demanded that the 'drift towards constitutionalism' should cease. At the same time the Muslim League whose feeble showing in the provincial elections had alarmed its leaders, now cooled towards federalism. Under the 1935 Act, there were four Muslim majority provinces out of the total of eleven (Bengal, Punjab, North West Frontier Province and Sind) yet the Muslim League was far from forming the government (or even sharing in government) in any of them. The Aga Khan was supposed to have told Linlithgow that 'the sugar had all come off the pill'. If the States' representatives were elected, the power of the Muslims and the States to block unwelcome Congress measures would disappear.

From March 1939 even those who belonged to the Chamberlain camp had to recognize that a clash with Germany was coming. Linlithgow's thoughts were still on federation; he advised Zetland to 'let the situation develop'; he still expected the Muslims to come in, he did not 'expect any serious trouble' (22 May 1939). Meanwhile, in Congress they were thinking about the onset of war. Nehru had visited Republican Spain and 'Free China'; he was a vociferous opponent of Fascism. On 1 May Congress passed a resolution insisting that for India to be committed to fight, the Indian people (which of course meant Congress) must give their consent. Congress withdrew its members from the central legislature at the end of August 1939. Hence, they were not present when the Assembly received the formal notification of India's declaration of war on 4 September. When Britain declared war on Germany, India was automatically in: this was certainly the formal constitutional position, but Linlithgow missed an opportunity to rally the country to fight Nazism. He met Gandhi on 4 September and they talked for nearly two hours. Despite his devotion to non-violence Gandhi declared his support for Britain. On the same day Linlithgow saw Jinnah who commented: 'I was wonderstruck why all of a sudden I was promoted and given a place side by side with Mr Gandhi'. On 11 September the Viceroy addressed the central legislature. He announced the postponement of federation though stressing that it was still the objective. On 14 September the Congress Working Committee met at Wardha. They were in some disagreement. Gandhi wanted to offer support to Britain unconditionally. Subhas Chandra Bose was invited to meet Linlithgow on 10 October (he was still Congress President). No record emerged, but soon after he insisted that India must utilize the war situation for its own advantage. That same day Congress passed a resolution stating that no decision would be taken precipitately: they waited to hear the British Government's aims in war and peace. On 17 October the Viceroy at last issued a statement: which an unorthodox ICS officer called 'a dreary prosaic statement on the situation and its political implications'. Once again it was emphasized that the goal was Dominion status; the Governor-General's Council could be at once expanded to include representatives of the political parties, while a consultative committee could be established to deliberate more widely on the political goal. Gandhi wrote to C. F. Andrews 'You will feel as much grieved as I do over the utterly wooden declaration' (18 October). The Congress High Command ordered all the Congress ministries to resign. With evident reluctance they complied. Section 93 government replaced ministerial government: instead of Ministers the Governors now had ICS 'Advisers'. They were back in the days before the Morley-Minto Reforms. The comment of an ICS officer who later felt compelled to resign is here pertinent. 'From every point of view...the Congress attitude was unfortunate except perhaps that of the successful prosecution of the war. But this was the aspect which at the time most impressed itself on the British.[4] Congress "cooperation" it was felt would take the form of daily and exasperating obstruction to which non-cooperation or even active hostility would be preferable. A section of British opinion therefore was not at all keen to have members of Congress in office during the war and secretly welcomed their departure....On short-term considerations there was much to be said for this view and whether deliberately or not, the Viceroy ensured that events would conform to it'.

There followed a silence in the Viceroy's House. From this time forward, Linlithgow's thoughts and actions were all directed to the war effort. On the outbreak of war he asked the India Office how India could help in the war. One division was earmarked for the Middle East. But Linlithgow had no reply to his message until March 1940. His views on political advance were that they 'would have the most serious reactions on the whole Indian position'.

Zetland was pondering on future political developments. On 1 December he wrote to Neville Chamberlain: 'War on the grand scale seems to be accompanied by the churning up of the ocean of thought...I do not believe that the picture of India moving towards the goal which we have set before her, by smooth, measured and leisurely stages—which is what we have hitherto had in mind—is likely to be realized'. Pondering on how progress might be made he brought up the forthcoming visit to India of Stafford Cripps. Late in December 1939 Cripps arrived in India on his way to Burma and China: he was a militant Socialist, expelled from the Labour Party in 1938, and not re-admitted until 1945. His main purpose was to meet the Congress leaders, especially Nehru with whom he had established a close relationship (as he thought). He also met Linlithgow and urged him to bring Congress and the Muslim League together. He told Nehru that 'The rather sphinx-like nature of the Viceroy made it difficult to find what is cooking in his mind....I don't think there is any question of his playing the Moslems against the Hindus—that stage has passed' (24 December 1939). However, the next move was made by the Muslim League. In March 1940 a resolution was adopted calling for 'independent states' in the North-West and Eastern zones of India. This was immediately dubbed the Pakistan resolution, though the whole plan was deliberately left vague by Jinnah who now took his place centre stage in the endgame.

Linlithgow still made political gestures, but without enthusiasm or, perhaps, much expectation that anything would come of any of them. When the Muslim League adopted the Lahore resolution, Linlithgow commented to Zetland: 'Silly as the Muslim scheme for partition is, it would be a pity to throw too much cold water on it at the moment, though clearly we cannot accept it....My only other reaction is that I am not too keen to start talking about a period after which British rule will have ceased in India. I suspect that day is very remote, and I feel the least we say about it in all probability the better' (5 April 1940).

On 10 May 1940, Winston Churchill replaced Chamberlain as Prime Minister. Zetland was replaced by Leo Amery. His father had been in the Indian Forest Service and his mother was Hungarian, which left the young Amery with a fascination for Austro-Hungarian politics. After serving as Colonial Secretary he was out of office from 1929. He had been hostile to Churchill's line on the Government of India Bill. However he had endeared himself to the great man by his demolition of Chamberlain in the debate after

Hitler's triumph in Denmark and Norway quoting Cromwell ('In the name of God go') expressing sentiments which Churchill in the Cabinet was prevented from uttering. Somewhat more progressive than Zetland he was a totally ineffective spokesman in Cabinet (one Minister admitted that if he came into a Cabinet meeting late, he always voted the opposite way to Amery). Although at Harrow School he had been senior to Churchill he was quite unable to stand up to the great man, who bullied him in Cabinet and out. He insisted on dealing with Linlithgow directly and also had all the telegrams between the Secretary of State and Viceroy shown to him. Amery's main ally in Cabinet was Attlee, who also found it hard to oppose the Prime Minister. The only opportunities came when Churchill went to the United States to meet Roosevelt, leaving Attlee to act in his place.

Towards the end of May Linlithgow obtained Cabinet approval for a Revolutionary Movements Ordinance which largely recreated the Rowlatt legislation. As a counterweight to this proposal for repression he suggested constitutional proposals which would give the Indian political leaders places in the existing scheme of government and also offered to accept a postwar constitution framed by the Indian political parties themselves. The Government of India was intercepting the letters of the Indian leaders and Linlithgow informed Amery that he must be 'prepared to take a chance and go fairly far' if any progress was to be made: 'If the Cabinet were ever prepared to go so far as the rough sketch which I suggested, and if that were to be published...the Working Committee might find themselves a little awkwardly placed' (1 July 1940). Meanwhile as the middleman Amery was somewhat awkwardly placed. The position in Cabinet now resolved into a standoff: Linlithgow was prepared to propose the scheme if it came to him with Cabinet backing; the Cabinet was prepared to accept the scheme if it had the Viceroy's backing. Churchill disturbed these delicate manoeuvres by inquiring from the Viceroy whether it was wise to make any move when the invasion of Britain seemed imminent. Linlithgow promptly pulled back. When he issued the 'August Offer' as it was termed (8 August 1940) the long term policy was almost entirely tentative, indeed the most memorable passage in this statement concerned the difficulty of obtaining agreement among the parties in India: 'His Majesty's Government could not contemplate transfer of their present responsibilities...to any system of government whose authority is directly denied by large and powerful elements in India's national life. Nor could they be parties to the coercion of such elements into submission to such a government'. The Congress responded with a resolution adopted at Bombay on 16 September 1940 with an expression of admiration for the bravery and endurance shown by the British people in the face of 'danger and peril' and then an indication they would follow the path of 'complete world disarmament'; a free India should 'be prepared to give a lead in this to the world'. A major cause of war was the domination of a country over another; India would 'peacefully labour' to attain the end of all this. The resolution was as devoid of meaning as that by the Viceroy a few months before. With the political future left undecided the British still expected that 'all parties, communities and interests will combine and cooperate in making a notable Indian contribution to the victory'. There was no British inducement to respond. Congress launched a campaign of individual *satyagraha*: not a very positive method of countering the British, as most recognized. Some 23,000 *satyagrahis* were jailed, but there was no effective disruption of the national life. A member of the High Command wrote a long note condemning what was called the 'policy of drift': if Congress had 'adopted a wholly bargaining attitude, specifying its terms for a whole hearted support of the war effort' this would have improved its own position and that of the Indian people. The High Command was split into different groups: the most moderate advocated a return to parliamentary government (Rajaji, Satyamurti, Asaf Ali and Bhulabhai Desai); another group proposed an all out mass struggle (Subhas Bose and the Forward Block, the Congress Socialist Party, led by Jayaprakash Narayan, and the Communist Party); while yet another wanted *satyagraha* but recognized the need to build up India's defences (Nehru and Azad). Gandhi's actions and words were confused. On 24 October 1940 he admitted to Nehru 'It is Do or Die. There is no turning back'.

The policy of centralization was deplored by many Congress Leaders. Dr Satyapal, veteran of the Amritsar tragedy resigned from Congress: he alleged 'Congress men are pestering jail authorities for release on parole'. He went on 'Congress has suspended its constitution and converted itself into a rigid dictatorship'. The climax of this phase in the Congress was a meeting of the High Command at Bardoli in Gujrat which issued a resolution on 30 December 1941. The *satyagrahis* had been released; Pearl Harbour had been bombed. Once again the Congress expressed its 'sympathies [with those] fighting for their freedom', but reiterated the demand for Indian freedom. Linlithgow could afford to bide his time: but pressures were growing from other directions. Amery found the Viceroy a tedious colleague: 'He seems quite incapable of saying anything simply and clearly and I am not surprised his negotiations with Indians come to nothing'. British political initiatives faded out, along with those of Congress. Nevertheless, Linlithgow's period in office was extended. Amery began sounding out the names of possible successors in 1940, but nothing came of it; doubtless Churchill was too absorbed in immediate problems to give the matter thought. Linlithgow's tenure was extended; first for one year and subsequently for a second, although those who met the Viceroy reported that he was tired and his correspondence became increasingly testy. British political initiatives faded out, along with those of Congress. During the early part of 1941 it became possible for the British people to look beyond siege conditions. In North Africa, the British forces under Wavell's command inflicted heavy defeats on the

Italians. The two Indian Divisions played a major part in the British success, and in Eritrea formed the main thrust in the attack which ended the Italian hold on Ethiopia. These successes were largely negated by Churchill's instructions to Wavell to commit most of his forces to a campaign in Greece where the arrival of German divisions to attack the Balkans shattered the best of the Commonwealth divisions in the Middle East. The unexpectedly robust Russian stand against German attack had some impact on India. Nehru and some other leaders declared their support, and the Communist Party of India, hitherto hostile to the war between Imperialists now rallied to the cause. Amid all this, Wavell, the architect of victory in North Africa was relieved of his command and sent to India as Commander-in-Chief. During 1941, the expansion of the Indian Army really gathered pace and by the end of the year there were about 900,000 men under arms: recruitment was drawn mainly from the traditional recruiting grounds, especially Punjab.

Amery was only marginally brought into these developments. The Government of India decided that there was no longer a valid reason for holding the *satyagrahis* arrested the previous year. As usual, Churchill proved difficult. He mounted 'a fortnight of irritation, excitement, argument' before he accepted these proposals. Amery blamed Linlithgow for much of the fuss: 'He deliberately invites interference by all the volume of argument and counter-argument which he sends home. If he had only announced that...he had decided to order the release of the prisoners...leaving it to the Cabinet to override him...the thing might have gone through much more easily' (Amery Diary, 22 November 1941).

So the world approached the moment when Japan would carry out the long awaited 'advance to the south' (nanshin). The objectives were strategic raw materials: oil, rubber, tin. Already French Indo-China was within the Japanese sphere: now, in rapid succession, Hong Kong, Malaya, Indonesia and Burma were invaded and occupied.

At the beginning of 1942 a group of distinguished Indian Liberals led by Sapru appealed to the Prime Minister to re-open the political dialogue. Churchill's initial response was eccentric even for him. He cabled Attlee from Washington: 'The Indian Liberals though plausible have never been able to deliver the goods. The Indian troops are fighting splendidly but it must be remembered that their allegiance is to the King Emperor and the rule of Congress and Hindu priesthood machine would never be tolerated by a fighting race' (7 January 1942). Quite independently Linlithgow sent an 'appreciation' of the situation to Amery. He abhorred any political move at this juncture. He detected quisling feelings in Bengal and Eastern India generally: 'Cabinet will I think agree with me that India and Burma have no natural association with the Empire...from which they are alien by race, history and religion, and for which, as such, neither of them have any natural affection...lip service is given' (21 January). Acting as stand-in for Churchill in London, Attlee was disgusted with this effusion, which he called 'distinctly disturbing' and 'defeatist' (24 January). He followed this letter up by a memorandum for the War Cabinet: he called the Viceroy's telegram 'an astonishing statement....more like an extract from an anti-imperialist propaganda speech. If it were true it would form the greatest possible condemnation of our rule in India....but it is not the whole truth....The history of at least a hundred and fifty years has forged close links between India and the United Kingdom....I find it quite impossible to accept and act upon the crude imperialism of the Viceroy, not only because I think it is wrong, but because I think it is fatally short-sighted and suicidal. I should certainly not be prepared to cover up this ugliness with a cloak of past sentiment about liberty and democracy....A renewed effort must be made to get the leaders of the Indian political parties to unite. It is quite obvious from his telegram that the Viceroy is not the man to do this. Indeed his telegram goes far to explain his past failures....My conclusion therefore is that a representative with power to negotiate within wide limits should be sent to India now, either as a special envoy or in replacement of the present Viceroy and that a Cabinet Committee should be appointed to draw up terms of reference and power'. This powerful blast was received by the Cabinet with bland assurance. Sir David Monteath called Attlee's memorandum 'near a motion of censure on the present Viceroy' (which indeed it was). But Attlee was not listened to: the Cabinet invited Amery to prepare an alternative draft statement.

All this took place while Singapore awaited its downfall and Burma was invaded. Linlithgow went on firing off telegrams as though the outside world did not matter: 'The Viceroy has been ill-used in this business and I most devoutly hope that he may count on the Secretary of State who is his natural protector to see that nothing of the kind should occur again' (13 February). 'I am carrying here an immense responsibility. Indeed I do not think it is to exaggerate to affirm that the key to success in this war is now very largely in my hands. I am debarred from...consultation with any considerable number of persons....Deprived as I am of the help of Laithwaite [through illness] I am dependent on Hodson and Maxwell [Home Member]....With these slender means I am invited at the shortest notice to comment on a scheme...I am forced to regard as dangerous and amateurish to a degree....The manner in which I have been used over these past ten days is not in tune with the treatment which anyone holding my charge is entitled to expect' (16 February). This outburst was occasioned by the decision of Churchill to broadcast a message on India: a decision which was shortly cancelled. Amery did not respond: perhaps he was becoming blasé about the Viceroy's problems. He resumed his favourite pastime of devising a constitution. He cabled Linlithgow:

> We cannot go back...on our 1940 pledges to Moslems and Princes, or beat about the bush in answer to the questions that are bound to be asked. On the other hand Congress and many

people here will say that in insisting on agreement we are in fact inviting a recalcitrant element to blackmail the rest of India by vetoing all progress unless it gets its full pound of flesh. Is not the right ultimate solution really to be sought on the lines which we have followed in the case of every previous federation and which in fact were adopted in the present Act with regard to the Princes, i.e. to let Federation be formed as soon as a sufficient number of the federal units have agreed, leaving the dissidents to stand out for the time being and possibly altogether? (22 February).

Nobody else agreed with this approach, yet it was to be embedded in the proposals offered to the Indian leaders.

An important new element was the entry of Stafford Cripps into the War Cabinet from 19 February, having served as ambassador in Moscow from May 1940 to January 1942. He was credited with reaching an accord with Stalin and stiffening the resistance. Appointed leader of the House of Commons he introduced a series of austerity measures; at a time when Churchill's star seemed to be setting, his was high in the sky. Already accepted as an authority on India he became founder member of the new India Committee of the War Cabinet. Churchill took the chair at its first meetings, but thereafter he left it to Attlee. At the second meeting they considered a draft declaration presented by Amery. This acknowledged that India would become a Dominion('Equal in every respect to the United Kingdom'). Among the many provisions was this which declared that 'Provinces or States where not prepared to adhere should stand aside'. This ambiguous proviso was accepted by the India Committee without comment, Cripps being among those who assented. In the usual fashion the draft was endorsed at several subsequent meetings, all attended by Stafford Cripps.

In a comment on the declaration as it was evolving Amery asked Churchill to 'support me against being rushed by Cripps and Attlee', he added 'I think Linlithgow may well feel in any case that he was being unfairly rushed. I should not be altogether surprised if he talked of resignation. Cripps and Attlee are very eager to secure this anyhow—and there may be much to be said for a new man to carry out a new policy' (2 March).

Linlithgow steadfastly opposed the provision for a province to stand aside (described under the innocuous term 'local option'). He addressed a series of telegrams to Amery between 2 and 6 March. The only other strong opposition came from Smuts with his memories of the negotiations over the Irish muddle in 1921 which had led to the partition of Ireland. He urged Churchill to drop 'local option' which might 'be taken as a British invitation or incitement to partition'. He suggested that instead the British Government should announce it would 'use all the influence at its command to compose such differences' (5 March). Amidst these difficulties, Amery noted 'Winston's complete inability to grasp even the most elementary points in the discussion....He seems quite incapable of taking in even the simplest point...and then rambles on inconsecutively....He is very tired and losing his grip altogether' (Diary, 26 February). Next day Amery noted that at a meeting of the India Committee 'I was glad to find that Cripps and the rest of them [were] prepared to accept my view...that any province which disliked the new constitution could stand out. This gives the Moslems the power to have their Pakistan if Congress is not prepared to meet them but, on the other hand does not hold the rest of India up indefinitely' (Diary, 26 February).

Linlithgow continued to oppose 'local option' totally, but Amery was adamant on this point and the other members of the India Committee could not see how adverse this provision would be to any chance of Congress accepting the scheme with their belief that they represented all-India. Finally, on 9 March Linlithgow sent a flurry of telegrams to Amery all urging cancellation of 'local option' which he believed would be seen 'as a virtual promise not merely of

Pakistan but of Sikhistan also'. He pushed his opposition to the point of resignation, that he would 'telegraph to Winston my resignation in a form suitable for publication'. Speculating on the effect on public opinion he suggested he might fly back 'ostensibly for consultation', putting in Lumley, Governor of Bombay, as acting Governor-General until permanent arrangements were made. All this was ignored by Amery who continued to send out long minutes on details of 'his' plan. Two days previously Cripps had told the India Committee that 'someone' should go out to India, and this was taken to be an offer by Cripps himself (as was almost certainly intended). Amery took Linlithgow's telegrams to Chequers to show to Winston: 'Looking at the first [he] threw the whole lot down indignantly and refused to read them'. Winston had now become convinced that he had framed the declaration which was a 'masterpiece...firmly determined not to consider the matter any further' (Diary, 8 March). When Linlithgow's resignation arrived, Amery showed it to Winston, Attlee and Cripps. Winston replied by assuring Linlithgow that no announcement would be made before the departure of Cripps who would put the agreed document to the Indian parties: if they should reject it then 'our sincerity will be proved to the world', he admonished Linlithgow: 'Do not therefore think of quitting your post at this juncture for this might be the signal for a general collapse in British Indian resistance with serious rupture of political unity here'. The latter worried Cripps most. The same day (10 March) Amery cabled Linlithgow assuring him that the policy entrusted to Cripps was 'fairly conservative': 'As for Congress...they [will] discover that...the nest contains the Pakistan cuckoo's egg....It is for them to find a compromise which will induce the Moslems to drop Pakistan'.

Apart from the desperate situation in the war, a major element pushing forward the mission initiative was the force of American criticism. According to Neville Butler of the Foreign Office, the British were seen not just as 'Imperialists, but bungling Imperialists'. A long report from the Washington Embassy ran: 'The British are imperialistic. They do not believe in the equality of men. British Colonial policy has been oppressive, stupid, inefficient and insulting to the natives with the result that Malays and Burmese have been conspicuously disloyal'. Later in the year the embassy reported that there was much anti-British feeling in the new military training camps. All this appeared to help Cripps in his search for a formula. He arrived in Delhi on 23 March. Almost simultaneously, 'Colonel' Louis Johnson arrived as Roosevelt's 'Personal Representative with the rank of Minister' (the letter informing Linlithgow of this appointment was signed in Washington on 19 March, five days after Cripps left London). Roosevelt intended to hustle negotiations along: neither he nor Johnson had any notion of how tortuous Indian negotiations could be. Cripps held a press conference on 23 March when he announced his intention to stay in Delhi for two weeks, not visiting other centres. Somewhat hopefully he expressed his 'confidence' that the press would not prejudice a settlement by 'untimely speculation'. No kind of intimacy was to develop between Cripps and Linlithgow. As R. J. Moore comments, although they were very different 'Among the characteristics which he [Cripps] shared with Linlithgow were piety and self importance so that their conflict of political philosophies was almost certain to produce a counterpoint relationship'.[5] At this delicate moment the imperturbable Laithwaite was unwell and the Viceroy was having to work with a Bengal Civilian, L. G. Pinnell, who did not have the negotiating experience of Laithwaite. Cripps intended to launch straight into discussions with the politicians but Linlithgow insisted that courtesy required him first to meet the Executive Council. Here Cripps had quite a rough ride, though perhaps the most difficult question was posed by Linlithgow: 'His Excellency enquired whether if Bengal and Punjab only went out [of the new federation] they would have a central government to which Sir Stafford replied that what was contemplated was that they would form separate dominions'. This was an ominous beginning. When Cripps began to meet the politicians they responded on predictable lines: Jinnah 'was surprised in the distance it went to meet the Pakistan case' (25 March). Already the contents of the proposed declaration were being circulated and Cripps told London that he would release the plan on 30 March. He met Gandhi three days before then; the Mahatma went straight to the great defect in the plan from the Congress point of view: 'He started by asserting that the document was an invitation to the Moslems to create a Pakistan'. Cripps tried to reassure the Mahatma: 'I had always understood that the attitude of the Congress was that once the British Government was out of the way...it would be possible for the Congress and the Moslems to come to an agreement'. Gandhi implored Cripps not to publish his plan before they had the opportunity to negotiate confidentially.

Many difficulties arose from the differences between the Congress leaders. Gandhi would not budge from the doctrine of non-violence; Nehru, Rajaji, Azad and some others were for participation in the war effort, providing that a substantial degree of power was transferred to the Congress; other important figures like Patel adopted a pragmatic approach. Cripps assumed that the Nehru attitude was what mattered and began to juggle with the way in which his demands might be met without upsetting the Viceroy and Commander-in-Chief too much.

When Cripps had an interview with Nehru and Azad on 29 March he noted that Nehru 'was tired and not well...he left me in complete doubt as to whether Congress was more or less decided not to accept it [the plan] and that it was not worth arguing or pressing for any alteration'. At a large and disorganized press conference the same day, Cripps went far 'too far' in recognizing the possibility of Pakistan. He was asked 'Supposing there are two or three non acceding provinces what is the procedure? Do you offer to them a new dominion?': he replied 'Provided it is physically possible'. He envisaged working out the new relationships by means of a treaty with Britain. The conference lasted an inordinate length of time; and not infrequently Cripps showed his irritation. His replies were often abrupt and not at all conciliatory. The previous day the Press had reported that Nehru was asking whether the Defence Department would control the Commander-in-Chief or vice versa. Asked 'Who is going to give the Commander-in-Chief his orders?' Cripps replied 'The War Cabinet; it would be dishonest to say that the India Defence Minister was responsible for defence'. Asked in conclusion when he would leave he replied, 'I expect to leave on the date on which I said I would leave'. At a later interview he declared that he 'intended to force a decision on Wednesday and then clear out, probably by next Monday' (6 April). Next day Cripps invited Nehru to dinner. He conveyed the impression that the Working Committee would not accept the proposals. The same day a 'draft declaration' was published: the only new feature was that any non-acceding provinces could obtain 'a new constitution giving them the same full status as the Indian Union'. Next day, Cripps met Linlithgow, stating that he 'realized he was finished...the general response was so poor that he would not be justified in recommending HMG's plan and that he was going back'. Nevertheless, Cripps plodded on with interviews to all and sundry. Relations between Viceroy and envoy were still amicable, Linlithgow told Amery: 'If the signs are not at this moment favourable...this is certainly no fault of Cripps for he has handled a difficult and wearing job with outstanding skill, courage and imagination'.

Thus far the United States had not attempted to intervene, though Roosevelt came up with the proposal that 'complete autonomy, including power to raise armies should be given to the provinces'. Bajpai, to whom this extraordinary proposal was made tried to explain that 'the need is for greater unity rather than disintegration of effort—but the President is not a good listener'. Nehru now made contact with 'Colonel' Johnson. He seemed to believe (mistakenly) that Roosevelt had sent a personal letter to the Congress leaders. Nehru spoke 'of hitching India's wagon to America's star and not Britain's.' According to Johnson's report (neither conjunction seems likely to accord with Nehru's political philosophies). Johnson assured Nehru that 'America would have the leading place at the peace table [and] that her attitude towards India...would be determined by the Indian war effort'. Nehru informed Johnson that the Congress leaders 'did not like the present Commander-in-Chief though they expressed admiration for his predecessor'.

While this peculiar dialogue went on a proposition was put by Cripps to Congress for a division of defence functions with the Commander-in-Chief retaining virtually all control over the military apparatus and an Indian member in charge of a 'Defence Coordination Department' which would have been little more than a welfare job. Stranger yet was the procedure now adopted.

On 4 April Nehru came to meet Wavell and his Chief of Staff, Lieutenant-General G. N. Molesworth. According to the latter, Nehru launched into a whole series of demands; Wavell listened in silence, until in a pause he observed 'If that is your position then we have nothing more to discuss'.[6] Molesworth was appalled; he realized that Nehru was adopting a maximalist position and it was up to Wavell to reduce the distance between them. But Wavell never understood that Indian politics was all about bargaining; Nehru went away disgruntled, and never attained any kind of understanding with the gruff old soldier. Cripps handed his letter about defence to Johnson who gave it to Nehru as his own suggestion! When Linlithgow learned of this on 8 April his tone changed: 'I at once protested against Congress having been shown the draft...the fact that Johnson had shown it to them made the position all the worse given the USA position in the business. Cripps generally glozed over the incident'. Linlithgow was further upset by a cartoon in the *Hindustan Times* showing Roosevelt taking a hand in solving the deadlock and a headline in the paper 'Will America intervene in time?'

The marginal role of the proposed Indian Defence Member had now been amplified. Linlithgow told Amery of his anxieties, and on 9 April Churchill entered the scene, adjuring Cripps: 'You must not commit us in any way as at first sight it seems most difficult to understand'. When Churchill brought up the whole issue in Cabinet (9 April) he insisted that Johnson 'was not the President's personal representative in any matter relating to Indian constitutional issues': 'It was felt that we were in danger of being drawn away from the clear position which had been explicitly stated'. The proposal put to Congress was called 'obscure'. Cripps replied by listing the functions of what was now called the Defence Department in very general terms. The functions of the new War Department were sketched in even more vaguely. In a further telegram to the War Cabinet (10 April) Cripps stated: 'I am sorry that my colleagues appear to distrust me over this matter, and I am quite prepared to hand the matter over if they would rather someone else carried on the negotiations'. After a meeting of the War Cabinet, Churchill cabled Cripps: 'We sympathize with you in your difficulties but we have our own responsibilities as well as you' (10 April). By now, Laithwaite was back at work, sustaining Linlithgow in his increasingly exasperated response.

The Congress High Command came in with their very different interpretation of all these negotiations. From the Indian side the leaders threw in their hand, believing that the game was up. On 9 April Nehru wrote a parting letter to Johnson after a last talk with Cripps:

> I am very sorry to say that the talk was entirely unsatisfying....The whole picture that emerged from our talks took me aback and I suddenly discovered that the very premises on which we had been discussing this subject during the last four days was unjustified. The whole structure that we had

tried to build up laboriously in our minds was without any real foundation.

This was really the end, though Cripps tried to squeeze something out of the muddle for another day or so.

Azad reminded Cripps that 'you had referred both privately and in the case of public statements to a National Government and a Cabinet consisting of Ministers. These words have a certain significance and we had imagined that the new government would function with full powers as a Cabinet with the Viceroy acting as a constitutional head; but the new picture that you placed before us was not really very different from the old!....It would just be the Viceroy and his Executive Council with the Viceroy having all his old powers....The picture thereafter placed before us is not essentially different from the old one....We cannot fit into it'. Azad went on to reaffirm their intention to form 'a Cabinet government with full power' but their suggestions were 'the very minimum'. He concluded that these suggestions 'may be the unanimous demand of the Indian people' (10 April).

Linlithgow's response to the breakdown was to cable Amery that he would contact the Congress and League leaders 'to tell them that we have left the old world and its quarrels behind us for ever' (11 April). Cripps too tried to make something out of the failure to agree: 'Nehru's fighting statements and speeches should be played up' (11 April). Similarly, Congress leaders tried to salvage something from the debacle. Azad insisted that they were 'not in the wrong': 'What we were told in our very first talk with you is now denied or explained away. You told me then that there would be a national government which would function as Cabinet' (11 April). He went on 'Even in this grave hour of peril the British Government is unable to give up its wrecking policy'. Without doubt everything was much worse than before Cripps came. He left on 12 April, and never again commanded the full confidence of the Congress leaders.

Most of the British community in India accepted the official view of Indo-British relationship but not all. Foss Westcott, Bishop of Calcutta and intimate friend of C. F. Andrews addressed a plea to the British community in India, criticising 'the calm assumption of superiority inherent in the British race...[resulting from] lack of knowledge and appreciation of the culture and civilisation of the East accentuated by that insularity which is characteristic of many British people' (*The Times*, 20 April 1942). The government could not do anything about Bishop Westcott, but they were able to silence the Anglo-Irish editor of *The Statesman*, Arthur Moore, whose editorials increasingly served to break ranks. He survived the Cripps mission, but his response to the August disturbances was deemed intolerable. He was removed after pressure on his master, Lord Catto.

The departure of Cripps left Indian politics in limbo. Sapru delivered his verdict in a letter to the journalist Shiva Rao dated 12 April 'Cripps began badly but ended well. Congress began well but ended badly....Cripps' greatest mistake was to have assumed from the very beginning that the only body which mattered in India was the Congress and the only person in the Congress who mattered was Jawaharlal!...He must have realised by now that the Congress cannot be depended upon for settlement'. As if to illustrate his analysis, Gandhi now took up the running. As early as 26 April in *Harijan* he called on the British to withdraw from India. The High Command met next day despite a body of opposition—Nehru, Rajaji, Bhulabhai Desai, Asaf Ali and Satyamurti—they passed a resolution on Gandhian lines. However, nothing happened. Commenting on all this, Amery told Linlithgow 'It is certainly cheering to know that Congress is in a desperate position and "beaten to a pulp"....I certainly see no reason for helping them out of their difficulties and nothing could be of greater benefit to India...than that Congress should disintegrate' (28 May 1942). Curzon's comment that Congress was 'Tottering to its fall' seemed to be believed forty years later. Linlithgow was not so sure; by the end of June he was putting together a plan to deal with a Congress revolt. His Olympian view of his own position was unchanged. When told that Vernon Bartlett wanted to visit and interview him Linlithgow replied that the population 'continues to regard the Viceroy with something of superstitious awe. I doubt whether we should do well...in an Oriental country to run the risk of destroying a mystery built up over so many decades' (30 June 1942).

The first major response by Congress came in a resolution issued from Wardha. This repeated the Gandhian interpretation of current events. Nehru and other dissentients now accepted his leadership: 'There was a rapid and widespread increase of ill-will against Britain and a growing satisfaction at the success of the Japanese'. Following the meeting of the High Command, Gandhi made a statement: 'After all, it is an open rebellion'. Nehru acquiesced: 'It is Gandhiji's feeling that Japan and Germany will win. This feeling unconsciously governs his decision'. He even welcomed this outcome: 'If I continue to wait I might have to wait till doomsday....I must ask the people to resist slavery. Not everyone was content to take this line'. Rajaji resigned from the Working Committee, announcing 'My resignation is not surrender but protest'. However, Rajaji was in a small minority. Gandhi's correspondence increasingly turned towards militancy: he was moving as far as ever he did towards condoning violence. As Vijaya Lakshmi Pandit wrote to a friend: 'Gandhiji's instructions are to completely paralyse the government in any way possible, short of murder....I am working with the rest of the people here. Publishing leaflets, and distributing them - making propaganda ....Policemen are more or less on the borderline and with encouragement they can be made to change over'.

The political militancy growing in India, was accompanied by critical pressure in the USA. The British Government had hoped that Cripps' visit would have demonstrated to the Americans that Britain was sincere in desiring political progress and also how unreasonable Congress was.

Unfortunately many Americans could not see why independence could not be conceded at once; they believed that this was the only way to mobilize full Indian support for the war. The Government of India representative at Washington informed Delhi that the State Department considered that 'American criticism of the Congress rejection of Cripp's proposal was premature and the sinister distrust of British promises of post-war Dominion Status was justified by the slow and grudging character of past British attitude to Indian pleas for freedom' (17 July 1942). American pressure was reinforced by a steady stream of denunciation from Chiang Kai-Shek which Roosevelt relayed to Churchill. Thus, 'The wishes and most enlightened policy for Britain to pursue would be to restore to India her complete freedom and thus to prevent Axis troops from setting foot on Indian soil'. Linlithgow bitterly resented the American politicians who visited India, all wanting to talk to Gandhi. He was particularly concerned to warn off Wendell Willkie, the Republican contender for President in 1940. His heavy hints were successful, and Willkie did not stop in India on his tour of the Far East in mid-1942. This did not prevent a blistering attack when Willkie returned to America.

The only response produced by Linlithgow was an expansion of his Council and introduction of an increased Indian element to try and show that they were going ahead with Indianization. The convention had been established in the 1920s that the Viceroy's Council comprised seven members: four British (including the Commander-in-Chief, the Finance Member and the Home Member) and three Indians roughly duplicating the set-up in the Dyarchy provinces. Early in 1942 the Council was expanded to twelve Members, a majority being Indians. On 2 July it was reconstructed with fourteen Members; one additional post was that of Defence, held by Firoz Khan Noon. His responsibilities were similar to those adumbrated when the question of splitting the tasks of the Commander-in-Chief were discussed with Cripps. The new Indian members were men of distinction, drawing heavily on the Princely States; but they represented no constituency, as Jinnah refused to allow Muslim League representatives to join and of course Congress would not cooperate: though one former Congress Chief Minister, M. S. Aney took on the Department of Indians Overseas. The new Councillors were probably of higher calibre than the representatives of the parties could have been, but the role of the distinguished individual in Indian politics (exemplified by Sapru and Sastri) was no longer credible. One of the new men, Sir C. P. Ramaswami Aiyar took charge on 3 August; decided that his department was a 'sinecure' (19 August) and resigned on 20 August. Though Linlithgow treated his Indian Councillors with courtesy he firmly suppressed any tendency to independent action. They had less responsibility than the Durbar of an Indian Prince. Amery who regarded himself as a constitutional expert, was quite taken in by these cosmetic changes: 'The present Executive is our real bulwark in India today, and I find myself fighting...those members of the Cabinet, Labour as well as Conservative, who will not realize the extent to which the Indianization of the Executive has altered the de facto constitutional position' (Diary, 13 August). Linlithgow did not really believe in the policy he was promoting. He told Amery on 3 August: 'There is little if any sign of personnel of the requisite quality; there is precious little indication of any desire to face unpopular decisions or to carry responsibility; and I have not the least doubt that progressive Indianization is leading...to a substantial deterioration of quality which acquires momentum every year' (3 August).

All these cross currents welled up in the great wave which swept India consequently on the All India Congress Committee adopting the 'Quit India' Resolution on 8 August. This reinforced the Wardha resolution of the High Command of the previous month. It called upon every Indian 'who desired freedom and strives for it' to fight for 'the ending of British rule in this country'. On this will 'depend the future of the war and the success of freedom and democracy'. The resolution merged together Gandhian non-violence and Nehru's anti-fascism. Anticipating a British response the resolution concluded: 'A time may come when it may not be possible to issue instructions...and when no Congress Committees can function. When this happens every man and woman who is participating in this movement must function for himself or herself...along the hard road where there is no resting place and which leads ultimately to the independence of India'.

However, the High Command were not prepared for the speed with which the British responded. Next morning at 5.00 a.m. the whole leadership was arrested and transported to the detention centres previously prepared: most of the Working Committee went to Ahmadnagar Fort but Gandhi, and his secretaries and Sarojini Naidu were installed in the palace of the Aga Khan at Poona. Though their followers were temporarily stunned by the disappearance of their leaders, resistance very soon acquired a terrific momentum. At first Bombay city was the centre of the storm and the Governor's reports were 'gloomy' but elsewhere the troubles were described as 'sporadic disorder'. This diagnosis had to be changed rapidly as it became clear that the whole of Bihar and the Benares Division of UP were right out of control. These were the centres of the 1857 revolt, they were also areas where, because of the permanent settlement of land revenue, the district administration was very thin on the ground. Gradually, reality began to penetrate the Viceroy's House where Linlithgow presided in remote authority. An indication of this separation from the world of India was given to Amery by a member of the Bengal Legislative Council and President of the European Association of India, Sir Edward Villiers on 13 August. He said that 'the personality of Linlithgow had something to do with the present difficulties'. He was inaccessible and in Council 'things were very much cut and dried and the Executive expected to sign on the dotted line. Europeans and Indians generally complained that the Viceroy kept to himself, Laithwaite and a very small circle'. Amery recorded this damning indictment 'with a grain of salt': after all, he was even further removed from reality.

Linlithgow's confidant, Laithwaite, was almost equally out of touch. On 25 August he sent a private telegram to Monteath at the India Office, recording his conviction 'that Parliamentary Government with political unity in India is beyond the capacity of a self-governing India and likely to remain so for many years to come' (25 August). Meanwhile, the security situation remained tenuous and the great Tata steel works was on strike; they returned to work early in September. The reports which the Viceroy sent to London played down the severity of the crisis though at the end of August he informed Churchill: 'I am engaged here in meeting by far the most serious rebellion since that of 1857, the gravity and extent of which we have so far concealed from the world for reasons of military security. Mob violence remains rampant over large tracts of the countryside and I am by no means confident that we may not see in September a formidable attempt to renew this widespread sabotage of our war effort....If we bungle this business we shall damage India irretrievably as a base for future allied operations....Throughout this most anxious crisis I have managed to hold together the Indian members of my Executive Council though several of them are in mortal terror of the possible consequences to themselves of their having supported me in arresting Gandhi' (31 August). Doubtless Linlithgow did well to persuade his Council to agree to unpopular measures, but the picture drawn of a Viceroy leading his team as John Lawrence led the Punjab administration in the Mutiny is distinctly overdrawn. The task of suppression was the responsibility of army officers, and district officers, as well as railwaymen, policemen, communications workers and all the other people in the field. The Viceroy just sent reports to London. Linlithgow was always seeing himself as a world leader; second only to

Churchill in the load he had to carry. This was evident in his communications to the Secretary of State as when he insisted 'We shall have to stand firm over the general Indian business as against the USA unless we are prepared to throw our hands in altogether' (21 September). As regards the imprisoned Congress leaders he concluded 'They will have to stay in for some time to come...as long as proves practicable....I do not believe that any one can do business with any of them while the war lasts'.

The next move from the Congress side was an announcement from Gandhi that he intended to undertake a fast. Linlithgow told him bluntly: 'I regard the use of a fast for political purposes as a form of political blackmail (*hinsa*, "violence") for which there can be no moral justification'. Gandhi stated explicitly that this was not intended as a fast unto death, but the non-Muslim politicians who had joined his Council were intensely worried and urged that the Mahatma should be released—at any rate for the period of the fast, which began on 10 February 1943. One week after the fast commenced, three Council members submitted their resignations—which Linlithgow accepted. The three were M. S. Aney (whose departure Linlithgow specially regretted), N. R. Sarkar (the longest serving Member) and Sir Homi Mody (a Parsi). There was a typically Churchillian response: 'What did it matter if a few blackamoors resigned? We could show the world that we were governing'.

The fast was ended on 3 March without a noticeable deterioration in the Mahatma's condition. By then, Linlithgow had gone off for a weekend, shooting snipe; they shot 661 birds. 'Almost a record', noted the Viceroy. In passing, on 18 March he cabled the Secretary of State: 'The food situation in India generally is at present much improved. This improvement is due mainly to increase in public confidence....Until recently there were long queues outside the grain shops from early in the morning. These queues no longer exist'. Early in May he was 'uneasy about the rice position and the Bengal position in particular is most unsatisfactory...They have been extremely slow in getting any sort of organization together'. Whereas the good news was cabled back, the alarming Bengal report was sent by letter. There was still no decision about Linlithgow's successor, as the months went by. Linlithgow had to accept a second extension of his tenure. Early in June, Amery approached Churchill yet again, suggesting the names of possible candidates. The *Daily Worker* had a cartoon showing an empty throne with a small dog—the Secretary of State—on guard. Amery gave Churchill the view of James Holburn—*The Times*' correspondent in India—on the departing Viceroy: 'His actions are challenged, the honesty of his motives is never impugned. It is a pity that he does not have the flair for personal contacts which Willingdon had, and which are so important here. But one cannot have everything'. This accorded with the account given to Amery by Sir Zafrullah Khan, a Judge of the Federal Court, who in conversation 'contrasted his handling of the Executive [Council] unfavourably with Willingdon's free and easy manner and encouragement of general conversation. Linlithgow...began straight away with the successive items on the agenda, asking everybody formally in turn from the Commander-in-Chief downwards and never disclosing his own views till he knew what everybody else thought and even then often keeping them back....I am afraid that this is a true criticism' (Diary 8 January 1943). His weariness was beginning to show through. When Amery made the suggestion that when Linlithgow might return home to Scotland 'you will not be free from a good many domestic problems even there', Linlithgow noted petulantly: 'All together they won't trouble me as much as L. S. Amery. Besides, Leo may be having a holiday by then!' (presumably a suggestion that his time at the India Office might be near its end).

At last on 9 June, Churchill sent a telegram to Linlithgow giving his decision ('I have never in my life had to solve a more puzzling appointment'). The choice was Wavell, whose name had not come up previously in the hunt for the next Viceroy. However, Linlithgow had four months to run before his departure.

Meanwhile, the situation in Bengal was attaining crisis proportions, as even the Governor was realizing. On the eve of a Food Conference in Delhi he wrote to the Viceroy 'I must invoke all my powers of description and persuasion to convey to you the seriousness of the food situation in Bengal' (2 July 1943). Linlithgow noted 'I wonder how far he is right about the Bengal situation'. In reply to Herbert he wrote 'I quite realize your anxieties. You will by now have a full report on how things went in the Conference. I dare say that Bengal could have wished that...the outcome of the Conference had been rather different' (11 July). 'I gather on paragraph eight of your letter that your food drive has located 155,000 tons of rice [Herbert had actually identified 100,000 tons]...that is a very satisfactory result and shows how much food is in fact available'. In actuality Linlithgow was highly critical of the regime in Bengal: 'One fatal defect in which Herbert suffers in extreme degree is that he will insist on doing all the talking himself. I am told that his Cabinet meetings consist very often of little more than an interminable and rather muddled homily by the Governor'. The Regional Food Controller in charge of rationing was H. B. L. Braund. He reported that 'There exists no adequate organization at present to supply or feed or ration Calcutta, the second largest city in the Empire...and that no provisional organization exists' (to Amery, 10 August 1943).

Herbert was in fact a sick man and had to go into a nursing home. The Governor of Bihar, Sir Thomas Rutherford was put in to act for him (from 6 September) and it soon became evident that Herbert would not return. Meanwhile, Linlithgow was infuriated by an article contributed to the *New Statesman* and *Nation* by Edward Thompson comparing the punishment meted out to the villagers of Chimur in Central Provinces with atrocities in

Czechoslovakia; the article was 'Characteristically one sided and my sympathies are with the local government'.

Linlithgow was beginning, mentally to disengage; reporting a conversation with the Premier of Punjab to Amery he replied to Khizar's expectation that he would still try to look after Punjab when he retired. Linlithgow 'made it clear to him that once I had laid down my office I had nothing more to do with these matters'; an attitude which Reading or Halifax would have found incomprehensible. His last communications with the Secretary of State affirmed his conviction of his success in his regime: 'Largely owing to efforts of Government area of serious distress [i.e. food shortage] are confined to certain districts (not whole) of Bengal, Travancore, Cochin and certain parts of the Deccan where autumn crop has failed two years in succession' (10 October). He indited a long valedictory epistle to Amery: 'It has been a very long spell of office, and a very heavy one....My serving for half as long again as the normal term of a Viceroy....It has enabled one to test out the organization of the Governor-General's own Secretariat which came into being for the first time in 1937....I leave the country in pretty good trim. It is true that there is the so-called deadlock on the political stage. But no human ingenuity on my part could have avoided that deadlock....The leaders of that section which alone...desires to see us out of the country...have neither programme nor policy. The Working Committee are in jail and forgotten....The Muslims who have immensely strengthened their position during the last three or four years are solid, more bitterly communal than ever....So far as the war effort goes, as you know, India has made an immense contribution and everything is in admirable running order....We are going to be under a very heavy strain once the South East Asia Command gets going...we shall have the same trouble with the Americans as their interest in this area grows....The one thing which I am definitely disturbed about is the food position, and I shall have to leave that to Wavell in an untidy state: though by the time he takes over we shall have bought a good deal of the experience that I suspect always has to be bought in handling a situation of this sort'. Presumably this was meant to suggest that one could not make an omelette without breaking eggs! Whatever he meant, his days were nearly over. On 20 October, the new Viceroy was sworn in. Linlithgow greeted Wavell at the top of the steps in front of the Viceroy's House with the words 'I am glad to see you. I do not think I have ever been so glad to see anyone'. His return to Britain lacked the pageantry of previous Viceregal arrivals. Despite their convergence of views on so many occasions, Churchill ignored the former Viceroy after his return. He died in January 1952.

NOTES

1. Linlithgow to Hoare, now Lord Templewood, 13 July 1953.
2. Jawaharlal Nehru, *The Discovery of India,* 1946.
3. Gowher Rizvi, *Linlithgow and India,* 1978, p. 85.
4. Penderel Moon, *Divide and Quit,* 1961, pp. 24-5.
5. R. J. Moore, *Churchill, Cripps and India, 1939-45,* 1979.
6. G. N. Molesworth, *Twilight on Olympus.*

Chapter 10

WAVELL: NEARING JOURNEY'S END

There is no evidence that Wavell wanted to be Viceroy: his desire was to end his career with another active military command. But it always seems to be the fate of those holding high rank in the early days of a war to be relieved when the going becomes tough: they are required to pay for the refusal of the politicians to face realities when peace crumbles into war. One week after he returned home in April 1943 for consultation on the operations in the Far East he composed a poem about a picture remembered through

> Long years of battle, bitterness and waste
> Dry years of sun and dust and Eastern skies

The lady in the painting was one reason why 'I go back to fight'. But, as he later added, he was 'not allowed, after all, to go back and fight', but went to govern India until further notice.

Linlithgow had been due to relinquish the Viceroyalty in 1941 and almost as soon as Amery took office he began to inquire about the next Viceroy. On 24 September 1940 he had some words with Churchill: 'He was in favour of John Anderson, of whom to discredit I should say I have never thought, but not ruling out Sam [Hoare] though he is obviously very conscious of the 'old gang' talk that would be raised' (Diary, 24 September 1940). Churchill thought of many names: he constantly returned to Anthony Eden who showed no enthusiasm (he had no Indian connections). For a long time Churchill favoured the Liberal leader Sir Archibald Sinclair, Secretary of State for Air, and an old pal of the Prime Minister. Amery told Linlithgow, 'He has a good presence, speaks well, has I think a reasonable courage and an adequate wife' (27 August 1942). Speculation reached a point where Sinclair issued a disclaimer that he was considering going. He too was cool about India. Another Liberal who was mentioned was Gwilyam Lloyd George. One who lobbied hard for the post was Sir Miles Lampson, High Commissioner in Egypt, favoured by Churchill who asked Smuts for his advice. He advised that Lampson should be left in Cairo. Amery suggested himself, but received no encouragement, another political suggestion was Attlee, but he could not be spared: Anderson was ruled out for the same reason. There was even a suggestion that Halifax might go back for a second term. When Wavell paid a visit to London, Amery told Linlithgow that he had been to tea and 'I could do no more than extract a few non-committal monosyllables' (22 April). With commendable loyalty Linlithgow replied 'he is excellent company and most interesting once he starts to talk. But it is not always easy to get him started' (10 May). On 29 May, Churchill informed Attlee from North Africa: 'In the opinion of Brooke and Ismay, Wavell aged considerably under the many strains he has borne during this war and I am sure he would not be the best man to command the East Asia front which it is urgent to establish. On the other hand Auchinleck would seem far better qualified to deal with the much magnified Indian Army. I should be sorry to leave Wavell unemployed as he had justly acquired a high reputation'.

This was the situation when Churchill left for yet another meeting in America. This time the military organization of the return to South East Asia was the main item. Should the commander be British or American? Should there be a unitary, combined command for South East Asia? Or should the Air be separated from the ground command? All this was thrashed out at Quebec, where the decision was made to install Mountbatten as Supreme Commander. Wavell might have well expected to be offered this appointment. He had to be accommodated. Also there was Auchinleck, removed from his command in the Middle East. It was advised that an officer who had been Commander-in-Chief in India could not be employed in a subordinate position. Hence, the suggestion that he might become Inspector General of the Indian Army would not be possible. How to fit in this outstanding soldier and also find a place for Wavell? The solution produced was rather like a jigsaw puzzle. The key piece was Mountbatten, as Supreme Allied Commander South East Asia, with operational responsibility for the war against Japan. Auchinleck was restored to the post of Commander-in-Chief, India, which had been his from 1940-1. Wavell became Viceroy. All this was settled in a few days in June, having been left undecided for a year, in the case of Auchinleck, and two years in the case of the Viceroyalty. The final piece in the jigsaw, Mountbatten, was not fitted in until his appointment was announced on 25 August. Wavell himself wrote 'a very curious chain of circumstances'. 'When forced on him [Churchill] my appointment as Viceroy as the only way out of a difficult place....I accepted the Viceroyalty in the spirit of a military appointment - one goes where one is told in time of war without making conditions'. Born in 1883, Wavell was just in time for the Boer war in which his regiment—the Black Watch—'trekked wearily and reluctantly over the veldt'. He spent five years in India as a subaltern: 'some of the best in my life' he later said. In the Great War he was in the retreat from Mons and lost an eye in battle. His glass eye gave him a forbidding appearance and contributed to his remoteness as a person. In conversation he was laconic—'I see' and 'Very well' were all he said. He served under Allenby in the conquest of Palestine. His chief's personality was not dissimilar to his own: he was outwardly ferocious, yet the private man led a simple life and engaged in gentle pursuits, notably bird watching. Wavell was to write the biography of his chief: *Allenby, a Study in Greatness*. The first volume covering his military career appeared in 1940. But Allenby went on to become High Commissioner in Egypt and *Allenby in Egypt* (1943) told a very different story. Appointed to quell the rise of nationalism, Allenby made terms with Zaghlul, the leader of the Wafd, though he repudiated the agreement and was banished to the Seychelles. Allenby negotiated with the younger nationalists, much to the displeasure of London, and a new constitution was forged. Churchill, of course, remembered only the daring soldier.

Posted to Cairo in 1937, Wavell brought his small force to a high state of readiness. During 1940-1 he enjoyed a series of spectacular successes at a time when Britain badly needed some good news. On the orders of Churchill and Eden he committed some of his best troops in Greece. When the Germans intervened, this led to catastrophe. In the desert, his weakened forces faced Rommel with a powerful tank arm. The British were driven right back and evacuation of Cairo was considered. Wavell kept a file labelled 'Worst Possible Case': this was not even opened in 1941. When Churchill came to survey the situation he deduced that Wavell was played out. So in July 1941 he was relieved by Auchinleck and sent to Delhi. When the Japanese launched their conquest of South East Asia, Wavell was made Commander of ABDA (American, British, Dutch, and Australian forces in the West Pacific) with headquarters in Java. This was an impossible task and in February 1942, Wavell returned to Delhi. During the brief ABDA period he endeavoured, without success, to arouse his commanders to overcome a mentality of retreat. Back in India he launched a limited offensive in Arakan, employing greatly superior numbers against the Japanese: again to no avail, within two months the British-Indian forces were back on their start line.

This was the man who now sat down with his new Private Secretary, Evan Jenkins, in a room in the India Office to work out his programme for the new era. Churchill thought that in appointing a soldier he was suspending any change in India: he was wrong. The departing Viceroy Linlithgow shared the assessment of the Prime Minister: 'All may go well even if one does...wish that it had been possible to find...a front rank politician with Cabinet experience. But if Wavell can get through the war and early post war period that will clear the way for the future' (29 June 1943). Wavell gave Amery advance proofs of his second volume on Allenby; he noted that Churchill would not 'Have been so keen about Wavell as Viceroy if he had realised how thoroughly Wavell backs up Allenby's policy of sympathy with Egyptian nationalism. I should not be at all surprised if Wavell went a long way in trying to find a solution to the Indian problem' (Diary, 28 June 1943). This was a better forecast than most. His was different from the general expectation that with Wavell's appointment all prospect of reform would be deferred. Linlithgow had not anticipated change: 'The fact is that none of these people know what to do. The Muslim League have no wish to do anything, the Congress are completely at a loss': 'There is precious little interest in any radical change in the system of government, and a fairly considerable and growing reluctance to face the chaos and misery that would come with the end of British rule' (2 August). Considering all this the *News Chronicle* commented that the Government of India was a virtual dictatorship. When Wavell first discussed prospects with Amery he suggested that the two courses open were 'to stand on the position that nothing could be done...or whether to make some attempt at progress in the near future'; he was thinking of 'a renewed attempt to secure a provisional government at the Centre containing the party leaders....on the main lines of the Cripps proposals....There would be a great relaxation of political and communal tension with the disappearance of the present sense of frustration'. The details might be worked out later....But Amery saw the opening for a constitutional disquisition, and launched into the question of whether 'the British parliamentary executive was a suitable form of government for India'. Wavell halted this diversion; realistically he suggested there was a fifty per cent chance of success: 'The main reason for the failure of the Cripps offer had been the conviction in India that we were losing the war'.

At this juncture, Attlee reconstituted the India Committee: its first meeting was on 17 September. Those invited, besides Attlee, Amery and Wavell, were Lord Halifax (temporarily absent from Washington), Cripps, Sir John Anderson, Lord Simon, and Sir James Grigg. The last two, especially Grigg, were the real Diehards. Wavell laid a long memorandum before them. The first section concerned the Executive Council: 'An official government the members of which are respected not as popular leaders but because they exercise authority and distribute patronage....It could not in any circumstances plan and execute political and constitutional reforms'. So long as this government continues any change would be limited to 'palliatives'. The alternative was a Council of leaders selected 'for their representative character and for their influence with the Indian people....I can see no halfway house'. There were dangers—'Gandhi and Jinnah are both dictators'; however Wavell hoped they might create a 'constructive partnership'. The discussion was not very positive. Cripps who might have been expected to make a helpful contribution did not attend, Amery gave very qualified support: 'the chances of acceptance of the plans were perhaps even less favourable than Lord Wavell had estimated'. Halifax was the most helpful 'it was important not to allow the present deadlock to continue'. Grigg was 'opposed to any offer on the lines suggested'. Attlee made the debating point that Cripps had proposed first that a Constitution-making body should be set up after the war, and that only if this were agreed would the politicians be invited to participate in the 'counsels of their country'. The present proposal reversed these two stages 'and the reversal was in his view a fundamental and most serious change....He asked whether the radical changes would not greatly weaken the responsibility of the Viceroy and of the Secretary of State'. Simon seized on this point; it would create a 'Very difficult, uncertain and indeed dangerous position'. Attlee came back to emphasize 'the difficulty of having any dealings with Gandhi. He deprecated 'having negotiations with the leaders of the political parties....We were more likely to make a successful approach...if the Centre was built up out of elements drawn from the Provinces and the Indian States rather than from the political parties'. After this Diehard declaration there was not much more to be said. Wavell produced a modified version of his proposal to meet the objections raised: the new draft included an appeal to the Indian leaders. 'You are being asked to cooperate in the formation of a Coalition Government...for the performance of administrative tasks which require political leadership. There is no question of any constitutional commitment by any party at this stage'. The revised draft again went to the India Committee on 29 September. Cripps, present on this occasion said that he 'agreed generally with the memorandum'. Sir John Anderson disagreed that an approach be made to the Indian leaders; Grigg said that such an approach would be 'disastrous'; they should not try to negotiate with Congress 'During Gandhi's lifetime'. Wavell curtly replied that if the British Government did not want to make any attempt at reform during the war 'he should be authorized to state this definitely'. Cripps offered support: the plan 'would help to prevent feelings in India becoming embittered'. Attlee deduced from the discussion that, apart from Grigg, they all thought Wavell should be able 'to make a fresh approach to the Indian political leaders'. Anderson responded to an invitation by Attlee to state his case by suggesting they must obtain 'an assurance of the goodwill and cooperation of the Indian leaders'; then they might be willing to consider 'some provisional interim arrangement whereby the recognized leaders of the Indian political parties would be entrusted with a greater degree of responsibility'. Simon gave this assessment modified support. Wavell, clearly losing patience replied that this approach 'would wreck all chances of a successful issue of the approach suggested'.

After further confabulation, Attlee 'pointed out that no reference had been made...to our responsibility for minority communities', Anderson emphasized 'the responsibility of Parliament', and Grigg reiterated that 'he remained opposed to any approach to the Indian political leaders during Gandhi's lifetime'. Wavell called this meeting 'Rather a depressing experience'. In his diary Amery recorded 'Wavell held his own very well' and concluded 'I backed up Wavell stoutly'.

The discussion was further revolved at a Cabinet meeting on 7 October. This began with a note from Grigg: 'I am in complete disagreement with the recommendations'. This negative tone was reiterated in the conclusions of the Cabinet: 'It was doubtful whether any advantage was to be gained by laying down at this stage too precise and definite a case of action'. The Conference leaders must disavow their 'present attitude': they were not prepared to negotiate with Gandhi: this 'would be attended by grave inconvenience'; Churchill would prepare a revised draft of the statement. This emphasized 'the defence of India' and not much more. From this unpromising material Attlee constructed some kind of statement 'I can only ask the Indian people to have patience'.

Meanwhile, a farewell dinner was given for Wavell. Churchill turned up late; inclined not to attend but persuaded to go by his wife. When his turn came to speak, according to Amery he 'made a pure Diehard speech glorifying our past record in India'. Churchill did praise Wavell 'one of our foremost citizens and one of our greatest soldiers, a man of the highest courage...capable of wielding the pen with almost equal effect to the way in which he wields the sword'. Wavell produced an equally polished and Delphic reply: 'I have had three difficult but most extraordinarily interesting years under a remarkable war leader...India will be just as difficult...our aim is the summit, the goal of a self-governing India'. When Wavell had departed the Prime Minister 'declared that he was going to be the greatest failure as a Viceroy that we had ever had' (according to Amery's diary, 5 November). He could not have been more wrong. Wavell completely altered the Viceregal style: no top hat, no special white train, no elaborate ceremonial. Within his first week in India he flew to Calcutta to see the food situation for himself: 'grim enough to make official complacency surprising'. He was disappointed in the acting Governor, Rutherford—'no fire in him'. he arranged for the refugees to be moved off the Calcutta streets into special camps, supplying military personnel and vehicles to carry this out. All this was hailed by Gandhi with high praise: 'As a great soldier, Lord Wavell has gone straight to Bengal'. Unhappily this note was not sounded again.

Wavell was appalled by what he found in Bengal; not only was the Muslim League ministry self-serving and corrupt, as well as inefficient, but the administrators had lost heart and were concerned merely to keep things from getting any worse. The acting Governor, Rutherford, was going the way of his predecessor, Herbert, and was unable to cope with the problems. Losing heart 'he went away to Darjeeling to recuperate and never really took hold again'. Soon after his arrival Wavell appealed to Amery to find a really first class man from outside. Churchill was able to suggest R. G. Casey the Australian politician who was Minister Resident in the Middle East which was becoming rather a backwater in the war. Casey was a good man, but he seemed unable to understand that the need was urgent. It took him over two months to get from Cairo to Calcutta and on arrival he went down with fever (not his fault, of course). Another appointment which was delayed was that of a new Finance Member of Council. Raisman's time was up, and he was showing signs of fatigue. Wavell wanted to show his confidence in Indian leaders by shifting Sir Ramaswami Mudalier from Commerce to Finance. The Cabinet refused to agree, believing that Finance must remain a British responsibility (their main concern was the mounting debt which the UK was incurring with India on account of supplies and troops supplied, mainly to the Middle East). Wavell refused to accept anyone connected with the Bank of England and a fatuous suggestion was made for appointing a junior Canadian expert. When the question was considered in Cabinet, Attlee was in the chair as Churchill was overseas as was so often the case. Attlee made no attempt to argue in favour of an Indian appointment; he simply recorded the 'predominant view' of the Cabinet against appointing an Indian. Among other questions on which the Cabinet refused to accept Wavell's suggestion was his recommendation that the Ministry in Bengal be superseded by direct rule by the Governor. It became clear that their main argument was that because it was a Muslim League minority it should not be relieved of office. Wavell's imperative was to ensure that Bengal did not undergo another famine in 1944; to this end he also badgered London to provide ships for imports from Australia, Canada, etc. Lord Leathers, the Minister in charge of shipping was totally unimpressed. Wavell must have doubted if the Cabinet would ever adopt his proposals. There was a core of opposition—Grigg, War Minister and former member of the Viceroy's Council, Simon, now Lord Chancellor, and on most questions Anderson, now Chancellor of the Exchequer (former Governor of Bengal), with Churchill of course when he was not away on his frequent jaunts to the United States and the war zones, leading the pack. Wavell received some support from Cripps, ideologically committed to reform but not sympathetic to Wavell personally. When Attlee was in the chair he took the obligation for impartiality to the extent of siding with the majority and at best offered lukewarm support. Thus, over Wavell's proposal to appoint Mudalier he said 'it was clear that the predominant view of the War Cabinet was not in favour of the appointment at this juncture of an Indian as Finance member' (6 January 1944). Amery backed up the Viceroy but his contributions were brushed aside. As Wavell put it 'nothing he says goes down very well' (19 July 1944). In his next letter to the Viceroy he would launch into some irrelevancy; thus, writing on 6 January, he did not mention the rejection of Mudalier but enlarged upon a plan to recruit selected Indian boys for service 'as the Turks conscribed Christian boys' as janissaries. Then he went into a plan for co-opting Dominion judges to sit on the Judicial Committee of the House of Lords and vice versa. As an afficianado of Alice, Wavell must have found himself in wonderland when these effusions reached him instead of practical plans. Wavell was not altogether content with the working of the Government of India. He reduced the time-honoured habit of holding a meeting of his Council once a week to that of a fortnightly meeting: sometimes lasting half an hour. He also cut the number of telegrams to London by a half, observing that the India Office was also bad, quoting one telegram about the status of Bajpai, Indian Representative in Washington 'which asked at inordinate length questions to which answers must be known to you already' (30 November 1943). Doubtless the King was all in favour of brevity but not Monteath and Amery to whom these telegrams were a major raison d'etre.

The main event of 1944 was the release of Gandhi from detention. He underwent a coronary thrombosis, and on 4 May Wavell informed Amery that he had instructed the Bombay Government to release the Mahatma at 8.00 a.m. on 6 May. It was interesting that having consulted the Cabinet about so many less important suggestions he should have taken this major decision without prior deliberation, though the move was dressed up to appear to be in response to the decision of the Cabinet. Surprisingly, Churchill treated the news as comparable to the reconciliation with the Boer leaders after the British had fought them. He added, that 'the greatest mistake of the Cripps offer was that it came on top of all our disasters in the East'. A salutary conclusion. When Gandhi approached Wavell to reconsider a national government, the Cabinet re-drafted his letter of reply in terms which the Viceroy considered discourteous. He protested and urged them to return to his draft. Cripps made the comment that their telegram 'was the outcome of discussion in full Cabinet' and was 'a deliberate decision that the reply...should be in firm and uncompromising terms'. He deprecated any compromise: 'the matter was clearly one that could not be finally decided without further reference to the War Cabinet'. Butler was more helpful 'to try to guide both parties out of this impasse'. Wavell came back again. The next time, Attlee was in the chair, the decision was unchanged. Only Amery spoke up for Wavell, asking for his dissent to be recorded. With the progressive minority in the Government joining the diehards the Viceroy had only one ally—Amery. Amid all the problems of India and Empire there were family worries. Archie John Wavell went into Burma with a Chindit column. He was severely wounded and lost his left hand. The Wavell's were a close knit family, and Wavell was specially close to his only son. Wavell had been among the few supporters of Wingate. Now he was dead and the Chindits had passed under the command of the American Stilwell, who was callous in squandering his men's lives. Young Wavell's column, formed from the South Staffs was to suffer 800 casualties before taking their objective Mogaung: Wavell's son was among the earliest. He was left behind until the most seriously wounded were evacuated. Then he too went back, to the unfamiliar splendour of Viceroy's House. Amid all his troubles, the Viceroy received constant support from his wife who he recorded as 'an outstanding success....The atmosphere in the Viceroy's House is friendly without loss of dignity'.

Wavell was continuously looking ahead to the postwar India. On 24 October 1944 he addressed a lengthy letter to Churchill on the postwar plans for India, writing: 'I feel very strongly that the future of India is the problem on which the British Commonwealth and the British reputation will stand or fall in the postwar period'. Yet, within Wavell's experience, 'vital problems of India are being treated by His Majesty's Government with neglect, even sometimes with hostility and contempt'. As regards immediate problems, 'we should be able to hold the food position, but only just'. 'In the longer term, we cannot reverse policy of political reform; we cannot hold India down by military force; there must be acquiescence in the British connection if India is to remain in the Commonwealth; we cannot go on with the present situation'. 'We have every reason to mistrust and dislike Gandhi and Jinnah and their followers', but 'We have had to negotiate with similar rebels before, e.g. De Valera and Zaghlul'. They should make the move before postwar problems make India 'unsettled and discontented'. Any move should 'be such as to capture the Indian imagination'.

At the year's end he summarized his impressions; he pondered his political proposals. Could he set India on the right road? 'I am afraid that the hopes are slender. I have less opinion than ever of the Indian capacity for leadership and statesmanship and common sense: nor do I think that I have a strong enough personality to put through the almost superhuman task of persuading India to be a nation'. He was doubtful: 'Few of them see beyond their own personal or sectional interests. There is no greatness about India yet....Has India a great future or is her great future already behind her?' Already Wavell was considering the prospects for a visit to London and meeting the Prime Minister and Cabinet. His proposal to the Prime Minister elicited no response; but he was not put off. He continued to badger the Secretary of State. Amery was fearful of propositioning the Prime Minister directly, but he approached Cripps to intervene: 'We cannot allow it to become known that we refused even to consider his proposals'. 'As leader of half the Coalition you can make it clear to him that you cannot afford to be put in the position of having acquiesced in the postponement' (2 December 1944). Four days later the India Committee agreed that Wavell must be invited home: the India Committee agreed that to send out a negative response 'would expose His Majesty's Government to criticism and grave misunderstanding' (6 December 1944).

All this led Amery to mount his hobby horse and suggest that the root of the problem was the belief that India must necessarily adopt the Westminster pattern. He submitted an enormously long memorandum to the India Committee, inviting comments from colleagues. Several responded at length. The main innovation suggested by Amery was that full internal self-government should be established before not after constitutional change. Cripps replied on 1 January 1945, suggesting that the new polity should be for 'a very loose federation...the very minimum possible'. He envisaged Hindustan and Pakistan [sic]: 'I feel that Pakistan has become so much the slogan of the Moslems that it is no use working out anything to start with that does not proceed upon the basis of its future existence; though whether it will ever come into being is quite another matter'.

Meanwhile, Wavell was planning his London visit and requested Amery to let him see 'a record of the discussions on the Indian constitutional problem in the India Committee'. Amery sent round this request as a matter of course to Attlee and received a totally negative reply. Attlee observed (28 December) that 'it would be quite wrong to send the Viceroy the minutes, the report or even a summary of the discussion of the India Committee'. He observed that 'even the composition of Cabinet Committees is, as a rule, not communicated to Parliament'. He finished this chilling note by suggesting that 'the making of this request is, I fear, only another example of having a Viceroy with no political experience'.

The request had been taken to Attlee's office by Monteath. That stickler for constitutional correctness was astonished by this response. Wavell had already met the

India Committee before his installation as Viceroy: he knew very well who were its members. As Monteath pointed out, Wavell had been specially sworn of the Privy Council and as such was 'eligible to participate in Cabinet confidences'. With great restraint, Monteath concluded: 'It seems a little pedantic to refuse to let him know how the views of the Committee are developing before he actually meets them face to face'. Attlee's complaint seems particularly peevish when we recall that the man he chose to succeed Wavell—Mountbatten—had even less knowledge of British politics. Nevertheless, Wavell's supposed lack of political expertise was to become a fixed part of Attlee's stereotype of the Viceroy. Wavell arrived back in Britain on 23 March. His first meeting with the India Committee took place on 26 March with Attlee in the chair. There was a full attendance, including the new Labour parliamentary Under Secretary Lord Listowel, though he was silent. Wavell began with a general survey of the Indian situation. Regarding the Governor-General's Council he observed that its character had changed markedly: it was now a body of fifteen with only four European members: the Viceroy had a veto but neither Linlithgow nor he had been required to exercise it. He was asked about the attitude of the British Indian politicians. Gandhi was now very frail; Jinnah 'would of course never commit himself'. Attlee asked whether the new political council might have to accept the Viceroy's veto, or else the Viceroy 'would rapidly move into the position of a Dominion Governor-General'. Wavell replied that the real safeguard was the communal balance: 'he thought a walk-out unlikely'. Attlee feared that under this scheme there might be deadlock: 'Lord Wavell agreed that there was a risk. But it was not in his judgement so great as the risks involved in sitting still and letting things get worse'. The Committee agreed to meet again next day. Attlee began by asking if Wavell envisaged constitutional change? Not for some time, replied Wavell. After a lengthy discussion Attlee observed that 'he was frankly horrified at the thought of the substitution for the present government of a brown oligarchy'. A government responsible neither to Parliament nor to a legislature 'would leave His Majesty's Government powerless to protect the Indian masses which would be defenceless'. The Council would be 'responsible only to party caucuses'. Wavell replied that the new Council would be more responsible than the existing Council: 'The people of India were incapable of exercising the power of election and to suggest that there was any real power in India of choosing or electing was a fiction; but the government 'had after all been ready to take a chance in 1942'. This upset Cripps who insisted that his negotiations had depended on 'acceptance by Indians of his proposals as a whole'.

The Committee met again on 29 March without Wavell present. Anderson 'remained as apprehensive as ever', yet realized that Wavell could not return empty handed. Grigg said that the decision had been made to Indianize the whole Indian Army: 'It would take twenty years to bring that about....We must face the facts'. Cripps observed that any constitutional change 'must in present circumstances be done by His Majesty's Government: thereafter we should say quite plainly what we intended to do'.

The Committee next met on 3 April with a poor attendance. Attlee declared that 'there was too great a tendency to consider the India problem in terms of Gandhi and Jinnah': he went on to observe that he 'disliked the Viceroy's suggestion for informal conversations with party leaders who might well carry us further than we wished'. Wavell was not impressed by the return to the Cripps offer: 'a further repetition would, in his opinion, have no effect whatever'. He criticised the other proposals, Attlee retorted that under Wavell's plan 'all these things of which he expressed himself uneasy would come to pass by the mere pressure of the situation'. Afterwards Wavell recorded that even his cool, equable Private Secretary was depressed 'we are heading for an impasse' (9 April). The next India Committee meeting went ahead without Wavell. With his customary bluntness Grigg insisted that 'there was nothing for it but to send him [Wavell] back to India to stonewall'. Amery retorted that Wavell had returned to the United Kingdom to discuss his own proposals: they could not send him back with Simon's plan, 'or to explore the situation. He doubted, indeed, if Lord Wavell would return on that basis': 'We must either accept or reject the Viceroy's scheme'. Attlee objected: 'Lord Wavell seemed to have no conception of the constitutional implications of his plan'. Amery finally observed that 'He could not understand why the Committee seeing how far they had been prepared to go in 1942...should now hesitate over the Viceroy's proposals.'

Attlee declared that 'he was dismayed that we should hand over the people of India to a few very rich individuals who could control the caucuses without responsibility to anyone. (When the Cabinet Mission surveyed the scene a year later, these doubts were forgotten). 'Nor was he satisfied either that the situation in India was as acute as had been suggested'. Grigg from his extreme right wing perspective agreed: 'we were in danger of handing over India...to two party caucuses and fastening a most oppressive tyranny on the Indian peasant'. Amery mildly retorted that 'We were committed too far to make it possible for us to change our policy'. Cripps emphasized that whatever was done should be done 'in a very formal way': any announcement 'should be made first in Parliament and not in a broadcast by the Viceroy'. Despite all their caution the Committee decided to transfer external affairs to an Indian Minister. They also agreed to the appointment of a UK High Commissioner mainly to safeguard British economic interests in India.

With his habitual optimism, Amery informed Colville, as acting Viceroy that 'the difference between the Cabinet Committee and Wavell have narrowed down more to points of method than of real substance' (12 April). Amery continued to pour forth a stream of notes on constitutional powers, mainly drafted by the indefatigable Monteath. About the next meeting on 18 April, Wavell noted in his diary

'Attlee started attacking me at once...John Anderson complained that I would not admit that I was making a radical change in the constitution. Cripps was absent, Grigg and Simon were definitely hostile....An hour and a half of desultory and rather acrimonious discussion got us nowhere...' Next day Wavell talked it over with his Private Secretary: 'thinks we have failed....Evan says the India Office officials are against my proposals....They are a poor lot anyhow I think'. To his diary Amery confided 'Attlee began by barking at Archie...after which we had a futile wrangle....However, after a lot of irrelevancy we got down to his (Wavell's) specific suggestions and ended by practically adopting all of them'.

To Wavell, accustomed to military conferences and the Viceroy's Council where he was in the chair it must have seemed like a bear garden: but to those accustomed to Cabinet meetings under Churchill where a monologue alternated with a general altercation it was much as normal. To Colville, Amery wrote: 'We get on by degrees and Wavell holds his own extremely well against a great deal of theoretical and to my mind often irrelevant argument'. On 3 May Amery told Colville 'the India Committee after many sittings has practically come back to Wavell's original plan, subject only to its being launched by a formal declaration in Parliament'. So much for the labours of six weeks. He still hoped to reach a decision in about ten days. The India Committee's report went to Churchill on 27 April: Attlee had departed for San Francisco and Churchill was wholly absorbed in the problems arising from the ending of the war. The War Cabinet gave the report cursory consideration at their meeting on 30 April. About the only helpful comment came from Bevin who termed this 'a small step' but recognized it was 'a further move in the right direction'. The India Committee then plunged into the consideration of British commercial interests in India.

Amery wrote to Churchill about the delay in 'taking' India on 8 May but received a brush-off from the Prime

Minister. Exasperated, Wavell addressed the Prime Minister (24 May), reminding him that his proposals were given to the Cabinet six months before he returned home. He complained that the last meeting of the India Committee he attended had been over one month previously: 'I have had no communication from yourself since you saw me shortly after my arrival home'. The delay had made his task in India more difficult. Although annoyed, Churchill was at last goaded into a response, ungracious like so many of his communications: 'I did not consider that your visit to this country was necessary at the present time'. Amery assured Wavell that all was well: he could make arrangements to return to India. By now, the wartime Cabinet had been replaced by a 'caretaker' Conservative Cabinet: this made little difference to the tone of the discussion. However, the old Churchill re-asserted himself and a further meeting was announced for 6.30 p.m. that evening with Churchill 'in his most truculent mood and very difficult'. Amery insisted that after waiting two months Wavell must have the opportunity to state his views. Another Cabinet meeting was held on 31 May where Wavell made a lengthy statement. This time Churchill conceded virtually everything (only reserving certain parts that Wavell had never liked but inserted to please Anderson). There was still another India Committee meeting that same afternoon and yet another Cabinet meeting later in the evening. The minutes read that Churchill 'Thanked the Viceroy warmly on behalf of the Cabinet and expressed their cordial good wishes'. Amery recorded that Churchill expounded the Wavell scheme 'as his own conception'. Amery much later conceded that the failure of the Simla scheme was due 'to the long delay...and to Winston'.

The Viceroy got back to Karachi on 6 June. Wavell's terms for a political Executive Council laid down a 40:40:20 ratio with equal numbers from the Muslim community and the 'Caste Hindus'. The Muslim League quota was limited by Wavell's insistence that one Muslim nominee must be from another party. He envisaged a Punjabi Unionist representative, of course. While Congress had been attempting to sabotage the war effort and Jinnah had stood ostentatiously aloof, the Punjab under Unionist leadership had given unstinted support. Wavell issued a broad list of invitations to attend the conference. Everyone except Gandhi accepted. The Mahatma objected on two counts: he was not a member of Congress (having not paid his subscription) and he rejected the identification of 'caste Hindus' and by implication its application to Congress, which he insisted, represented all the peoples of India. Nevertheless, he agreed to come up to Simla to make himself available for consultation.

The conference formally opened on 25 June and adjourned four days later. Wavell almost at once had to confront Jinnah's obduracy. The party leaders were asked to submit nominees for the new, representative Executive Council. Jinnah insisted that he would accept no formula which did not acknowledge the right of the Muslim League to nominate all Muslim representatives. The conference took place while the election campaign was being waged in Britain. A Cabinet meeting was held on 10 July with a very limited attendance. They could not resist instructing Wavell not to go beyond the terms already laid down, though even Amery described them as 'rather pernickety' and wanting the proposals to break down. Jinnah reinforced his demands, and informed Wavell that 'they could not cooperate'. Knowing that the Cabinet would react badly to any deviation, Wavell took this as the signal to close down the conference. Congress had behaved very reasonably, and submitted a list which included non-Congress names. When the Conference met for the last time, Wavell took the blame for failure on himself. Azad, as President of the Congress would not accept this: 'With his usual sincerity His Excellency took all the responsibility which really rested on other shoulders'. Azad went on: he hoped 'His Excellency would not misunderstand when he said that the British

Government could not absolve itself of the blame for the present communal problem. So long as there was a third power the two parties were like pawns which could be moved one way or the other'. When Jinnah came to speak he reported that 'the Congress stood for a united India whereas the Muslim League stood for Pakistan'. He asserted that the League 'had repeatedly offered their hand of cooperation for the prosecution of the war' (a highly dubious proposition) and he complained that Pakistan had been 'Put in cold storage indefinitely'. In Wavell's words 'he actually seemed to claim grant to the Muslims of equality with all other communities taken together in an interim government'. Wavell was unimpressed, but he thought Muslims were fearful 'that Congress would combine with other minorities [sic] in any interim government to settle finally with the League'. Wavell concluded: 'Jinnah would have done better to say nothing'. There was a good deal of breast beating and Rajaji was unusual in suggesting that a way forward might be to reform the provincial governments and choose a Council from among them. Wavell reviewed this disappointing result to Amery observing that their failure had narrowed the field for future negotiations: it was not clear what Jinnah would accept 'short of Pakistan'. Gandhi told Wavell that the British Government 'would have to decide sooner or later whether to come down on the side of...Congress or League since they could never reconcile them'. A discouraging comment but true...(15 July).

Wavell's decision not to challenge the League was influenced by the negative attitude of the caretaker government in its dying days. Had Wavell gone ahead and announced an interim government without the League—as he was to do in September 1946—Jinnah would certainly have realized that he must come in or be marginalized. V. P. Menon recorded: 'At no time in my experience of over thirty years has a Viceroy had such universally good press and good will...Congress was most anxious to form a National Government...Gandhi approached Jinnah to find a compromise....It was a great achievement to have got the Congress to agree'. However, the war was still on and Winston was still Prime Minister.

However, the days of Tory control were almost at an end, and figures such as Grigg and Simon disappeared from the scene (though not the arch-Tory, Churchill). The incoming government included several figures who had made their debut in Victorian and Edwardian times, such as Lord Stansgate, Addison, Secretary of State for Dominions (b.1869), former Secretary of State for India Wedgwood Benn, and Pethick-Lawrence (b. 1871), and now Secretary of State for India. As Mr Lawrence he had married Miss Pethick and they had combined their names on marriage. Both were fervent supporters of women's suffrage and both went to jail for the cause. When his wife was jailed, Pethick-Lawrence announced that he would contribute one pound for every day his wife was kept in prison—something which amused irreverent persons. A Conscientious Objector in the Great War, he defeated Churchill at the 1923 election in the contest at Leicester. He was in and out of parliament and in 1929 became Financial Secretary to the Treasury. He was a delegate to the Round Table Conference in 1931. He held no ministerial office during the war, 1939-45. He and his wife had long been supporters of self-government for India.

Would the advent of Labour make a great difference? In a speech to the Labour Party conference at Blackpool Bevin stated: 'If Labour is returned we would close the India Office and transfer Indian business to the Dominions Office....This act would give them confidence that they are no longer governed from Whitehall' (23 May 1945). Yet in the Labour Party manifesto on which they had fought the election, 'Let Us Face The Future', there was only the statement that India would obtain Home Rule (a curious Gladstonian echo). Some in Congress were persuaded that there would be a fundamental change, but both Nehru and Patel were highly sceptical, alleging that neither in 1924 nor in 1929 had the advent of Labour made any difference. Labour certainly began carefully, picking up where the previous government had left off. At the start of the new parliament, Attlee replied to a question by Woodrow Wyatt about transferring Indian affairs to the Dominions Office by declaring that he had 'no statement to make' (21 August 1945).

The three Ministers mainly concerned with India were not a homogeneous group. Attlee was a gradualist: he had not submitted a minority report with the Simon Report and repeatedly referred back to that document. He genuinely intended to advance India to self-government, but hoped this would be in the framework of the British Empire (as the Commonwealth was still described). Pethick-Lawrence was mainly a social reformer; Cripps was the only real Socialist. Expelled from the Labour Party in 1938 for advocating a Popular Front he was not readmitted until just before the 1945 election. He was austere and also arrogant: a combination which made him highly comparable with Nehru. They were in frequent communication. At the first meeting of the new India-Burma Committee on 17 August, he urged his colleagues 'If we act quickly in the right way we have a great opportunity.' He did not attach undue importance to Muslim feeling, since his information was that the 'Muslims were now tending to desert Jinnah'. The first move by the new government was to announce the appointment of Fred Burrows, previously President of the National Union of Railwaymen, as Governor of Bengal in place of Casey, who returned to Australian politics. Wavell protested about this appointment when it was announced with no prior reference to him, but as soon as he met Burrows he warmed to him. He was a Company Sergeant Major in the Guards during the Great War and he was 'straight'; and in Wavell's book this was high praise. Despite his faults Amery had been straight. Wavell bestowed this term on no other politician: Cripps certainly was not straight, although he was a Wykhamist like Wavell. The Viceroy was called home yet again to discuss the future: his visit (August to September) did not involve waiting about, as before. Cripps had prepared a statement to be announced on Wavell's return which Wavell found unsatisfactory: he was insistent that the first priority was to confront the Muslim League with the implication of their plan, which must entail the division of Punjab and Bengal. Cripps admitted that Muslims 'might not cooperate...in that case the Constitutional Assembly would have to devise a constitution for Hindustan' (the short-hand term for the non-Muslim majority areas). In return Cripps declared that 'the Viceroy's draft statement would be disastrous' (4 September). Despite these differences the visit went off amicably.

The Cabinet decided that the next move should be to send a parliamentary mission to India; on a fact-finding tour. Its members were selected to give predominance to Labour: they provided six members, five were Conservatives with one Liberal. Professor Robert Richards, the leader was a veteran who had been Under Secretary in the 1924 Labour government and had not subsequently held office. He was somewhat out of touch and disconcerted his Indian audience on arrival by assuring them that India 'was certainly entitled to a measure of Home Rule'. The most informed member was Reginald Sorensen, a leading light in the India League. A Unitarian Minister, Sorensen was one of those attractive eccentrics who once adorned the Labour Party. There were grave doubts about his inclusion, expressed by Attlee and also Herbert Morrison. He was suspected of being in the pay of Congress. Before the date of departure Pethick-Lawrence met a group of Labour MPs, led by William Dobbie, former railwayman and also a member of the India League. Rather charmingly Pethick-Lawrence explained that in the first days of his office certain important points had become evident to him. One of these was that the 'Viceroy was not an ordinary civil servant and that his views must be taken into account'. On their return the delegation met the Prime Minister on 13 February 1946. Almost all insisted on the need to face up to the Pakistan issue: Sorensen called the Pakistan idea 'wholly irrational' but admitted that it was necessary to accept this in principle. He still anticipated that a Central Government would retain 'the essential federal functions'. In a separate memorandum he noted 'Lord Wavell is held in general respect; the Government of India is not held in general respect'.

Meanwhile Wavell's relations with the Cabinet and the Prime Minister had become chill. At the India-Burma Committee it was observed that 'the Government of India seemed to have no clear conception of their policy and consistently failed to obtain adequate publicity for their point of view. This was in part due to the nature of the Government which did not contain the necessary political spokesmen'. This was astonishing coming from a group of men who had refused to face the Viceroy's constant insistence that they must confront the Pakistan issue even though they privately agreed that 'we might have to contemplate a division of India into Hindustan and Pakistan as the only solution' (19 December).

Wavell was facing an increasingly unstable situation: Nehru led the revolutionary rhetoric: 'India must prepare for a mass battle for freedom which may come sooner than people expect' (12 November 1945). The Viceroy met the revolutionary leader and warned him that 'the preaching of violence must eventually lead to violence'. This prediction was very soon to be fulfilled. Among the armed forces the Indian Army with its long tradition remained stable (apart from marginal mutterings in the support services); the Indian Air Force, enlisting more educated Indians was affected and observed the example of the RAF in India who had mutinied to obtain release more quickly. Finally there was the Royal Indian Navy which was based on the great ports with their politicized population. On 18 February the navy at Bombay began a violent protest. This quickly spread to Karachi. For several months Wavell had been warning the Congress leaders that violent speeches would produce a violent reaction. He negotiated with the mutineers and within three days they surrendered. Unfortunately for Wavell he had regarded the mutineers as within Auchinleck's sphere. He left it to the Commander-in-Chief to inform London. This was done on the day after the mutiny erupted. However, the report was delayed in transmission and was not received until 3.30 p.m. on 21 February, by which time the matter had been raised in London in Cabinet. Pethick-Lawrence cabled to Wavell: in moderate terms. The Prime Minister informed Wavell: 'Your failure to reply to the Secretary of State's telegram asking for information on the situation in Bombay places us in serious difficulty here. Information should have been sent by you without even a request from here. I must demand an immediate statement'.

Wavell did not answer the Prime Minister's intemperate outburst but he cabled the Secretary of State with a bald message. In his diary he noted (23 February) that Whitehall was in a 'flap'. Meanwhile he had a game of golf and wrote in the diary that he 'played well'.

Meanwhile the electoral process had started. The central assembly was still elected under the 1919 franchise and voters were limited to the middle and upper classes. They proved susceptible to the politics of community: the Provincial elections followed, the pattern was similar though less clear cut. The League was entirely successful only in Bengal where they won nearly all the Muslim seats (113 in a total of 119). They were able to form a ministry with the help of the independents. In the other key province, Punjab, the League largely replaced the Unionists winning 79 of their 86 seats, while Congress captured 51 seats, including most of the Jat constituencies previously loyal to the Unionists. The Sikhs split three ways, with 23 of their 31 seats going to the Akalis. The Muslim League was clearly the main party, but could not furnish a majority. In Sind the League made no gain and Congress doubled its representation. However, the Governor, Sir Frank Mudie, was pro-League and installed a minority League government. On the Frontier the League failed to oust Dr Khan Sahib and his Red Shirt followers, allies of the Congress. The League could claim to speak for the Muslim community yet reaped no reward in obtaining office, although they polled rather more votes than the Congress on the Frontier (146,158 to 135,885)

On 24 May Wavell recorded in his journal: 'The three Magi have arrived. They are pleasant and friendly but I am still doubtful whether they have got any definite plan in their heads'. Actually, their plan was to extract proposals from the Indian leaders. However, they remained as divided as ever. The approach of the Secretary of State irritated the Viceroy: 'He is inclined to be sloppy and long-winded and makes little speeches instead of asking questions'. (Wavell called it 'slopping goodwill all over the place'). Cripps is of course an expert and incisive cross-examiner but for some reason he makes lengthy notes all through an interview' (Journal: 2 April).

The Secretary to the Mission, Frank Turnbull, who had accompanied Cripps in 1942 gave his impression to Sir David Monteath: 'He was a bit stiff at first but is now quite happily at home with the three. I think he really thought they had come to put something big across him....Stafford is a good deal changed since 1942. Much more disposed to listen to a case and much more responsible I think'. Sir William Croft, the senior India Office man with the delegation was more appreciative of Pethick-Lawrence than Wavell: 'Winning golden opinions all round, he seems to have the liking and respect of the Viceroy which I should say was hardly true in the case of Cripps....So far he shows no sign of wear and tear....Although I should guess that there was not much love lost between Cripps and the Viceroy there has been no serious clash so far'. Croft noted that the question of precedence was solved by Wavell and Pethick-Lawrence taking the two central seats of the table with Cripps and Alex on the outside. A photograph taken later in June shows Wavell looking quizzical, Pethick-Lawrence somewhat exhausted, Cripps staring fixedly and sternly and Alex raising some point with his Secretary. They did get through without open disagreement.

The meetings with Indian political leaders followed predictable lines, with Gandhi elusive and Jinnah inflexible. When the Mission arrived, Nehru was on a visit to Malaya where he fell under the spell of the Mountbattens. Among the provincial politicians, Dr Ambedkar was detached from the Hindu-Muslim confrontation though bitterly conscious of the misery of his own Untouchable brethren. "He wondered whether Pakistan was a permanent or a passing mood among the Muslims. Quite probably it would pass. But it was impossible to wait and see'. He thought that 'if India became independent it would be one of the greatest disasters that could happen' (5 April). A less sombre note was struck by the Premier of Punjab. He had been a soldier in his younger days. 'Sir Khizr asked what was the Delegation's plan of action. Sir Stafford Cripps replied that they had no plan as yet, only a determination to succeed. Sir Khizr said that this was a pity....The Delegation must be able to produce something definite in order to remove the prevalent impression of indecision' (5 April). Wavell noted 'It was obvious that he had no belief in Pakistan; and said in effect ...that the British had no business to go till they could hand over to something much better than Congress'.

At an early stage the suggestion that Congress and League differences might be resolved by a three tier set-up with a minimal centre and 'groups' of Muslim and Hindu provinces was proposed. Wavell became increasingly irritated by his colleagues' tactics: on 11 April he described the proceedings as 'a pure waste of time'. They all went up to Simla for intensive sessions and on 16 April 'the critical interview with Jinnah went about as badly as it could'. Pethick-Lawrence 'began with ten minutes rambling platitudes and would-be sympathetic stuff about "the welfare of the world", "advancement of India's interests" etc. which had not the slightest effect on Jinnah....At the end of two hours we had made no progress whatever....I don't think [Cripps] approves of the Secretary of State's methods or mine, but hoped that a lawyer-to-lawyer approach would be successful' (11 May): dreadful day according to Pethick-Lawrence 'vague and benevolent generalities'. As spokesman for Congress, Nehru increasingly took the lead: he too expressed the view that the conference had lasted too long: 'the last month had been entirely wasted. On 11 May Wavell recorded 'This is where the conference should have ended' as they plunged into another wrangle. The unfortunate Secretary of State was accused by Gandhi of writing 'in the best imperialistic style which I thought had gone for ever' (22 May).

Negotiations with Gandhi reached a dead end, though Pethick-Lawrence and Cripps were loath to recognize this. Disillusionment came on 20 May when Wavell and the mission met for a private meeting which was electrified by a letter from Gandhi which demolished most of the propositions on which their elaborate attempt to create a framework for proceeding to independence rested. Alexander was indignant: 'It grossly misrepresented the Delegation's position. If this letter represented Mr Gandhi's attitude then the Delegation had better go home'. Even the benign Pethick-Lawrence was shaken: 'No one should see Mr Gandhi apart from the other members of the Mission and without a note being taken. Sir Stafford Cripps said that he thought the best thing might be to see Azad and Nehru'.

However, if a deal was still not in sight, some kind of scheme was needed. They returned to the 'breakdown plan' which had first been propounded by the Viceroy's Private Secretary Abell. This had postulated that the two alternatives were 'repression' and 'scuttle'. It was realized that repression (or long-term British rule) was unrealistic. Auchinleck in London for the Victory Parade, was telling the Cabinet that three or four additional British divisions would be necessary, and these divisions did not exist. A halfway house was suggested, whereby the British would evacuate Central and South India and remain in the 'Pakistan' provinces. On his return, Auchinleck said bluntly that 'The British troops in

India were quite insufficient to deal with the situation and could only hold the ports and Delhi. He did not think it was practicable to stay in Pakistan for any length of time after evacuating Hindustan. The British Government in India rested entirely on its prestige and if three quarters of India were evacuated there would be no prestige left'.

This was the nearest thing to recognizing that British rule had been based upon bluff: upon the willingness of large numbers of Indians to subordinate part of their feelings to a commitment to an alien power, as well as what Gandhi called the 'pathetic contentment' of the rural masses. These supports were now beginning to falter. The Mission seemed to be breaking up. Cripps had to enter hospital after combined physical and nervous exhaustion. Sir William Croft surveyed the situation in a letter to Monteath (30 May): 'I have never been optimistic about the prospect of our being able to bring the parties together....The possibilities are becoming clearer, and the clearer they are the less inviting they look. Alexander...has been taking an increasingly active hand in things and has been contributing a useful element of solidity and good sense....The Secretary of State has stood up to the rigours of the climate marvellously well. But one sees some signs that it is beginning to affect his mental vigour and I think he will have had about as much as he can stand in a week or two's time. The Viceroy seems to have inexhaustible reserves of character and he stands up to the double job of running India and dealing with the Constitutional problem and he faces a cheerless future with remarkable imperturbability'

Meetings with the political leaders continued. On 10 June Nehru was utterly intransigent: 'The Congress were going to work for a strong Centre and to break the Group system and they would succeed. They did not think that Mr Jinnah had any real place in the country'. Wavell recorded in his diary 'Nehru struck me as a little unbalanced'.

For the League, Jinnah took the decisions; and only Jinnah. For Congress there were three alternative leaders

Gandhi, Nehru and Patel. Gandhi continually insisted that he was an outsider, but when he used his authority no other could challenge him. At last it seemed that an agreement was in sight, but Gandhi stood out for a Nationalist Muslim among the Congress members of the new, political Council. 'It mattered not that the principle had ceased to have practical significance now that Jinnah had won almost all the Muslims to his side. It mattered not that insistence on it would infuriate Jinnah whose cooperation in any unitary form of government was essential and would disrupt, with unpredictable consequences the delicate web of negotiations spun by the Cabinet Mission....Dismay in Cabinet mission circles was intense and intense too the indignation against Gandhi. It was he who had wrecked the Cripps mission in 1942. Now he had done it again'.[1] There was Nehru, breathing revolution and defiance, and unwilling or unable to consider compromise, although in private conversations he could be charming, and then there was Patel, whose position was indistinct to the British negotiators. He was actually the realist who took the hard decisions. Early on 23 June Pethick-Lawrence had a conversation with him at Gandhi's prayer meeting: 'Patel said that we gave way to the Muslim League demands at every point. The Secretary of State replied that this was not the case, that Mr Jinnah had made several important concessions and in particular had accepted the Statement of May 16 which the Congress had not done. Patel said that the Congress had certainly accepted that Statement and added that the Congress were going to work the long-term plan in any case however the Interim Government were settled. The Secretary of State had said that it was news to him that the Congress had accepted the Statement'. At a formal meeting later in the day with Nehru, Azad, Patel and Rajendra Prased present the Cabinet delegation once again went over the whole situation. Patel said very little, and his observation of the previous day was not repeated, although the following day a meeting with Rajaji and Amrit Kaur produced the news that 'Patel now wanted the Congress to accept the statement of May 16'—a less clear-cut position but giving some hope. The meetings went on. Pethick-Lawrence wrote to his wife on 22 June: 'The political barometer has gone so up and down that I really don't know from day to day what the final result will be....People start coming to interview me at 7.00 a.m. and the last doesn't leave much before midnight. And nothing whatever comes of it! And the heat is stifling'. At length, in the last days of his presidency, Azad addressed a lengthy exordium to the Viceroy which ended with the declaration that 'While adhering to our views we accept your proposals and are prepared to work them with a view to achieving our objective': i.e. a united India. Wavell noted to his Cabinet colleagues 'Congress manoeuvres have now put us in a very difficult position'. He asked 'whether the Delegation propose to regard the Congress acceptance of the Statement of 16 May as genuine in spite of their declared intention to evade at least one of its essential provisions' (grouping). When they met, the Ministers agreed that 'although cleverly worded the last paragraph of the Congress President's reply must be regarded as an acceptance of the long term proposals'. Alexander commented that Congress 'could say later that they had only accepted subject to their own interpretation of the Statement if it proved convenient for them to do so'. Pethick-Lawrence thought 'it would have been a great mistake to have exacerbated Mr Gandhi....The Viceroy said that he thought an acceptance by Congress which they meant to break was worse than a refusal'. In his private journal Wavell pointed the finger at Cripps who, he noted, has assured them that they would never accept the 16 May statement: 'I am afraid I would not put it past Cripps to have suggested to Congress in one of his many talks that they would put themselves in a better tactical position if they did so'. When Wavell tackled Pethick-Lawrence on this he defended it on the grounds that to get the Congress into the Constitutional Assembly was such a gain that he considered it justified'. As Wavell had written about the Simla Conference on 11 May, this was really the moment when the Viceroy should have decided to end it all. Wavell was becoming slightly paranoid on the subject of Cripps and Pethick-Lawrence, who now returned to an earlier suggestion that he should consult Gwyer, the Chief Justice of India. Wavell was not impressed and replied that 'I had to rely on my own judgement for a long time before the Mission came, but if His Majesty's Government or the Prime Minister would prefer to replace me by someone with more political experience that would be quite all right by me'. The Mission departed on 29 June. Wavell and Cripps were not any more on speaking terms. When they reached London, onlookers thought that Pethick-Lawrence had aged ten years in the last two months.

Wavell recorded his impressions of the talks. He deplored the absence of a 'definite plan of action'; he found the Congress leaders clever but lacking statesmanship. Azad he described as 'honest, moderate and a gentleman'; Nehru as 'sincere...personally courageous but lacks balance and political courage'; Patel 'is more like a leader than any of them'. Among the League's leaders he singled out Jinnah, 'Too uncompromising...but he is straight compared with Congress and does not constantly shift his ground, as they do, though he too drives a hard bargain'.

When the Congress High Command met, Nehru made a speech on 7 July which effectively put paid to the Cabinet Mission scheme, though it remained policy: Nehru declared 'We are not bound by a single thing except that we have decided for the moment to go to the Constitutional Assembly'. Patel called Nehru's speech 'emotional insanity' and Azad pronounced that he was 'carried away by his feelings' and that his utterance had 'changed the course of history'. Wavell persisted with the plan for an interim government. Jinnah responded by withdrawing the League's acceptance of the Cabinet Mission constitutional scheme. Jinnah was sulking after his rebuff by the Mission. Wavell went ahead with the short-term plan to bring in an Executive

Council of politicians composed mainly of Congress and League. His invitation went out on 22 July. On the same day Attlee addressed one of his astringent communications to Wavell. He put his remarks into the framework of the Simon Commission—his preferred baseline—and suggested that Wavell had: 'a great lack of the kind of experience on which it is necessary to draw in political matters....We have perhaps put you in an unfair position in not having provided you with someone of experience in these things'. 'The name occurs to me of Sir Maurice Gwyer who is quite exceptionally well qualified'. Attlee said that his suggestion was 'the result of nearly twenty years fairly close connection with the Indian problem'. Quite why Attlee like Pethick-Lawrence was so keen on Gwyer is not clear: he had been a member of the Indian States Enquiry Committee in 1932 and Parliamentary Counsel to the Treasury before his appointment as the First Chief Justice of India in 1937 under the abortive Federal constitution. Since 1943 he had only been the Vice Chancellor of Delhi University. If Attlee was so concerned about appointing a person with political experience, why for his two gubernatorial appointments in Bengal and Madras did he choose a railwayman and a military staff officer? And why, when he came to replace Wavell did he go for a naval officer? The only explanation seems to be that there was a personality clash between Attlee and Wavell. Wavell replied to Attlee, declaring that he needed no intermediary in dealing with the Indian leaders: 'If I may be frank, I think that the late Cabinet Mission had too many unofficial advisers and indirect contacts'. He understood that Attlee might 'rather have a politician than a soldier at the head of India at present and if you wish to recommend to His Majesty to make a change I shall of course accept your decision without any question'. He concluded 'I have no personal ambition, I have already reached a position far above my expectations or merits....but as I think I must be allowed to exercise my own judgement in the matter of the advice I give to His Majesty's Government. I do not believe it has been so very far wrong up to date' (1 August 1946). Attlee did not follow up Wavell's invitation to change horses, though he already had Mountbatten waiting in the wings. His reply was unusually mild, ending 'All good wishes' (20 August).

Meanwhile, the Indian leaders continued to try Wavell's patience. On 23 July, Nehru wrote to decline entry into an interim government: 'So far as I know the mind of the Congress they would want the political independence issue settled before they can enter any government'. Two weeks later he wrote again (10 August) announcing 'I have accepted the advice of my colleagues...I am therefore in a position to place before you our proposals for the form of this government'. Jinnah's immediate response was to declare 18 August as 'Direct Action' day. In Bengal, this was observed as a public holiday, which the Governor thought would be conducive to calm. His first report reflected this assessment 'though I am unable as yet to say that we have passed the worst' (16 August). The killing continued out of control for four days, and then evaporated: not before over 4,000 persons had been killed and nine battalions deployed on the Calcutta streets, five of them British regiments. A strange feature of the whole business was the immunity of Europeans from the communal imbroglio.

Burrows requested Wavell not to come to Calcutta while the killing was still going on, but the Viceroy paid his visit soon thereafter. He endeavoured to repair the damage to the limited extent possible. On his return to Delhi he met Gandhi and Nehru: according to the Viceroy 'The old man was in a legalistic and malevolent mood and Nehru was full of hate against the League' (Journal, 27 August). According to the official transcript Wavell asked the Congress leaders to make a statement that Congress would agree that the provinces 'must remain in their sections until after the first elections under the new constitution'. Gandhi replied that it was for the Interim Government to decide; Wavell answered that it was a matter for Congress as they had challenged the statement of the Cabinet Mission; he then went off into long legalistic arguments about the interpretation of the Mission statement. 'I said that I was only a plain man and not a lawyer and that I knew perfectly well what the Mission meant and that compulsory grouping was the whole crux of the plan. The argument went on for some time, and we did not make much progress....Gandhi said that if a blood bath was necessary it would come about in spite of non-violence. I said that I was very shocked to hear such words from him'. Next day Gandhi replied. He was clearly shaken by the tussle but he gave no ground. 'Your language last evening was minatory. As a representative of the King you cannot afford to be a military man only, nor to ignore the law, much less the law of your own making. You should be assisted if necessary by a legal mind enjoying your full confidence'. It was interesting that his arguments were so close to those of Attlee. Reporting the letter to Pethick-Lawrence, Wavell wrote: 'It is to my mind convincing evidence that Congress always meant to use their position in the Interim Government to break up the Muslim League and in the Constitutional Assembly to destroy the group scheme....Provided we are firm over this we may still have an outside chance of getting a coalition government' (28 August).

Probably still seething from this encounter, Wavell addressed an uncharacteristically rough letter to Attlee in reply to his letter of 20 August: 'I am afraid I cannot regard it as an adequate reply to mine...From your silence on the matter I assume that you wish me to remain in my present post....I feel I must put before you certain matters on which I feel strongly. I think that it is essential that I should know your mind more fully as regards India, and also that I should have a definite policy from His Majesty's Government....I cannot be responsible for affairs in India if some members of your government are keeping in touch with the Congress through an independent agent behind my back, as they appear to be'. Wavell then enclosed an intercepted telephone message between Patel and Sudhir Ghosh in London. Wavell added that Ghosh had obtained a priority passage to England by favour of Pethick-Lawrence, and over Wavell's head. Wavell ended by declaring 'matters simply cannot be allowed to drift' (28 August).

Attlee then composed three draft replies, each a little longer, insisting that 'I should have thought our policy definite enough'. None of these drafts was issued and the letter eventually despatched on 6 November was entirely free of the tone of the headmaster: in effect he said 'Wait and See', the formula to which so many politicians have had recourse.

Meanwhile Wavell was having to live with his new political Executive Council. Nehru had no doubt about who was now running the government: he was. His first Council (which took office on 2 September) was composed of Congress supporters with two non-political members—Dr John Matthai (Finance) and C. H. Bhabha (Commerce). Defence went to the Sikh, Baldev Singh, a former Minister in the Punjab Government. There were three Muslims from outside the League. Wavell rejected the suggestion of including the renegade Bengali politician, Fazlul Huq in the Council. The new men all looked to Nehru rather than to Wavell. Nehru's position was that of Deputy Leader of the Council, but he appropriated the title of Prime Minister. Before each Council meeting, the members were asked to come to his room, and the policy for the approaching meeting with the Viceroy was laid down. From this time the actual Council meetings were more formal, though Wavell refused to rubber stamp Nehru's plans. As Bevin observed in London, 'The relationship...between the Indian Government and the UK Government had been radically altered... notwithstanding the fact that the constitutional functions of the Viceroy have not been brought into line with these new realities' (16 September). Attlee was already considering curbing Wavell's powers as Viceroy. On 22 December 1945 he wrote to Pethick-Lawrence to suggest someone who might take over from Wavell in negotiating with the Indian leaders. He came up with an extraordinary suggestion: 'There is one man in our ranks of outstanding capacity who has the confidence of people of all political views and who has proved himself a most skilful reconciler of contending factions, Tom Johnston' (a veteran of the crisis of 1931). Johnston knew nothing of India, but Attlee proposed to give him Sir Maurice Gwyer for 'Technical' advice: 'But essentially it should be a one man job'. Pethick-Lawrence agreed that Wavell was restricted by 'the aloofness of his official position' though 'he won confidence of Indian leaders because of his sincerity'. He promised 'further consideration' to the Prime Minister's suggestion, but nothing more was heard of the plan.

Meanwhile Wavell's effort to draw Jinnah produced a result: on 13 October he signified that the League was ready to nominate five candidates for the Executive Council. Wavell reported to Pethick-Lawrence 'This looks more promising than I had expected....Please do not count either on the League acceptance or on Congress complaisance. Both are on the knees of strange gods'. The background was a communal explosion in Eastern India. People who had lived together for centuries went mad. First in Eastern Bengal in Noakhali District where Hindus were the victims and then in Bihar where from 1 to 6 November about 5,000 Muslims were killed. The new ministries tried to halt the killings but once again it was only the arrival of the army which brought the slaughter to an end. Nehru's priority was to convene the Legislative Assembly. On 20 November Wavell issued invitations to attend and Jinnah instructed the League members not to go, emphasizing that their rejection of the Cabinet Mission plan still applied. Wavell was beginning to feel the strain 'not sleeping properly and letting these wretched people worry me. However, some courage and a sense of humour usually returns with the morning ride' (Journal, 24 October). Wavell was all too aware of the perils of the situation and sent to London what was described as 'A Policy for India'. This was an updated version of the Breakdown Plan discussed with the Cabinet Mission. However, the Cabinet in London rejected the plan and also Wavell's proposal that an announcement be issued 'not later than 1 March 1947' that the British would withdraw from India 'by the summer of 1948' even if the Interim Government and the Constituent Assembly were functioning. Pethick-Lawrence replied 'We feel that we should carry on as long as possible giving every assistance we can to secure orderly transfer of power' (28 September). Wavell was not impressed; 'It is my responsibility as the man in charge on the spot to advise you....If HMG consider that my advice shows lack of balance and judgement, or that I have lost my nerve, it is of course their duty to inform me of this and to replace me. But they take a very grave responsibility upon themselves if they simply neglect or disregard my advice....The trouble is that I do not know what long-term policy HMG is pursuing...To carry on without any more definite programme than to hope for the best, they will inevitably place themselves, gradually or almost at once completely in the hands of the Congress'. Wavell ended by asking for answers to the overall questions: 'Were HMG committed to leaving India shortly, did they accept that eighteen months was the maximum period Britain could effectively exercise power?' 'If HMG is unable to accept my plan, on what plan am I to base our withdrawal?' (23 October). In an undated note, Attlee wrote that there could be no reversion to staying on under any circumstances. Subsequently Stafford Cripps prepared a long draft.

Inevitably in reconstructing the Council Congress refused to give any of the big departments to the League (External Affairs, Defence, Home Affairs) though after considerable pressure they agreed to hand over Finance believing that a Muslim would make a mess of this task. Wavell was only one among many feeling the strain: the Inspector General of Police in the UP was forced to resign because in response to Congress irregularities he issued an order which was called 'a minor error of judgement': the Viceroy told the Secretary of State 'This is beyond doubt a test case. If measures cannot be protected your protection of the services is proved to have ceased' (30 October).

These disputes were only the surface evidence of the deep split in the government. Nehru's insistence that grouping would not be accepted, and the League's refusal to rescind their denunciation of the Cabinet Mission Plan continued. Wavell was nettled by what he called the 'well-known act of injured innocence' by Congress 'whenever I have been compelled to resist their manoeuvres'. He resisted Congress demands that the Constituent Assembly be convened until in a desperate effort to break the deadlock, Wavell asked colleagues in London to bring the politicians together to discuss grouping. On 30 November he left Delhi for London, arriving in London on 3 December. Nehru had first said he could not go, but eventually accepted; Patel absolutely refused to leave.

The same day Wavell left Karachi, Cripps received a 'Personal and Private' letter from one of his confidants Major 'Billy' Short. In reply to Cripps he expressed surprise at 'How different Wavell had become', but added that 'It would be fatal for you to replace him': evidence of one line of thinking by Cripps; 'It is here that the finest is needed'. Short made the odd suggestion that the British ambassador in Washington, Lord Inverchapel, could take over 'since the perfect Viceroy is now so crucially needed'. However, Short concluded 'Once there is a positive policy of withdrawal such as I advocate...Wavell will be a changed man....For Wavell like Churchill is susceptible to history....The effect would be to bring such comfort to Wavell that he would become more comfortable to deal with'. Short was a simple man and to evoke such a misunderstanding of the actual situation, Cripps must have passed on a perverted account of their dealings.

The London talks were fruitless. It was clear relations between Wavell and Nehru were bad. Concerning progress,

Nehru observed that 'naturally there was tension. The viceroy said that a total of several thousands killed indicated something more than tension'. Nehru accepted that there was disharmony but he declared 'The Muslim League was a fly in the balance compared with the vast human forces in India as a whole'. He told Cripps 'The Muslims would come in anyhow, sooner or later, provided that they felt that the Constituent Assembly was going ahead'. He could not see why the Muslim League should not come in and put the question of interpretation to the Federal Court. 'The only other test was the test of battle' (4 December).

Meetings with Jinnah and Liaquat went no better. Liaquat refuted Nehru's charges of non-cooperation 'All that they refused to do was to attend so-called "Cabinet Meetings" over which Pundit Nehru purported to preside as Premier and the decisions of which were to go by majority'.

A meeting the next day between Attlee, the Cabinet mission team and Wavell produced an unexpected alliance between Wavell and Cripps who observed that 'there was a strong case for a declaration now that we would only stay a year or eighteen months in India'. The Viceroy then said that 'within the last few months we were for the first time in the position that we could not prevent even the most outrageous things from happening'. All this talking led nowhere. Nehru returned to India for the opening of the Constituent Assembly. The Muslim leaders stayed on as the League was boycotting the Constituent Assembly; which actually only met to elect a President, Rajendra Prasad. Wavell also stayed on, though unwillingly. He trotted out his gradual withdrawal plan again and this was considered, inconclusively, at two meetings of the India-Burma Committee on 19 and 20 December. Wavell's plans were submitted to a full meeting of the Cabinet on 31 December. There was vigorous opposition to any plan which gave the appearance of forced withdrawal led by Ernie Bevin; Alexander (now Minister of Defence) also expressed his dislike of any policy announcement which seemed to 'excuse our withdrawal: we should rather claim credit for taking this initiative'. In the end 'The Cabinet decided to defer for the present their final decision about the timing of the proposed declaration'.

Next day Bevin wrote strongly to Attlee. Cripps, he suggested 'Is so pro-Congress that a balanced judgement is not being brought to bear...while on the other hand, probably, the Minister of Defence is too pro-Moslem'. Bevin said he 'did not think that the facts justified the pessimism which seemed to pervade the whole Cabinet, I am against fixing a date....I cannot get it out of my head that there must be millions of Indians who as a result of the murder incidents of the last few months would welcome a strong and courageous lead'. Bevin saw the trend in India being repeated throughout South Asia: 'I do beg of you to take a stronger line and not give way to this awful pessimism'. Bevin said he was expected as Foreign Secretary 'to make bricks without straw' yet within the British Empire 'we knuckle under at the first blow...even if it does involve a certain risk, to take it' (1 January).

Attlee replied next day 'I agree with you that Wavell has a defeatist mind and I am contemplating replacing him, but...he has the support of the most experienced Civil Servants in India. I am not defeatist but realist'. He went on:'It has been common ground with all of us who have had to study the Indian problem that there are millions of Indians who do not wish for a change of government, but they are passive. The active elements in the population including practically all the educated classes have become indoctrinated to a greater or lesser degree with nationalism. We are seeking to fulfil the pledges of this country with dignity and to avoid an ignominious scuttle. But a scuttle it will be if things are allowed to drift...If you disagree with what is proposed you must offer a practical alternative. I fail to find one in your letters'. So the headmaster was back, rebuking a thoughtless prefect.

A voice from another age was heard when Lord Hailey interviewed the Secretary of State (it seems appropriate to phrase it that way). Hailey 'did not disguise from me that those with whom he was in contact were feeling a loss of support amounting to neglect by the Secretary of State and were gravely troubled about their future prospects' (Pethick-Lawrence to the Prime Minister, 6 January 1947).[2]

On 18 December 1946 Attlee asked Mountbatten to get ready to be the next Viceroy. It does not appear that he informed the Secretary of State or anyone else. On 8 January the Prime Minister informed the Cabinet that Congress had decided to drop Nehru's minimalist interpretation of the Cabinet Mission Plan. Partly because the situation was so confused the Cabinet decided to ask Wavell to pay another visit to London in the near future. It would appear that Attlee and Cripps hoped to use this as a device to get Wavell to go quietly. If this was a trap, Wavell declined to be drawn in. He countered with a proposal that he return in March or April and then take home leave 'since I have had no rest for a long time' (17 January). Both Attlee and Cripps informed Mountbatten that the letter from Wavell was in a 'very "difficult" form'. They were 'considering the next step': the delay was 'very irritating', but they would 'let you know as soon as possible...I am so sorry not to have more definite news for you'. It was all very different from their treatment of Wavell.

The situation in India was in flux while Attlee finalized his plan to oust Wavell. On 4 February the Viceroy received his letter of dismissal: 'Not very courteously done' as he recorded. In his reply, Wavell told the Prime Minister that 'so summary a dismissal of His Majesty's representative in India is hardly in keeping with the dignity of the appointment'. He asked that his departure would not be expected before mid-March 'to avoid the indignity as well as the inconvenience of a scuttle'.

The announcement of his departure was given to Parliament at 3.30 p.m. on 20 February. This was equivalent to 9.00 p.m. in India when the changeover was simultaneously announced. The timing was intended to take place after the marriage of Wavell's daughter, Felicity, that same day. Wavell and his wife must have experienced very mixed emotions during the wedding.

Attlee's statement to parliament was a compound of half truths and untruths. Wavell's viceroyalty was 'a wartime appointment', and it was now time to 'terminate this wartime appointment'. Churchill made the obvious comment that the war had been over for eighteen months: were there 'differences or disappointments' between Viceroy and government? Attlee claimed that this statement would remove uncertainty; he denied that they would hand India over to chaos. A debate was promised for the following week, but this did not take place. It was left to Willie Gallacher, the sole Communist MP, to inquire whether the name of a Labour or Trades Union candidate for Viceroy had been considered. There was no response.

Some members asked if Wavell would make a personal statement in parliament on his return: Curzon, the only previous Viceroy to leave under similar circumstances made a lengthy statement. When he read the account of the debate, Wavell assured Attlee that he would say nothing. The Prime Minister's private secretary observed that this was 'a very fine telegram'. Attlee had to agree.

The reaction of the Governor of Bombay, Sir John Colville was dignified and what the Viceroy would have called 'straight'. 'I am so unhappy and disappointed about the manner of Wavell's retirement and out of sympathy with the step that has just been taken...I admire very greatly his courage, vision and patience....I feel that the Government owe him more than any other public servant....I regret that the statement has been made at this stage when I think that further negotiation was possible'.

Wavell's remaining years were somewhat melancholy. His wife wished to live in London, so they took a flat. Wavell spent much of his time on the affairs of his old regiment, the Black Watch. Also he conducted a one-man campaign on behalf of those British officials who did not belong to the Secretary of State's services. Wavell described 1948 as 'an aimless, pointless, unprofitable year'. He became President of the Royal Society of Literature, but was unable to write very much. His most important writing was a chapter in the last volume of the Cambridge Modern History: *The Era of Violence, 1898-1945*, surveying the development of armies in war. This appeared posthumously (1960) for he died in May 1950. His family declined a grave in Westminster Abbey and he was buried in the cloister of Winchester College where he had been a scholar.

NOTES

1. Penderel Moon, *Divide and Quit*, 1961, p. 54.
2. His *The Times* obituary (3 September 1961) declared that Attlee and Cripps 'had taken matters of high policy in respect to India very much into their own hands'.

CHAPTER 11

MOUNTBATTEN: THE FINAL CHUKKER

An Australian historian of the postwar record in South East Asia Peter Dennis writes: 'Mountbatten was determined that history should record his achievements, that his central role in great events should be recognized. His version of these events did not always accord with the evidence'.[1] Mountbatten took an over-dramatic view of those events and of his own role. One of his favourite expressions was that he was 'absolutely staggered' by someone or something which he would almost invariably describe as a 'bombshell'. He was prone to drop bombshells himself and would be upset if the reaction was other than favourable. Some of these occurred during the re-occupation of Burma when Mountbatten transformed British policy towards Aung San and his anti-fascist movement. Many of the civil affairs officers, who had to deal with the results of his policy, were appalled. Mountbatten called them together at Government House, Rangoon, on 15 January 1945 and administered what he would undoubtedly call a rocket. He alleged that this policy 'Had been repeatedly sabotaged: it is confined to a few people whom I am watching carefully, I should like to make it clear that if one of them slips up and is caught out I will immediately court martial him'. He went on: 'I have detected a strong tendency to...express the prejudices of the intermediary, even when the enclosed report is widely at variance with them. This...has of course only been necessary where the report bore out the wisdom of the policy I had laid down'. Writing to his Chief Civil Affairs Officer, Major General Rance (who had adopted Mountbatten's policies) he added 'You and I at least have the satisfaction, when history comes to be written in a few years' time of being proved absolutely right'. This conviction of rectitude applied retrospectively as well. A leading Civil Affairs Officer wrote to Rance 'The most important point is to destroy the impression that SAC [Supreme Allied Commander] is unwilling to listen to facts other than those which support the correctness of his policy'. Colonel Wallace went on 'There are indications that Aung San and his friends are playing for time and wish to avoid the disbandment of the Patriotic Burmese Forces if they possibly can'. At his next meeting with the Civil Affairs Officers Mountbatten declared 'He wanted the unvarnished truth at all times and had no use for "yes men".' Several of those present took Mountbatten's words at face value and revealed their experiences in the districts. Mountbatten gave soothing answers but did not really take in their comments. He had his own plan to introduce suitable PBF men into the regular army, including Aung San who would receive the rank of Brigadier. This plan was presented to Aung San and his lieutenants at Kandy in September 1945, and produced what was called the 'Kandy Agreement' signed by Aung San and the leader of the underground movement, Than Tun. Negotiations were dragged out and by December 1946 had not been resolved to satisfaction. Some elements of the PBF became part of the Burma Army as separate battalions under their own officers: in effect an army within the army. Those who were not accepted were formed into para-military units, the People's Volunteer Organization. When Burma became independent they were the main force in the country.

These affairs demonstrate the Mountbatten technique, which in the language of today may be described as a 'quick fix'. Sometimes it worked: often it did not, but Mountbatten usually did not stay around to reap the consequences of his fix.

All this was not just the result of his impetuosity and (in the view of some) his lack of candour. Mountbatten was emotionally and intellectually committed to colonial freedom. At this time his politics belonged to the extreme left. Mountbatten was at Cambridge ten years before the spies; and it confounds one to imagine him among their number. But his most intimate, and lasting Cambridge friendship was with Peter Murphy, an impeccably upper class man who joined the Communist Party and who was in the 1950s denounced as a Soviet agent. He implanted the radical views which Mountbatten was to uphold beyond middle age.

Mountbatten's background was peculiar. The Battenburg family were royal, but through morganatic marriage had been excluded from the close-knit circle of those who could marry among the Protestant dynasties of Northern Europe. Queen Victoria was not constrained by these taboos, and did not discourage her youngest daughter from marrying Prince Henry Maurice of Battenburg. Battenburg was irked at being always at the royal court, he went off to the Ashanti war and died on the way home (1896). His youngest son died of wounds in action, October 1914. The elder brother also entered British service in 1868 and rapidly rose to high rank through his own ability. In 1912 he became the First Sea Lord under Churchill at the Admiralty. The anti-German outcry which also saw off Haldane caused his resignation in 1914. It seems evident that the man who sacked so many commanders in World War II felt that he had let down his First Sea Lord.

Lord Louis joined the fleet in 1917. His ships included the *Lion*, Beatty's flagship, where Mountbatten as a midshipman fell foul of the sub-lieutenant in charge of the gunroom who was a sadistic bully. Probably he perceived the son of the discarded First Sea Lord as his special prey. At any rate Mountbatten had to submit to constant beatings which left him with a hatred of this form of punishment all his life. When the war ended Mountbatten was given the opportunity to go to Cambridge, like his distant cousin 'Bertie' the King's second son. At Cambridge he fell under the sway of Peter Murphy, son of a family, comfortably off if not wealthy—an ex-officer of the Irish Guards who had embraced Left Wing views. Murphy found Mountbatten 'progressive' and encouraged his inconoclastic opinions. After Cambridge Mountbatten was invited by the Prince of Wales to join his entourage for an overseas tour which took in Australia and New Zealand. Then the Prince of Wales was told to visit India, and Mountbatten accompanied him. He had met and fallen for Edwina Ashley, an heiress, one of the richest women in England, thanks to her gigantic inheritance from Sir Ernest Cassel, her grandfather. Edwina had decided to visit India and as a matter of course was asked to stay with the 'temporary' Viceroy, Lord Reading. Mountbatten caught up with her at the Viceregal House in Delhi and proposed marriage. He was accepted and six months later they were married in the society wedding of the year. Mountbatten was already better off than most naval officers but now he was a rich man. India had given him expensive pursuits, especially polo, and expensive friends among the Princes. He did not return to the subcontinent for another forty odd years but he did maintain a connection with his princely friends like the Maharajas of Jaipur, Gwalior, and Bharatpur and the Nawab of Bhopal. He was on first name terms with them all, 'Dickie' to them, and they were known to him by the nicknames which almost all the Princes favoured.

Mountbatten steadily advanced in the navy. When war broke out he was in command of a brand new destroyer, *Kelly*, which he had some hand in designing. Unfortunately his impulsive response to any situation was to land *Kelly* into deep trouble. In October 1939, attempting to intercept a German battleship, racing *Kelly* through high seas, he took his ship into a roll which nearly sank her. Months in dry dock were followed by a return to sea when again the ship rapidly got into trouble, hitting another destroyer, the

Gurkha. They had to return to port for repairs again. With this record any officer without Mountbatten's royal connections would have lost his ship. But Mountbatten emerged from all this as a hero. A third blunder followed when with another destroyer *Kelly* went into action against the Germans. Mountbatten adopted a course which led to the loss of another destroyer. This time Mountbatten was heavily criticized but he was saved by the intervention of Churchill who 'staggered me' by suggesting an admiralty appointment. This was vetoed by the First Sea Lord. Back at sea, *Kelly* rammed a merchant ship and had another spell in dock. In April 1941 the ship was sent to the Mediterranean. They were right in the middle of the Crete disaster and Mountbatten's luck ran out: his ship was sunk, but some of the crew, including the captain were picked up.

His rise to the top continued, with promotion to the new post of head of Combined Operations. They had a number of small-scale triumphs and one large-scale disaster—the Dieppe raid.[2] For political reasons the assault force was mainly Canadian (they had been in England for two years and had seen no action while Australian and New Zealand troops were in the thick of the fighting in the Middle East). The raid took place on 19 August 1942. Resistance was fierce. Many never even got ashore and sixty-eight per cent of the Canadians were killed or wounded. Canada did not forgive Mountbatten: this included Beaverbrook and his *Daily Express*.

However, Churchill continued to favour him, and when a top level conference was convened at Quebec, Mountbatten was included in the party. A principal item was the appointment of a Commander for the new South East Asia Command. It was agreed that this should go to an Englishman, but he must be one acceptable to the Americans, who vetoed the first names suggested. However they had formed a very favourable impression of Mountbatten. When Churchill put the proposition to him Mountbatten told Ismay 'I feel as though I had been poleaxed'. To his daughter he wrote 'I still feel stunned'. The choice of the head of Combined Operations was logical: it was expected that the liberation of South East Asia would largely be a naval operation with an important air element.

They wanted to get away from the jungle fighting which had been so disastrous in 1942. The idea was to make SEAC a genuinely inter-allied command, with full British and American cooperation. It was therefore disastrous that Mountbatten's deputy was Lieutenant General Stilwell, nearly twenty years older than Mountbatten and fanatically anti-British. Mountbatten first set up his headquarters in Delhi, but his team rapidly outgrew their accommodation and he moved to Ceylon in April 1944, installing his 7,000 strong HQ in the botanical gardens at Peradenyia while his own quarters were in 'King's Pavilion' in nearby Kandy. The move was partly because of the expectation that the forthcoming operation would involve large-scale combined operations: but the landing craft required were retained in the Pacific and the Mediterranean. Mountbatten told the King 'This job is a pathetic farce and I wish they had let me go back to my aircraft carrier'. SEAC were out on a limb. Land operations were directed from Barrackpore by Sir Oliver Leese as Commander in Chief Allied Land Forces South East Asia, though actual operational responsibility rested with General Slim and the Fourteenth Army. The top layer of this military sandwich had little to do, and staff officers spent most of their time sending messages to each other. One of Mountbatten's senior staff officers, Major General H. E. Pyman observed 'It would be wrong to say that the machinery of command in Kandy is really efficient'; his chief political adviser, M. E. Dening wrote at the end of the war that SEAC HQ 'has now attained a standard of inefficiency which makes it a byword'.

Against all this must be set Mountbatten's insistence on seeing everything for himself and talking to as many men in his command as he could reach. Mountbatten, like Monty, realized that the British fighting men of 1939-45 were very different from their fathers of 1914-18. They were not prepared to die for king and country without knowing the reason. Mountbatten was at his best in man-to-man encounters with the other ranks. He was actively disliked by many senior officers, who viewed his technique as threatening discipline. His film-star charm formed an interesting contrast to Bill Slim's gruff, monosyllabic style, which was equally effective: both men were free of upper class mannerisms.

The liberation of Burma owed much more to Slim than to Mountbatten, though his intervention was vital in certain respects: as in retaining the services of American aircraft when they were under orders for other tasks. With the sudden Japanese collapse in August 1945, Mountbatten's responsibilities were expanded. MacArthur saddled him with the additional responsibility of French Indo China and the Netherlands East Indies. Just before the war in Burma ended, Leese arrived in Kandy with a proposal to relieve Slim from command of the Fourteenth Army, now preparing for the assault on Malaya, and his transfer to the Twelfth Army which had taken over the responsibility for mopping up in Burma. Mountbatten recorded in his personal diary 'Very important and not too easy interview with Oliver Leese'. Both emerged believing that they had carried their point. However, when Slim was told he declined the alternative appointment and informed the Chief of Staff accordingly. Brooke backed him up, and the situation had to be unscrambled: Slim took over at Allied Land Forces South East Asia. It was typical of Slim that he bore Mountbatten no rancour and typical of Mountbatten that with his quick fix dismantled he re-arranged the incident in his mental record of events. The unfortunate Leese 'carried the can': he went back to England.

Mountbatten returned briefly to Europe for the Potsdam conference. Churchill greeted him warmly: 'I have got plans in store'. Meanwhile, Mountbatten had to carry out post surrender tasks in South East Asia which proved as rigorous as any before. Mountbatten's instructions were to recover allied Prisoners of War and to disarm the Japanese. In Java this proved an appalling task. The departing Japanese had given arms to the Nationalists who were effectively the power in the land. When British-Indian troops landed they were opposed. Thirty battalions were sent in, of which only four were British the remainder Indian. Mountbatten was piggy in the middle. He was strongly opposed to Dutch efforts to re-impose their empire, but instructions from London were to support our allies and depose their enemies the Nationalists (regarded as Japanese collaborators). Wavell was negotiating with the Indian political leaders: he was fully aware of the political dangers of employing Indian troops. When the Secretary of State for War visited South East Asia he said that Britain had no intention of intervening. Attlee reprimanded him: 'Statements on policy should not be made by ministers travelling abroad' which evaded the question of whether Britain had a policy for the Netherlands East Indies. Without getting into this controversy, Mountbatten urged the Dutch to negotiate with the Indonesian leaders. He offered the Foreign Office two alternative cases: negotiation (Plan X) or punitive action 'Against known or suspected terrorists' (Plan Y). Bevin chose Plan Y, though Mountbatten was determined not to prop up Western colonialism whether in British, French or Dutch territories. He was much influenced by his old friend Peter Murphy, who joined SEAC in an undefined capacity and also by a new chum, Tom Driberg, the Left Wing Labour MP. It was against this background that Nehru paid a flying visit to Malaya in March 1946. The military authorities intended to cold-shoulder him but Mountbatten decided otherwise. On arrival he was driven directly to the Singapore YMCA where Mountbatten and Lady Edwina were present to greet him. He responded to their warm welcome and agreed not to carry out engagements which might raise the political temperature: he at once cancelled a visit to lay a wreath on the site of the

Indian National Army memorial (now demolished). He responded warmly to the Mountbatten charm.

Soon after Singapore and Malaya were returned to civil government (1 April). The Mountbattens had already left for a visit to Australia and New Zealand. This was a great popular success and Mountbatten was invited to become the next Governor General of Australia by the Prime Minister, Chiffley: but he was not interested in a purely ceremonial appointment. Mountbatten did not return to South East Asia; he was invited to attend the Victory celebrations in London. On the way he visited Nepal and was fêted by the Court. From Nepal he returned to Delhi, though he could have proceeded directly to Karachi. A dust storm had closed down Willingdon airport but Mountbatten insisted on landing. He intended to have talks with the Cabinet Mission, although this was not entered in the official record. Back in London he was the Man of the Hour. The Governor of Burma, Dorman-Smith had clashed with Aung San and the Anti-Fascist People's Freedom League. Dorman-Smith was recalled to London, where Attlee consulted Mountbatten about finding a replacement. Mountbatten had no hesitation in recommending his former Chief Civil Affairs Officer, Major-General Rance. Attlee hesitated, Rance was unknown, however eventually he accepted Mountbatten's advice. When Dorman-Smith paid a farewell visit to the India Office he was met by the Parliamentary Under Secretary, Arthur Henderson. Dorman-Smith wrote of the experience in a letter to a friend: 'Mountbatten's name came up. Henderson in a jocular way said that it was sometimes difficult to know whether Mountbatten was living at the other end of St James' Park or in King Charles Street [the site of the India Office]....The hand of Dickie is very evident. It stands out a hundred miles that the Viscount of Burma [as Mountbatten became in the Victory honours list] takes his responsibilities towards Burma very seriously. It also would seem that the Lord Louis has the P.M.'s ear...It is more than most unlikely that Attlee would have even thought of Rance off his own bat...Dickie must have had a very real say-so in all this... and what does all that mean?...is it because Dickie is going to get some monumental appointment in the East and wants to have his own men around him? I just do not know, but I confess that the whole thing smells a bit'[3] (8 August 1946). Dorman-Smith was an erratic governor but he knew the world. As the new governor of Burma, Rance addressed a personal telegram to Pethick-Lawrence on 17 September indicating that Burma 'felt aggrieved' because they had not received a Cabinet Mission such as the Mission to India. 'A suggestion has been made to me that Mountbatten with his great prestige in this country might be sent out.' Pethick-Lawrence was impressed and addressed a paper to the India-Burma Committee supporting the plan: 'If we do send anybody it must be someone who will strike the imagination, and Lord Mountbatten might do this'. The Committee considered the proposal but argued that on the model of the Cabinet Mission they should send a Cabinet Minister. In the end they sent nobody. Nothing happened for several months. Mountbatten was engaged in preparing a 'Report to the Combined Chiefs of Staff by the Supreme Allied Commander, 1943-5' for which he assembled a research team and acquired a London headquarters—7 Richmond Terrace, Whitehall, right at the heart of decision making. However, this could not absorb the restless energy of the man. He spent the second half of 1946 manoeuvring, lobbying, projecting his personality on a London only too happy to accept him at his own evaluation. He cultivated the King in his own special way, giving His Majesty pen portraits of all those who had been his associates—Auchinleck, the Admirals, Dorman-Smith and the rest. Ostensibly, he could not wait to return to the navy—but the navy would be there whenever he returned, and he realized that India was about to blow up for a showdown. Attlee's invitation to Mountbatten to succeed Wavell came while the latter was in London, trying to persuade the Cabinet to adopt his scheme. On 18 December Mountbatten's diary records 'PM sent for me and staggered me'. Mountbatten's reply was somewhat unrealistic. He asked that he could 'go out at the open invitation of the Indian parties in a capacity which they would themselves define' (20 December). If Wavell had put up such an unrealistic proposal the Prime Minister would have been scornful, but Mountbatten was different. He now went off for a skiing holiday in Switzerland. He was recalled after a few days. On his return Mountbatten skilfully avoided a suggestion by Attlee that he should take Cripps with him to India (another version of the Prime Minister's belief that a Viceroy who was not a politician should have a political adviser). Mountbatten tactfully suggested that if Cripps accompanied him he would appear 'A mere figurehead' (3 January). He negotiated the attachment of General Ismay to accompany him as Chief of Staff. He also obtained the promise that he would remain on the Active Flag List and 'on loan' only 'for this short period'. He also received the promise of a personal aircraft—a York.

Most important, it must have seemed, was the directive he received on 8 February defining government policy: 'It is the definite objective of His Majesty's Government to obtain if possible a unitary government for all India through the medium of the Constituent Assembly....The date fixed for the transfer of power is a flexible one but you should aim at completing the process by 30 June 1948. If it appears certain at final [sic] that the Muslim League will not cooperate in the Constituent Assembly you should then at once advise HMG as to the best course for them to adopt in handing over power on the due date'. Mountbatten continued to address peremptory messages to Attlee. On 11 February he listed some of the more important members of staff he wanted to take. Cripps had urged that Abell should cease to be the Viceroy's Private Secretary: Mountbatten had the sense to ask for him to stay en poste 'at any rate for the present'. Among his junior new faces were a bevy of WRNS to act as typists, telegraphists, etc. Mountbatten was not happy with the existing security at the Viceroy's House. On 18 February Mountbatten wrote to Wavell: one of his 'charming' letters: 'I was most surprised when I was sent for by the Prime Minister and told that your period of office had expired and absolutely staggered when he told me that the Cabinet wanted me to succeed you'. He ended with 'most sincere congratulations on your Earldom'. He also said that he had badgered the War Office into uncovering the recommendation of a gallantry award to Wavell's son. In this case he had acted on behalf of the son of a distinguished man, but he behaved in this way for dozens of his subordinates who were of no importance. Certainly, the award of a Military Cross to Archie John meant a great deal to Wavell. When Mountbatten is judged, this readiness to put himself out for men who could not possibly advance his cause should be remembered.

There was an attempt to get Wavell to meet Mountbatten in Karachi, which he rejected. On the eve of his departure Mountbatten had a meeting with Krishna Menon on 13 March. He attempted to sweet-talk Mountbatten into accepting a 'constitutional' role before the Transfer of Power. No record was kept of their discussion: very unusual with regard to Mountbatten's meetings.

On his arrival in Delhi on 22 March he met with Wavell, Ismay, Mieville and Abell. Mountbatten indicated that the British Government expected 'a clear plan for transferring power by the 1 October 1947'. Thereafter Mountbatten called a staff meeting almost every day, on the lines of what are inelegantly termed 'bull sessions' with Mountbatten holding forth at great length. At an early stage (on 28 March) Mountbatten told his staff that he would like to hold a 'Country House Party' at Simla to bring all the leaders round the table. He also launched a series of meetings with the Indian leaders, beginning with Gandhi. It appeared that the Mahatma still pinned his faith to making Jinnah Prime Minister, and allowing him to form his own government. Mountbatten regarded this as quite impractical, and it emerged that the Congress High Command were unwilling to go along with Gandhi, so on 12 April he withdrew his plan and left Delhi. Mountbatten spent a lot of time with Nehru, the one Indian leader he found really compatible. Not until eleven days after his first meeting with Nehru did Mountbatten invite Jinnah to see him, having instructed his staff to draw up a 'List of Awkward Questions'. 'This was the man who held the key to the whole situation', Mountbatten noted. Jinnah's response was to demand 'a surgical operation' to which Mountbatten made the somewhat lame retort that first an anaesthetic must be administered. Realizing that he must try harder, Mountbatten saw Jinnah on successive days: 5,7,8,9,10 April. 'On each occasion [he] would call upon me to hand over power as soon as possible, province by province and let the provinces themselves choose how they would form themselves into groups.' 'On 10 April I warned Mr Jinnah categorically that if I finally decided to recommend to HMG that there should be a partition of India then that principle would be applied right through to the provinces, and the partition would follow the boundaries of the communal majorities'.

A little while earlier Jinnah would have refused to consider such a suggestion but he was becoming desperate and he replied 'I do not care how little you give me so long as you give it to me completely. I do not wish to make any improper suggestion to you, but you must realize that the new Pakistan is almost certain to ask for Dominion Status with the British Empire.' Jinnah was advised to talk to the UK High Commissioner 'Since I could not possibly recommend to His Majesty's Government that they take on as a member of the Commonwealth so severe a liability as Pakistan was likely to be'. In reporting on his meetings, Mountbatten declared 'I regard Jinnah as a psychopathic case': he told Campbell-Johnson that Jinnah had been 'apparently much shaken' when he 'failed to react in any way to his offer...to bring Pakistan into the Commonwealth'. Others might have questioned who was most shaken by this occurrence. When Mountbatten reported the incident at one of his staff meetings (22 April), Ismay suggested 'If forced into a position whereby only one part of India wanted to remain in the Commonwealth he felt that HMG might accept such an application'. At these meetings, Mountbatten's own familiars (Campbell-Johnson, Erskine-Crum and Brockman) usually accepted his line but Ismay felt free to differ, having stood up to Churchill in his time. Among Mountbatten's brainwaves was to take up the proposition that Dominion Status might be promoted as an interim arrangement to attract Congress in the hope that this might become permanent. Ismay had to remind him that Dominion Status was granted when the stage of independence was reached and not before.

Apart from Jinnah, Mountbatten's toughest encounters were with Sardar Patel who was grimly taking on the realities of power, placing his own men in the key positions. One such was a meeting on 24 April when Mountbatten questioned the manner in which a British Officer had been pushed aside in favour of R. N. Banerjee from another department. When this was queried Patel noted that a reference to the Selection Board would be 'pointless' after Mountbatten had suggested this course. Mountbatten ordered him to withdraw his Minute; Patel 'categorically refused. I then told him that in that case I would see Nehru and inform him that I was flying home to resign my appointment unless Patel left the Interim Government'. Patel allegedly queried whether Mountbatten would go that far; Mountbatten retorted 'I could be tougher than him': 'Patel suddenly realized that I meant business and completely collapsed and gave in'. Or so Mountbatten recorded. All this made no difference to the appointment of Banerjee, and at this same meeting Patel told Mountbatten: 'Since you have come out here things have got worse. There is a civil war on and you are doing nothing to stop it. You won't govern yourself and you won't let the Congress Government govern....Let us govern.' Somehow this passage reads much more convincingly than Mountbatten's account of Patel's collapse, though both are supposed to have happened together.

Before this incident occurred Mountbatten addressed his weekly Private letter to a new Secretary of State. Pethick-Lawrence at last departed, on 23 April. He was worn out, and tired of seeing Attlee assume his responsibilities: however the 'irresolution and disinclination to reach clear cut decisions' which his record had revealed (as *The Times* obituary was later to observe) were now very marked. He died in 1951. The new Secretary of State, was the 5th Earl of Listowel, six years younger than Mountbatten. His only previous positions were as Under Secretary for India in the Coalition government, 1944-5, and Postmaster General in the Labour Government. Clearly he would not pose any problems to the Viceroy.

A visit by Mountbatten and Lady Mountbatten to Peshawar (28 and 29 April) revealed the Viceroy at his best. Nehru had visited the Frontier with Abdul Gaffar Khan as his cicerone. The Governor had warned him to expect trouble, but he brushed aside this advice and was abused and slightly injured. He attributed his reception to the hidden hand of the Governor and his officials. The Mountbattens faced what was potentially worse trouble, but they faced it out, scrambling to the top of a railway embankment and responding to the hostile mob by waving cheerfully. For the moment, the North West Frontier Province remained as quiescent as ever it could be, but Punjab was erupting into something like civil war. Even the Congress leaders had to recognize that this must lead to breakdown and hints began to be offered that partition would not be opposed. Indeed, at a meeting on 25 April Patel discounted what he said was the British Government's idea that 'Jinnah could still be induced to accept the Cabinet Mission's plan' and went on 'If the Muslim League did not accept the Cabinet Mission's plan Congress desired partition;

Congress had reached the maximum limit of their concessions'. But what did the various parties intend? The same day Mountbatten appears to have rejected the idea that a British Governor-General might remain 'as a high level umpire with a small team of advisers': this would be 'fraught with frightful difficulties', Ismay observed, 'the greatest care should be exercised over this question'.

All this was a prelude to Mieville visiting the homes of the Indian leaders to show them drafts of the proposed plan for partition on 30 April. Jinnah seemed the most disturbed: 'He did not react favourably'. He suggested that if people found themselves placed under authorities not of their own faith 'they could move to their homelands if they wished to do so'. He said this in the same breath that he condemned the Viceroy's plan which would lead 'to confusion...and bloodshed'. Mieville reported that Nehru 'only made two comparatively small points'. He opposed fresh elections in the North West Frontier Province in view of 'the iniquitous behaviour of the officials in the province from the Governor downwards', and he objected to the procedure in Baluchistan where the choice would be made by 'a few feudal landlords'. Mieville deduced that the Viceroy's scheme would be accepted, though Jinnah would be recalcitrant.

According to Mountbatten the two leaders read the proposal and accepted, though neither liked the procedure laid down. But how carefully were they able to examine the scheme? Clearly they had not been given copies for their own use, as this plan still awaited the endorsement of the Cabinet in London. But were they given the opportunity to think over the implications of the plan? Jinnah as a practising lawyer might have mastered the details in the course of a limited examination: but what of the dreamer Nehru? On 8 May Mountbatten warned Ismay 'There is always the chance that Jinnah may spring a surprise by rejecting the plan at the last moment.' Ismay left for London on 2 May to take the draft plan for Cabinet perusal. Mountbatten was becoming less assured about the reception his plan would receive, and he revived the Simla House Party idea in a very different form. He invited Nehru and his confidant, Krishna Menon to stay at Viceregal Lodge and placed a copy of the plan in his hands. This nearly caused a disaster. Twice already Nehru had been persuaded to the brink of accepting a constitutional plan (the Cripps Plan in 1942, and the Cabinet Mission Plan in 1946) and on both occasions he drew back at the last moment. It was the same at Simla. He could accept a proposal on a rational plane yet refused to accept on the emotional plane. In 1942 Nehru's moment of truth was expressed in these terms: 'The whole picture that emerged from our talks took me aback and I suddenly discovered that the very premises on which we had been discussing this subject...were unjustified. The whole structure that we had tried to build up so laboriously in our minds was without any real foundation' (9 April 1942). Now at Simla he reacted similarly: 'The picture presented by the proposals produced a devastating effect on me. The whole approach to them appeared to me to be dangerous....They would encourage disruptive tendencies everywhere and chaos and weakness....Hitherto all British proposals and indeed all discussions have been basically on a united India, the inroads into such unity being confined...to giving the freedom to certain areas...to create themselves into separate states' (Simla, 11 May).

How far was this a real crisis or a storm in a tea cup? Elsewhere the latter interpretation has been offered.[4] The Cabinet were bewildered by the reports from Simla. Mountbatten cabled Ismay that the London plan had been a 'Bombshell' to Nehru (11 May). He asked for time to re-draft the proposals. Ismay retorted that Mountbatten's message had been a 'bombshell' as the Cabinet 'have made no changes of substance' to the plan he had brought home (12 May). Attlee was upset by the bewildering news from India: 'All we have done is to try to clarify the presentation of the case'. Nehru had reportedly said that HMG 'seem to function in an ivory tower of their own isolated from realities'.

Mountbatten cabled to Ismay again, almost at midnight telling him that the plan must be drastically recast: 'I can only hope, though after today I can be sure of nothing...' If not, then Mountbatten proposed to 'threaten' Congress by proposing demission of power to the provinces: the solution which Nehru feared most.

After further Cabinet conclaves Ismay cabled Mountbatten to report that they had decided that 'A Minister or ministers should proceed to India to discuss situation at first hand with you or alternatively that you should be asked to fly home' (14 May). Mountbatten was determined that there should not be a third Cripps mission and at once agreed to fly home. He made the journey to London as soon as the York had returned to Delhi and was ready to meet the India-Burma Committee on the noon of 19 May, with Ismay and Erskine Crum in attendance. Mountbatten introduced amendments, mainly designed to conciliate Nehru and mainly cosmetic. The important new element in the situation was the willingness of the Congress leaders 'To accept Dominion Status provided they could say that by this means the actual transfer of power would be secured substantially earlier than June 1948'. This would involve the division of the Indian Army. Attlee said that if legislation had to be rushed through it would be necessary to obtain the cooperation of the Opposition leaders 'with whom the matter should be discussed immediately'. When the meeting ended, Mountbatten went round the table in the Cabinet room and gathered up all the surplus copies of the plan so that there would be no temptation to insert alterations.

While all this was going on there was a move in Bengal, agreed between Suhrawardy and Sarat Chandra Bose to ask for a 'Free State of Bengal'. Burrows was very much in favour, insisting that the Eastern segment of a divided Bengal would be 'a rural slum'. Although not included in the Mountbatten plan, this possibility was accepted by the Viceroy and Cabinet as a viable option. The editor of *Dawn* commented: 'This plan has two authors—one has no past, Shaheed Suhrawardy, the other has no future, Sarat Chandra Bose. Their commodity therefore has no market.' So it proved: though it was paradoxical that the arrangement so bitterly opposed by Bengalis in 1905 should in 1947 receive their fervent support. Suhrawardy and Bose were given less than two weeks to obtain 'prior agreement' on their plan so that its failure was almost assured given Bengali prolixity.

There were further meetings between Mountbatten and the India-Burma Committee on 20 May. He indicated that any transfer under the Dominion Status formula must be completed 'not later than the early autumn of 1947'. The Lord Chancellor was consulted and advised that 'As soon as Dominion Status was granted to British India paramountcy would come to an end. The States would then become fully independent and would be free to negotiate new agreements if they thought it desirable to do so': a definition of States' Rights which was never fulfilled.

A further meeting of the India-Burma Committee was held on 22 May. This was mainly a 'Tidying up' session. The fourth item was on the future of the India Office, and other such matters. It was agreed that the Office would be shut down when Dominion Status came into effect. A knotty question was that affecting Britain and the Princes. The suggestion made by Mountbatten did not really address the problem at all. The Cabinet was equally baffled. The best they could do was to suggest 'that the Princes might retain the right of access to the King for a period, of say ten years, and that the position thereafter should be left as vague as possible'. Policy with regard to British India was clear in essentials, if not in detail. The position of the Princes was left in limbo. It might be said that they deserved no more: but this was not a situation in which the British could take any pride. For his part, Nehru expressed his unease: 'We consider these activities of the Political Department objectionable, harmful and discourteous to the Government of India....The Political Department has long been considered as being opposed to Indian progress and unity' (26 May).

Mountbatten was still in London on 29 May when the India-Burma Committee held an inquest on their deliberations. There was not much to decide. The Andaman islands came up as a probable point of contention. The Chiefs of Staff were anxious to get their hands on these islands as a valuable staging post in future Commonwealth strategy. Alexander stressed their importance, and even Cripps acknowledged that Congress 'might be prepared to take into account the disposal of these islands' if in return the question of the sterling balances could be favourably settled. The future of Bengal as a separate Dominion was by now not an issue.

On his return Mountbatten quickly secured the agreement of Nehru and Jinnah to his plan for partition. This was a great achievement, but thereafter Mountbatten's freedom of action and decision seemed quite restricted. The aloof role of the Viceroy was no longer possible. He was under pressure, especially from Patel, who set himself to place men he trusted—Indians—in key positions; wherever he could induce the Viceroy to make a change. The first to be ousted was Sir Olaf Caroe, Governor of the North West Frontier Province. He was required to go on leave and replaced by Sir Rob Lockhart, Commander of the North Western Army. Another key official was William Christie, Chief Commissioner of Delhi, whose substitute was an Indian. Similarly, C. F. V. Williams, Joint Secretary in the Home Department (under Patel's personal control) gave way to R. N. Banerjee from another department; a more compliant person. Mountbatten made no attempt to oppose these changes. However, the agitation to get rid of Jenkins, Governor of Punjab was unsuccessful. Almost immediately after the political leaders had acceded to Mountbatten's plan they were confronted by a paper on the administrative consequences of partition. This seems to have caused perturbation, most evident in Nehru. Jinnah disputed

Mountbatten's approach which was to give the Interim Government the responsibility for all the consequential changes. Jinnah insisted that the British Government was responsible, and under them the Governor-General. Mountbatten replied that he would 'consult the leaders': Jinnah answered that he could 'consult anybody that he liked, but it would be the Governor-General and not the Governor-General in Council who would issue the orders'. Patel retorted that London had promised that the Interim Government 'would function as a Dominion Government. If this authority was then challenged and its members insulted they were led to thoughts of resignation'. In these exchanges Nehru invariably flew into a passion and even Patel showed his anger: Jinnah achieved a certain superiority by keeping very cool. He teased the Congress leaders and sometimes Mountbatten, by his resistance to such innovations as calling the Viceroy's Council the 'Cabinet'. Thus on 3 June there was a discussion about Mountbatten's references to 'the Cabinet': 'It was then explained to Mr Jinnah that the Viceroy was referring to the Indian Cabinet or the Interim Government. Mr Jinnah complained that he had been misled. "You mean the Viceroy's Executive Council" A spade should be called a spade.'

While these arid exchanges were taking place at the Viceroy's House, Northern India was getting to boiling point. Punjab, largely free of the troubles in 1942 was the focus of the violence. The Governor, Sir Evan Jenkins, had to try to control the situation with an administration and police force which was divided on communal lines. The future of the Princely States became more and not less secure. Again, Mountbatten was responding to the pressures from Congress who made the statement on 15 June that 'The relationship between the Government of India and the States would not be exhausted by the lapse of paramountcy. The lapse does not lead to the independence of the States'. This was queried at the India Office where the niceties still counted for a lot. Nehru had taken the Congress view;

Jinnah had challenged him. Sir Paul Patrick observed 'we must avoid as long as possible taking a hand in the controversy [but] it will presumably be necessary to say before long that with the lapse of paramountcy the ties and engagements made under paramountcy lapse and the States become free agents'. Some at the India Office were recognizing that legal forms no longer counted but most still behaved as though they were still in the old days.

Meanwhile, Mountbatten was in his own ivory tower. He had conceived the notion that he might remain Viceroy of the whole subcontinent by persuading the leaders of the new India and the new Pakistan to nominate him as their joint Governor-General. Nehru was drawn to the plan, knowing that Mountbatten would always favour the new India. Jinnah remained discouragingly distant. But he had proved hard to woo before: and then acquiesced at the last moment. However, the legislatures of Bengal and Punjab, divided on communal lines, produced a majority for partition. What was Mountbatten to make of all this? His wife was advising him to hand over on the transfer of power; and so were his own buddies, the staff he had assembled. But Mountbatten, his wish to return to the Navy forgotten, wanting to demonstrate the success of his determination to preserve some kind of unity between Hindus and Muslims, clung to the concept of the joint viceroyalty, and persuaded London that this was going to be. Nehru with his dream of some kind of unity continuing encouraged Mountbatten, but it was all a fantasy.

On 4 June Mountbatten held a press conference attended by some 300 newspaper representatives. Devdas Gandhi was among his most persistent questioners. Someone asked when the transfer of power would take place. Mountbatten gave the off-the-cuff reply: '15 August', and this became part of the plan though not previously discussed: at this stage October 1947 was regarded as the target date. When asked later why he had chosen 15 August he replied that this was the anniversary of his appointment as Supreme Allied

Commander South East Asia. This was typical of Mountbatten's methods: he had actually been appointed on the 25 August 1943: but what did a few days matter? Asked if he expected a mass transfer of population in Punjab, Mountbatten replied that some movement would come about 'in a natural way, that is to say people would just cross the boundary, or the Government may take steps to transfer populations'. Later, the spokesmen of India and Pakistan solemnly assured that 'in no circumstances will violence be tolerated in either territory' (22 July). Penderel Moon speaks of the 'amazing and pathetic credulity with which these assurances were received'.[5]

The reality was expressed by Jenkins in a letter dated the 16 June to Mountbatten enclosing an account of a speech by Nehru on the Punjab in which he stated that 'the trouble was prevalent the most where there were British Officers in charge and divisions under the control of either Hindu or Muslim officers were comparatively quiet....The British are no longer interested because they were leaving....Some officers asked the victims who came to them for help to go to him (Nehru) or Sardar Patel for help'. Jinnah asked Mountbatten 'I should be glad to know how far his views are endorsed by His Majesty's Government and Your Excellency'. Mountbatten replied as soothingly as he could 'Nehru's goodwill is essential to me in this critical transfer period. He is appallingly overworked, is liable to lose his temper and generally shows many signs of extreme strain....I cannot hope to achieve very much'. Mountbatten called the allegations 'completely absurd' and not to be believed. He ended with the lame request to 'keep up the morale of the British members of the Service'. He did not press the matter with Nehru as he felt the need 'to avoid anything which tends to a break with the principal Indian leaders' (27 June). Writing to Listowel the same day he recorded 'The meeting of the Cabinet on 25 June was a very difficult one. I was violently attacked by leaders...for the complete failure of the "British" to maintain law and order under Section 93.

Nehru, as usual, completely lost control of himself and demanded the sacking of every official from the Governor downwards that same day. I had to reprimand him publicly for this irresponsible suggestion....Patel then ranted against the British....He said it was a case of the British covering up for the British. I told him I could not take such a slur'. However the Congress leaders now only accepted such instructions as suited them. When Liaquat asked that one of the six Government of India presses in Delhi be transferred to Karachi, Mountbatten appealed to Patel to accede. He retorted 'No one asked Pakistan to secede....We have no intention of allowing them to injure the work of the Government of the rest of India'. However, Mountbatten regarded Patel as much less extreme than Nehru. He was relieved to find that Nehru (Minister for Commonwealth Affairs and Foreign Minister) would not take the new States Department: this 'Would have wrecked everything. Patel who is essentially a realist and very sensible is going to take over.'

Despite all these frustrations, Mountbatten seemed determined to stay on as Governor-General after partition, becoming joint Governor-General of the new India and Pakistan. When this was put to Jinnah he replied that he would accept Mountbatten as an arbitrator, a sort of Supreme Governor-General, but that Pakistan must have its own Governor-General. Mountbatten urged the Secretary of State to amend the forthcoming Bill to allow 'one person to hold both appointments'. He devoted an inordinate amount of time to this question, and persuaded his staff to go along with his plan, which he insisted was acceptable to Nehru and the Congress. There were few indications that the Congress leaders wanted to maintain connections with the new Pakistan. When Jinnah asked that the first meeting of the Pakistan Constituent Assembly should be given the Council House in Delhi, Nehru, Patel, Rajendra Prasad and Gandhi 'All four absolutely blew up and said that in no circumstances would they agree'. All this boded no good for the Joint Governor-General. At first Lady Mountbatten opposed the plan and as late as 5 July she suggested that all the arguments were 'contradictory in themselves....An almost impossible situation', though she acknowledged that Mountbatten had 'let them understand that you would remain here to give your support after 15 August'. In the end Mountbatten had to accept that Jinnah would be Governor-General of Pakistan. He agreed to stay as Governor-General of the new India until 31 March 1948. When he informed Attlee of this situation he caused him to reply 'This news is indeed a surprise'. He concluded 'Whatever the outcome no one could have done more or better than you' (7 July). If Wavell had got into such an impasse he would have been sharply rebuked! But Mountbatten could do no wrong.

Mountbatten told Attlee 'I am most grateful for all the thought that the King, yourself, and the Cabinet have given to this question. In view of your personal appeal...I feel in these special circumstances that I cannot but agree to have my name submitted to His Majesty for appointment as Governor-General of the new Dominion of India during the transition period although I must confess I still have some misgivings' (9 July).

Mountbatten's response to this muddle of his own creating was most candidly expressed in a letter to his elder daughter: 'Mummy feels I should preserve my reputation for impartiality and go on 15 August....I'm in the wrong. In fact at last I've made a mess of things through over-confidence and over-tiredness....I'm so depressed darling because until this stupid mishandling of the Jinnah situation I'd done so well. It has certainly taken me down many pegs' (5 July).

Mountbatten's natural resilience soon put that right. He would become the titular head of the new India; still Governor-General though no longer Viceroy. Viceroy's House in Delhi now became Government House, like dozens of others thoughout the Empire. Mountbatten continued to fill most of the twenty-four hours with tasks, some important, some trivial. On 30 July he signed his Report as Supreme Allied Commander South East Asia. The sections on Burma were published in 1951, but those relating to Indo-China and Indonesia did not appear until 1969 in deference to French and Dutch susceptibility.

He devised new flags for the navies of India and Pakistan to replace the White Ensign. He kept a watchful eye on the proceedings of the boundary commission set up under the eminent British Counsel, Sir Cyril Radcliffe to decide in detail how the frontier between the two new states should be drawn, in Punjab and Bengal. Above all he endeavoured to persuade the Princely States to accede either to India or Pakistan, depending on which was adjacent to them. Many states with Muslim rulers were in the orbit of the new India and Muslim Kashmir, with its Hindu ruler, was next to the new Pakistan. It was not easy. The states were required to accede to India in respect of three subjects: defence, external affairs and communications. That did not sound too much to concede, and all the 500 odd states signed up except for Kashmir, Hyderabad and a statelet, Junagadh with a Muslim ruler and overwhelming Hindu population. Junagadh was quickly pressured into acceptance by means of a plebiscite. Travancore, another state with aspirations for independence hastily came to order after the Dewan Sir C. P. Ramaswami Aiyar, a statesman who had been a member of the Viceroy's Council was subjected to an assassination attempt, but even more vital was the question of defining the boundaries between the new India and Pakistan. All those concerned made their decisions on the expected lines. The Independence Act had laid down provisional boundaries, but Radcliffe's tribunal had to devise the actual lines on the map, and on the ground. The Act had allowed for the decision to be finalized either before or after independence. Meanwhile, District Officers were appointed to the frontier districts on a provisional basis. It was soon evident that the eminent Indian judges appointed to represent India and

Pakistan were totally at odds and the decision had to be made by Radcliffe alone. Mountbatten made much of his detachment from Radcliffe's decision making. However, Radcliffe was lodged in a house on the Viceregal estate and some communication was inevitable. There is evidence that a map showing the proposed boundary line was put up in Ismay's Office. There had certainly been discussion between Radcliffe and Burrows over an aspect of the Bengal award: the allocation of the Chittagong Hill Tracts to Pakistan. The population of these tracts was mainly tribal—neither Hindu nor Muslim. Their lines of communication all ran down to Chittagong and the decision was for inclusion in the new East Pakistan. Altogether the boundaries of the East wing were peculiar with the Muslim majority district of Murshidabad allocated to India and Khulna with a bare Hindu majority to Pakistan.

However, East Pakistan did not figure prominently in the calculations, whereas Punjab already troubled by bitter conflict seemed about to go up in flames. The Governor, Sir Evan Jenkins, did his best to be even-handed: he made it clear he would be departing on 15 August, anyway. He needed information on the future of the central area of the Province, where the Sikhs had their homeland: though they were the majority community only in one tahsil in central Punjab, Tarn Taran. Jenkins was quite clear that the logical solution was to hive off the Hindi-speaking districts (which later became Haryana) and to promote a Punjab in which the Sikhs would be a minority, but a homogeneous minority, able to look after their interests. As this was no longer a solution which was practical politics, there had to be bargaining based upon physical force. None of this had impinged on the Mountbatten plan which assumed that a line could be drawn which all the communities would accept. Radcliffe had to make some sense of this puzzle, and perhaps did not get it right. He was asked to give Jenkins some details before the plan was finalized and transmitted to Lahore by scrambler telephone on 10 or 11 August. In the centre of the Pakistan position there was a bulge of Pakistan territory into Indian Ferozepore, consisting of two tehsils. On 10 or 11 August Jenkins received a message from the Viceroy's office 'eliminate salient'. The award as finally given drew back the border to the river Ravi (the previous draft would have left Sections of the border along the Sutlej). This was to lead to the allegation that Mountbatten had used his influence to get Radcliffe to change his award. The subject was explored when representatives of India and Pakistan met with Mountbatten in the chair on 16 August and ventured their wrath against the award. Mountbatten noted 'It is quite clear to me that if we had not brought the leaders together to hear each others' indignation and thus regain their sense of proportion we might have had as serious a blow [up] as V. P. Menon feared'. Most of the Viceregal staff, including Mieville (in poor health) left on the very eve of independence, Campbell-Johnson observed that George Abell was the pivotal figure: 'He said that the contrast between Wavell and Mountbatten was striking. Each had what the other lacked, and each was a great man'. Most of the Governors left on 18 August on the *Empress of Scotland* along with many other ICS officers. One of them commented 'These people were once described as India's steel frame but now they are more like a cargo of scrap iron'.

Mountbatten had been Viceroy for less than five months; he was to remain Governor-General of the new truncated India for eight months. It appeared a strange juxtaposition, though as Viceroy he had exercised his role very much more from a level of equality with his Indian colleagues than any of his predecessors and as Governor-General he assumed a greater part in decision-making than any of his successors. The first positive effect came from the decision of both the new Dominions to remain in the Commonwealth. Mountbatten had worked strenuously to bring this off. The main effect was external. In Britain there was a response, part pride, part sentiment, which affected even Churchill.

The hardheaded Smuts declared 'It is a most unfortunate development' when India's membership was endorsed even when she became a republic. Churchill, so long hostile to Indian self-government responded: 'When I asked myself the question 'Would I rather have them in even on these terms or let them go altogether? My heart gave the answer I want them in'. Of more immediate consequence was the unplanned movement of populations across the new Punjab frontier in which thousands were killed. The troubles engulfed Delhi where, in Ismay's words 'for a period there was...complete chaos; the Muslims were systematically hunted down and massacred, the security services failed, and the public services were brought to a standstill.' The numbers who died have been computed very differently. Possibly the least sensational figure is that given by Penderel Moon[6] 200,000. Congress leaders tried to pin responsibility on Britain, and in particular on the British officers of the Indian Army. They insisted that the Punjab Boundary Force be wound up and the Joint Defence Council set up under Auchinleck as Supreme Commander be terminated: Auchinleck was told to go, by Nehru, and again Mountbatten made no attempt to stand up for the man he had placed in this impossible position.

The next crisis occurred over the status of Kashmir and Hyderabad. Both these very large states attempted to stand out of the process of integrating the Princely States into the new Dominions. Both issues came to a head while Mountbatten was still Governor-General. Hyderabad was most vulnerable, being surrounded by Indian territory, and its fate was sealed when Patel lost patience and ordered the Indian Army to take over the state in mid-September 1948. Mountbatten tried to disguise the extent of the takeover by talking of the 'ridiculous misunderstanding' of the outside world over India's action. Once again his PR capabilities achieved some success.

Kashmir was a more intractable problem. The Maharaja's

efforts to evade a solution finally gave way to Pakistan pressure. Pathan tribesmen, under orders originating with Liaquat or Jinnah were moved up towards Kashmir. Hastily, the Maharaja who had hoped to keep clear of both the new countries flew to Delhi and met Mountbatten, who formally accepted the Maharaja's accession subject to holding a plebiscite: 'It is my Government's wish that as soon as law and order have been restored in Kashmir and her soil cleared of the invader the question of the State's accession should be settled by reference to the people' (27 October 1947). This never took place, and the dispute between India and Pakistan erupted into war, no less serious for being undeclared. Open hostilities were only terminated in January 1949 at the insistence of the United Nations.

By then Mountbatten had departed—he left in June 1948, and was welcomed home at the airfield by Attlee, the Duke of Edinburgh, and other high dignitaries. It was a triumph. Or was it? Two Britons who stayed on as Governors, Cunningham on the Frontier and Mudie in Punjab, met at Peshawar in January 1948: both agreed that the post-partition troubles were largely due to the acceleration of the date for Independence from June 1948 to August 1947. The later date would have given time to organize the division of the army, the civil service and the police, and the fiasco of the Boundary Force and many of the subsequent massacres would have been avoided. The argument of which so much had been heard in the months preceding August 1947 that the administrative machinery in India was running down was in their view mainly false.[7]

On his return Mountbatten continued his seemingly effortless rise to the top. Appointed First Sea Lord in 1955, he was responsible for planning the Suez adventure. He wrote to Eden to protest at its maladroit conception and incalculable consequences (2 November 1956) but he made no attempt to back up his protest by resignation. That was not his way. He was promoted to Admiral of the Fleet, and in 1959 became the First Chief of the combined services.

He had become convinced of the folly of Britain's nuclear policy but made no attempt to influence the government of the day. Edwina died in 1960, and with her departure his earlier left wing commitment perished. When a Labour government took office in 1964 the new Prime Minister, Wilson, announced that he would abolish the 'so-called British so-called independent deterrent'. Mountbatten urged him to reconsider—which Wilson rapidly did. Twelve years after, when he was long retired, Mountbatten did come out with his condemnation of The Bomb. On 11 May 1976, speaking at Strasbourg he declared 'The nuclear arms race has no military purpose.' Even then he was content to issue his declaration and made no attempt to campaign on the issue.

One of Mountbatten's last ventures was to put together a museum at Broadlands devoted to his own career. It was opened by the Prince of Wales who was required to pay the entrance fee like everyone else—except that he was not carrying any money (as presumably Mountbatten was aware) and he had to borrow from his great uncle.

This extraordinary man was assassinated by the IRA in 1979. The theory that he was killed by M.I.5 because of his anti-nuclear stance is far fetched: but it might have appealed to Mountbatten.

NOTES

1. Peter Dennis, *Troubled Days of Peace; Mountbatten and South East Asia Command, 1945-46,* 1987, p. 230.
2. See *Eminent Churchillians* by Andrew Roberts, 1994, Chapter 2, 'Lord Mountbatten and the Perils of Adrenalin' for an astringent account of the Dieppe raid (pp. 64-8).
3. Hugh Tinker, *Burma: the Struggle for Independence,* Documents, Vol. I, 1983, p. 939.
4. Hugh Tinker, 'Jawaharlal Nehru at Simla, May 1947: A Moment of Truth?', *Modern Asian Studies,* 4, 4 (1970). Incident at Simla, May 1947—What the Documents Reveal: A moment of truth for the

historians? *Journal of Commonweath and Comparative Politics*, July 1982.
5. Penderel Moon, *Divide and Quit*, 1961, p. 293.
6. Ibid. p. 94.
7. Norval Mitchell, *Sir George Cunningham*, 1968, p. 151.

CHAPTER 12

THE LARGER PERSPECTIVE

'The scene in India during the early years of the present century when I lived at Delhi resembled that of the Roman Empire nineteen hundred years ago': so wrote C. F. Andrews in 1932. 'There was the same vast, unbroken imperial peace in external affairs and a settled order outwardly maintained. But within this area of apparent calm a surging, heaving ferment had suddenly begun to appear like volcanic lava cracking through the surface of the soil. Men called it the "national movement".'

Most British people in India did not probe below the surface, believing that the Indians were content to accept their British administrators. At the apex of the structure was the Viceroy and his Council. The Executive Council was entirely British, down to the time of Curzon, but even with the addition of the Legislative Council, numbers were still small enough for everyone to sit around a large table, presided over by the Viceroy, seated under a portrait of Warren Hastings. Under the Morley-Minto reforms their total number was increased to fifty-nine: the Viceroy still presided, though now the non-official members sat in a double hemicycle facing the chair. The legislature only attained some semblance to a parliament under the reforms of 1919 when it became bicameral. The Upper House, the Council of State was allotted a maximum of sixty members while the Lower House, the Assembly was given a minimum membership of 140.

When Lutyens began to design his grand new palace for the Viceroy he first incorporated a chamber for the legislature: however the 1919 reforms necessitated fresh thinking. A separate Council House was built in the 1920s: its first session was inaugurated by Irwin in 1927. The Council House contained three chambers: the Assembly, initially composed of 145 members, the Council of State with sixty members, and the Chamber of Princes which failed to gain a permanent place in the scheme of things (it later became the library). The design of the two legislative chambers was made to accommodate many more occupants than the original number: 400 in the Assembly and 200 in the Council of State: hence the two chambers were adequate for parliament after independence. The hemicycle arrangement was preserved with the members all facing the president of the House. The Council House was circular overall. Some compared its design to the Colosseum in Rome.

The Viceroy still formed the central pivot of the system and set the whole tone of government. However, there was a transformation in the relationship between government and people about 1920, largely due to the advent of Gandhi. The last era in which government and people were in full accord was the viceroyalty of Hardinge. The most striking example of accord followed the outbreak of war in 1914. There was a wholehearted display of loyalty to the British Crown which included even the radical element, the students. It was possible to withdraw most regular British soldiers from India. Their numbers were reduced from 60,000 to 15,000 until replacements came in: raw territorials, not fully trained. However, little was made of this 'loyalist' spirit, and there were no British political gestures, until far too late. The Rowlatt legislation followed by the Amritsar tragedy totally alienated India: the great mass of rural folk (whose 'pathetic contentment' so disturbed Gandhi) as well as political India. The political class became much more numerous. A small minority of Indians, even among the educated, remained loyalists especially in the rural areas. In the towns the active element in society, the political class now formed a power structure which rivalled that of the government (never very formidable). The strength of the political class varied a good deal among the various provinces. It was most important in the triangle between Delhi, Calcutta and Nagpur. The South, and also the North-West was quite different. Politics focused upon caste in the South and increasingly on religion in the North-West: Islam, the Sikhs and the urban Hindus. Within the central ambit of India, politics was mainly about the fight for independence, which meant removing the British from the Motherland. Yet even within this area there remained many who still regarded the British Raj as the arbiter. The tradition of government service was preserved from Mughal times. A caste like the Kayasthas had found no contradiction in working for the Mughal Emperor and transferred its capacity for administration to the British without too much heart searching. This reached its ultimate contradiction during the second world war when senior Indians in the administration spent their days conscientiously working for British victory over the Axis powers before going home to listen to the German radio foretelling inevitable British defeat.

The Viceroy continued to preside over the massive administrative machine. Not until after 1945 did this begin to falter under the strain. The 1942 Congress 'disturbances' severely tested the machine but except for a limited area in eastern UP and Bihar it did not break down. Survival depended more on the local administration than on the central government and its head.

Many Viceroys arrived with only a sketchy idea of what awaited them: though the last four, from Willingdon to Mountbatten had acquired some knowledge of what to expect (even if Mountbatten often found what he wanted to find in his encounters). The last two were wartime heads of government, less bounded by protocol than their predecessors for whom there was a set routine: Simla for six or seven months each year, 'entirely out of touch with Indian life', as Valentine Chirol observed, and for most of the rest of the year Calcutta, and finally New Delhi; also western outposts. Chirol proposed that the Viceroy could make up for the gaps in his knowledge and experience by utilizing the collective experience of his Council.[1] But as the focus of authority and legitimacy passed to the political leadership—which really meant Gandhi until Jinnah aroused the Muslims in the 1940s—the utility of the Executive Council to the Viceroy diminished: although paradoxically it was increasingly Indian. Wavell turned to his Council less and less while Mountbatten relied almost entirely on his kitchen Cabinet—Ismay and the former SEAC team, until he came to depend on the few politicians he favoured—Nehru, Krishna Menon, and V. P. Menon, increasingly a politician.

One puzzle about the evolution of the Viceroyalty in the last days relates to the social status of the man who held the office. Why did selections for the office devolve almost exclusively to the aristocracy? When John Lawrence was called to take up the post, *The Times,* still under the direction of John Delane and sensitive to middle-class values, responded applaudingly: 'To break through the charmed circle which has so long restricted the office of Governor-General to the peerage and to send out to the Empire which was formed by the exertions of Robert Clive and Warren Hastings not only a commoner, but a commoner wholly unconnected with any family of the English aristocracy...A man ...stamped by the hand of nature with the truest impress of nobility' (30 November 1863).

Yet, after that departure from custom only two viceroys were chosen from outside 'the charmed circle': Reading and Wavell. All the remainder were hereditary aristocrats, the heirs to broad acres, not otherwise specially distinguished for records of public service. By coincidence, the period covered by this book saw ten viceroys and ten prime ministers. The viceroys were all aristocrats except for two. Among the prime ministers were three aristocrats—Lord Salisbury, his nephew, Balfour, and Churchill. All the rest were middle class with professional or industrial origins except for two who were of peasant stock—Lloyd George and Ramsay MacDonald. The aristocracy were no longer the natural leaders of British society.

The last of the Viceroys, chosen by a Socialist prime minister came not from the aristocracy but from royalty. It was left to the solitary Communist MP, Willie Gallacher, to ask Attlee why no Labour or Trades Unionist leader had been considered.[2] He was not afforded a reply: presumably the advantages of a socially acceptable viceroy were self-evident.

Mountbatten was a special case, but one may also wonder why after John Lawrence no administrator was ever given the top appointment. There were a number of officials who had shown great ability in the affairs of India and then went on to impress their mark on a wider stage. Lord Meston had a brilliant career in India: 'A splendid fellow', as Minto had discovered 'determined to win the sympathy and invite the support of his province' he also possessed a wider vision as when he promoted the creation of the Royal Institute of International Affairs. Yet Asquith chose the colourless Chelmsford as Viceroy in 1916. Then, in 1936 Linlithgow was preferred when Lord Hailey was available, having given firm government to the two key provinces of Punjab and UP. He had stiffened Hoare's will throughout the perils of the Joint Select Committee. But his father was not a great landowner, simply a country doctor.[3]

Throughout the Colonial Empire the appointment of gentleman amateurs, so common in the 19th Century had been replaced from the start of the 20th Century by the selection of outstanding members of the Colonial Service. No colonial territory could be compared to India, but some were important, such as Ceylon and Malaya. Sir Arthur Gordon, Lord Stanmore, governed Ceylon, 1883-90, but thereafter middle class governors were the norm.

The concept of a sole, supreme ruler in India was obsolete by the 20th Century. Harold Laski predicted, writing on the eve of the second world war 'As the centre of decision moves from London to Delhi the viceregal position will tend to approximate more and more to that of a Governor-General of a British Dominion...the main field of his influence will be the necessary building of bridges between a self-governing India and the India of the Princes'.[4] This might have proved a shrewd prophecy if the ultimate phase of British rule had not been so unexpectedly telescoped in time. As it was, Mountbatten remained the supreme arbiter right to the end—and indeed beyond the formal date of the transfer of power. The imbroglio over Kashmir's accession to India continued to involve Mountbatten when he was supposed to have become a purely constitutional head of state, though Nehru adapted to the demands of supreme authority and command quickly enough. He took over the most prestigious mansion in New Delhi after Lutyens' great palace, the former seat of the Commander-in-Chief—the Jangi Lat, with its spacious apartments and delightful grounds. His personal style oscillated between familiarity with the humble and meek and great dignity when with the grand. He maintained the 'dignified' side of office as well as fulfilling the 'efficient' responsibilities of a chief executive. Some of his critics did indeed refer to him as 'the Last of the Viceroys'. His election campaigns were more like American presidential tours than those of ordinary politicians. Of course, in Pakistan Jinnah became Governor-General, not Prime Minister and set the stage for his successors who did the governing and treated the Prime Minister like a chef-du-cabinet dismissing him when he was deemed to have fallen short. This relationship appeared to come to an end in 1993 when the Supreme Court overruled the dismissal of Nawaz Sharif. However three years later Prime Minister Benazir Bhutto was dismissed by the President of Pakistan, despite further protests.

In India, Indira Gandhi did not follow Jawaharlal Nehru into the mansion of the Jangi Lat (maybe she had seen enough of its ponderous dignity while keeping house for her father) but she went beyond Nehru's style of government (and also beyond the limits observed by the British Viceroys) when she assumed Emergency powers and, in effect, governed by decree. For their part, successive Presidents have taken over much of the 'dignified' ritual of the Viceroys, with displays of martial might and Court ceremonial which reproduce many of the trappings of old—the bodyguard on sleek horses with lances and pennons—open carriages, known in Britain as victorias with outriders dressed in gold; and over the unassuming figure of the president a golden umbrella, symbol of oriental might, which the British took over from the Mughals. Long after the British Viceroys have departed the spectral memory of their vanished pageantry lingers on.

NOTES

1. Valentine Chirol, *Indian Unrest,* 1910, pp. 315-16.
2. House of Commons, 20th February 1947. Attlee made only one working class man a governor: Sir Frederick Burrows, Governor of Bengal.
3. The entry in *The Dictionary of National Biography* concerning Hailey states that he was considered for the Viceroyalty but because of his wife's notorious eccentricity he was passed over. The evidence is purely anecdotal. The Private Office papers of the Secretary of State contain no evidence that Hailey was among those considered.
4. Foreword to Advani B. Rudra, *The Viceroy and Governor-General,* 1940, p.x.

FURTHER READING

A bibliography of books about the Viceroys, and the subjects which specially occupied them, is almost endless. The list given below is limited to those books which have contributed most to this study and from which quotations have been taken. Those listed as 'general' cover a considerable period, or involve several viceroyalties. Some works cover just two periods of office, and in those cases the list is attached to the first Viceroy treated.

General

M. Bence-Jones, *The Viceroys of India*, 1982
Marquess Curzon, *British Government in India*, 2 vols, 1925
R.G. Irving, *Indian Summer, Lutyens, Baker and Imperial Delhi*, 1981
A. B. Keith, *Constitutional History of India*, 1600-1935, 1936
A. Lyall, *Rise and Expansion of British Dominion in India*, 1911
S. R. Mehrota, *India and the Commonwealth*, 1965
Viscount Mersey, *The Viceroys and Governors-General of India*, 1949
B. B. Misra, *The Administrative History of India*, 1970
The Indian Political Parties, 1976
Penderel moon, *Strangers in India*, 1944
British Conquest and Dominion of India, 1989
Jawaharlal Nehru, *Autobiography*, 1936
L. S. S. O'Malley (ed.), *Modern India and the West*, 1941
A. B. Rudra, *The Viceroy and Governor-General*, 1940
G. Schuster and G. Wint, *India and Democracy*, 1941

H. Tinker, *A New System of Slavery*, 1974
Separate and Unequal, 1976
The Ordeal of Love; C. F. Andrews and India, 1979
S. Wolpert, *Jinnah of Pakistan*, 1984
Curzon, *Leaves From a Viceroy's Notebook*, 1926

Curzon

Joseph Chailley, *L'Inde Brittanique*, translated as *Administrative Problems of British India* (W. Meyer), 1910
Valentine Chirol, *Indian Unrest*, 1910
Marquess Curzon, *Leaves From a Viceroy's Notebook*, 1926
D. Dilks, *Curzon in India*, 2 vols. 1969
M. Edwardes, *High Noon of Empire*, 1965
J. Bradley (ed.) *Lady Curzon's India-Letters*, 1985
W. Lawrence, *The India We Served*, 1928
P. Magnus, *Kitchener*, 1958
M. Menpes, *The Durbar*, 1903
N. Nicholson, *Mary Curzon*, 1971
Earl of Ronaldshay, *Life of Lord Curzon*, Vol. I, 1928
K. Rose, *Superior Person*, 1969

Minto

J. Buchan, *Lord Minto, A Memoir*, 1934
M. N. Das, *India Under Morely and Minto*, 1964
M. Gilbert, *Servant of India...Sir James Dunlop-Smith*, 1966
S. Koss, *John Morley at the India Office, 1905-1910*, 1969
Mary Countess of Minto, *India, Minto and Morley, 1905-10*, 1934
J. Morely, *Recollections*, Vol. II, 1917
S. R. Wasti, *Lord Minto and the Indian National Movement*, 1964
S. Wolpert, *Morley and India, 1906-1910*, 1967

Hardinge

Lord Hardinge, *My Indian Years*, 1948
J. Pope-Hennessy, *Lord Crewe; The Likeness of a Liberal*, 1955
A. Rumbold, *Watershed in India, 1914-1922*, 1979
H. Sharp, *Good-bye India*, 1946
S. D. Waley, *Edwin Montagu; A Memoir and an Account of his Visits to India*, 1964

Chelmsford

As above
M. O'Dwyer, *India As I Knew It*, 1925
S. Wolpert, *An Error of Judgment*, 1970

Reading

H. Montgomery Hyde, *Lord Reading*, 1967
Dennis Judd, *Rufus Isaacs, First Marquess of Reading*, 2 vols. 1945
Iris Butler, *The Viceroy's Wife*, 1969

Some Records of Viceroys

All the papers listed here are from the India Office Records. Most of the Viceroy's papers were deposited at the India Office, though not all. Minto left his papers to the National Library of Scotland, Hardinge's papers are in Cambridge University Library, The Mountbatten papers were in the archieve at Broadlands, though I understand that they are now in the Southampton University Library. Every collection of Viceregal papers was printed by the press which was at the Viceroys disposal. These collections were made up under different heads: Correspondence with the Secretary of State, Correspondence with Persons in India, Correspondence with Persons in England and Abroad. Technically, these papers remained the property of the Viceroy and he could take them away; with the passage of time they found their way back to the India Office Records.